# Madagascar
# & Comoros

a tra

**Madagascar & Comoros - a travel survival kit**
**1st edition**

**Published by**
Lonely Planet Publications
Head Office: PO Box 617, Hawthorn, Victoria 3122, Australia
US Office: PO Box 2001A, Berkeley, CA 94702, USA

**Printed by**
Singapore National Printers Ltd, Singapore

**Photographs by**
Robert Willox (RW)
David Curl (DC)
Gilles Gautier (GG)
Front cover: A ring-tailed lemur (DC)

Back cover quote: *Los Angeles Times* © Copyright 1989
Used with permission

**Published**
November 1989

Although the author and publisher have tried to make the information as accurate as possible, they accept no responsibility for any loss, injury or inconvenience sustained by any person using this book.

National Library of Australia Cataloguing in Publication Data

Willox, Robert.
  Madagascar & Comoros, a travel survival kit.

  Includes index.
  ISBN 0 86442 029 3.

  1. Madagascar - Description and travel -
  1981- - Guide-books. 2 Comoros -
  Description and travel - Guide-books
  I. Title

916.9'1045

### Robert Willox

Robert Willox is a Scottish Highlander by birth and by nature, although he still gets on reasonably well with the English. For the past eight years, however, he has made Australia his home.

A journalist since leaving school (at about four o'clock), Bob has worked for newspapers in England, Scotland, Northern Ireland and, most recently, in Australia for the *Sydney Morning Herald*. In between newspapers, he has enjoyed stints as a philosophy graduate, a Royal Marine officer, an Antarctic expeditioner, a professional actor and an author. He wrote his first book, at the age of 19, about the German bandleader James Last. But don't let that put you off; he now likes Mantovani.

Bob had not written much about his extensive travels until he crossed paths with Lonely Planet. Although his main connection with the Indian Ocean is City Beach in Perth, Western Australia, he is also the author of two other LP travel survival kits: *Mauritius, Réunion & Seychelles* and *Maldives & Islands of the East Indian Ocean*.

### From the Author

I would like to thank the following people for background information and for their assistance in my travels. For Madagascar: Bruno Sausseu, Eddy Uprichard, Markus Ruckstuld, Elyane Rahonintsoa of the Direction du Tourisme, Marlyse Rebert and Walter Wurm, Pierre Lhuillier and Pascal Drouin, Berti and Uschi Haffner, Air Madagascar, Madagascar Airtours, and David Curl – photographer, and scientist from Monash University's Department of Botany & Zoology. For Comoros: Dragan Crnjanski and Salim Himidi. Thanks also to Robert Bruns, and Achim Klüber and family.

This book is dedicated Janet Fife-Yeomans.

### Lonely Planet Credits

| | |
|---|---|
| **Editors** | Lindy Cameron |
| | Tom Smallman |
| **Maps** | Trudi Canavan |
| | Greg Herriman |
| **Design, cover design & illustrations** | Trudi Canavan |
| **Typesetting** | Gaylene Miller |
| | Ann Jefree |

Thanks also to: Michelle de Kretzer for copy editing, James Lyon and Sue Mitra for proofreading, Greg Herriman for paste-up corrections, and Sharon Wertheim for indexing.

### A Warning & A Request

Things change – prices go up, schedules change, good places go bad and bad places go bankrupt – nothing stays the same. So if you find things better or worse, recently opened or long since closed, please write and tell us and help make the next edition better!

Your letters will be used to help update future editions and, where possible, important changes will also be included as a Stop Press section in reprints.

All information is greatly appreciated and the best letters will receive a free copy of the next edition, or any other Lonely Planet book of your choice.

# Contents

# Introduction

When describing Madagascar, it's not fair to trot out phrases such as 'a unique travelling experience', 'a strange and exotic land', or 'a country of mystery and suspense, of beauty and adventure. . . with warm and friendly people'. It's not fair because these descriptions can apply to practically any country in the world, and Madagascar is different. Honestly! These are understatements. It's all these things and much more.

The 'land that time forgot' is nearer the mark.

Madagascar also seems to be the land that travellers and tourists forget. More likely, they are not aware of the delights this country offers them. Perhaps a few hundred hardy, adventurous French,

Swiss or German souls go each year, but hardly any from Britain, Scandanavia, North America or Australasia, unless they are anthropologists or zoologists.

Hopefully this guide will change that and open the way for many more travellers because Madagascar is a great travel experience, and an inexpensive one to boot. Every journey is an adventure on this huge island of contrasts whether it's by foot, boat, car, train or bus – especially bus.

You wouldn't think it was the world's fourth-biggest island. This is because on the map it stands ankle-high alongside Africa, and our awareness of it is similarly dwarfed.

To see it as part of Africa is wrong. That

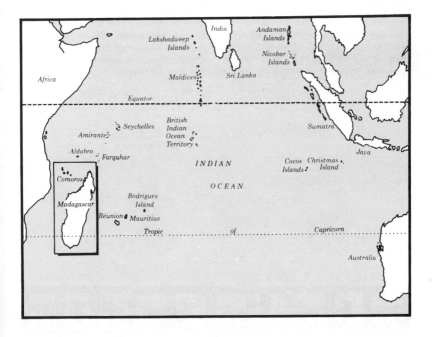

would be like seeing New Zealand as part of Australia. Rather, Africa is a part of Madagascar.

The ruling 'tribe' of Madagascar is more Asian than African, certainly in appearance. And there are a score or so of other tribes with varying customs and traditions which travellers will come across as they wander, or rather struggle from one territory to another.

The terrain is equally varied – from rainforest to desert, high plateau to tropical isles – and presents some amazing, natural, almost unnatural features. These are not well known, but the equally unusual creatures that live among them are.

On Madagascar, the wildlife evolved separately from Africa and the rest of the world. It was as if this was a testing ground for various species – nature's design laboratory, somebody called it. Maybe it was David Attenborough, who's been fascinating us for years with its natural wonders. All the time, however, we probably thought he was at the end of the earth, thousands of miles from civilisation, because he didn't tell us about the nation that was trying to evolve after half a century of French colonialism, nor the equally fascinating and friendly character of its people.

Well, now's your chance. If you've read this far, and you're either on your way there or thinking about going, push on. It will be good for you and good for Madagascar. The place needs a lot of attention.

Apart from suffering economic disaster, it is also facing ecological devastation, as the forests are desperately torn down to provide fuel and grazing or agricultural land. The top soil is washed away and voilá – nothing. The economy might recover, but the damage to the land is irreversible. 'A disappearing land' is another phrase we could trot out.

See it now. Save it now.

If you think Madagascar is a mystery, you should see the Comoros. You should. These four islands – three of which form an independent Islamic republic and one, Mayotte, which still belongs to France – are quite different from their big neighbour to the south-east. How? Well, the Comoros is a strange and exotic land, full of mystery and suspense ... with warm and friendly people.

# Facts for the Visitor

## VISAS & PERMITS

Make sure you get your Madagascar visa *before* you leave for the country. There's nothing you can do about the Comoros, however, until you land there.

Bring at least six extra passport photographs for possible visa extensions and other applications like national park permits. If you can arrange it, for Madagascar in particular, bring a 'letter of introduction' in French, or better still in Malagasy, and preferably on headed notepaper. This will help with accommodation outside the major cities.

An international driving licence is not necessary, but carry your regular one.

## MONEY

Travellers' cheques are best taken out in US dollars for Madagascar, and French francs for the Comoros. Other major currencies – UK pounds, Deutschmarks, Swiss francs, Italian lire – are acceptable. Australian, New Zealand and Canadian dollars and lesser currencies are useless in Madagascar. Don't bring other Indian Ocean island currencies or South African rand. (See the Money sections in the Factors for the Visitor chapter of each country, especially for Madagascar's currency controls).

Credit cards are little help in Madagascar, the Comoros and even the French territory of Mayotte, unless you are staying at the luxury hotels.

## COSTS

Madagascar is cheap to travel in; the Comoros islands are not.

The Malagasy economy has deteriorated in the past few years, and their franc has been greatly devalued. The tourist hotel rates have been increased to make up for the devaluation – and are charged in foreign currency – but a traveller should still be able to survive comfortably on under US$10 a day. Meals and local transport are also very low for foreigners not on a package tour.

The Comoros is an unexpected contrast. Its franc is tied to the French one, and the majority of hotels are foreign-owned and charge French Riviera rates. There are, however, a few 'budget' guest houses and if you get into them or the one old hotel (the cheapest), you could get by on under US$25 a day.

Mayotte is a French territory and while costs are similar to the other three Comorian islands, budget accommodation is even more scarce.

## HEALTH

The sun is the greatest general threat to your wellbeing, next to the Malagasy road traffic. Bring a good sun blocking lotion with you as the cost of sun lotions is high and the choice limited. You can tan easily and well within a week to 10 days, using a high-protection cream.

Don't underestimate the effects of the sun, even if you think you know your tolerance level. Drink plenty of liquids and keep salt intake up to replace that lost through perspiration. It's a good idea to wear a hat of some kind and sunglasses.

### Vaccinations

Vaccinations for hepatitis, tetanus, cholera, polio and typhoid should be considered if you are planning to go bush or travel around the region for a long period of time. Your government health department will advise you on which vaccinations are currently recommended. The only vaccination required for entry to Madagascar and Comoros is for yellow fever, if you have just been to a potentially infected area.

### Malaria

Madagascar and Comoros are both areas

where the chloroquine-resistant malarial strains exist. Chloroquine should still be taken, but a weekly dose of Maloprim or a daily dose of Proguanil should also be taken. You have to start your course of malaria tablets two weeks before you enter a malarial area and for up to six weeks after you leave.

Warning: Fansidar is no longer recommended as a prophylactic.

Mosquito coils or a non-aerosol repellent are useful in keeping the brutes at bay.

## Common Ailments

**The Traveller's Curse** I did not suffer any stomach upsets or diarrhoea, and met no traveller who had. But there were comparatively few other westerners around and maybe I was lucky. Consult your doctor about the best medicine to take for such problems.

If you do have an attack of diarrhoea the best way to treat it, however, is with no drugs. It's probably just your body's way of adjusting to a new environment and different food, so the most important thing to do is replenish your bodily fluids to avoid dehydration. A diet of bland foods such as rice, bread and weak tea is a good treatment.

If you have a fever, then your ailment might be something more serious, like amoebic dysentery, in which case you should see a doctor.

**Cuts** All cuts, no matter how minor, should be treated seriously and carefully if you're travelling in a tropical climate. Put mercurochrome on any cut or scratch, keep the wound clean and dry and check for any sign of infection. Deep or large cuts should be treated with antibiotic powder.

## Travel Insurance

It is a good idea to take out travel insurance. Look at a few policies to see what you will be covered for; some are better than others for certain activities, like diving or motor cycling. Make sure you're adequately covered for medical expenses, for the cost

of getting home for treatment, life insurance and baggage insurance.

## Medical Kit

Carry a basic first aid kit with an antiseptic agent (dettol), antibiotic powder and cream, bandaids, a gauze bandage, small scissors, burn cream, insect repellent and seasickness pills.

Don't forget any medication you're already taking, contraceptive pills or condoms if necessary, and women should bring a sufficient supply of tampons.

## DANGERS & ANNOYANCES

Because of the worsening economic crisis in Madagascar, crime is on the increase, particularly in the capital Antananarivo. There's also the occasional riot to get the heart going. We're not talking New York or Beirut here, but just take extra care.

## Security

A waterproof money belt or kidney pouch for your passport, flight tickets and travellers' cheques is worth considering. Use a day backpack to carry your camera and valuables, as well as the bits and pieces you'll need for the day.

Don't leave vital documents, money or valuables in your room or in your suitcase while travelling. Don't sleep with an open window which is accessible from the outside, or with the door open or unlocked.

## FILM & PHOTOGRAPHY

Film will be much more expensive on the islands than in the duty free shops, so stock up before you leave home. There are photographic and processing only shops in the capitals. Remember to take spare batteries for cameras and flash units.

Use Kodachrome 25 or 64 transparency (slide) film, rather than Ektachrome. The cost of the film usually includes processing and you can mail the rolls back to the labs in the envelopes provided. Rewrap the package to disguise it and send it registered if you don't trust the post

(I wouldn't in Madagascar). Kodacolor 100 film is the most popular print film and is fine for most general photography in the tropics.

Don't leave your camera for long in direct sunlight, and keep it protected from dust and sand. Don't store used film for long in the humid conditions, as it will fade.

The best times to take photographs on sunny days are the first two hours after sunrise and the last two before sunset. This brings out the best colours. At other times, the harsh sunlight and glare washes everything out, though you can use filters to counter the glare.

Photographing people, particularly dark-skinned people, requires more skill than snapping landscapes. Make sure you take the light reading from the subject's face, not the background. It also requires more patience and politeness. Many islanders, particularly the older Muslims and Hindus, are offended or frightened by snap-happy inquisitors. You should always ask first, ingratiate yourself, or film discreetly from a distance.

Don't take photographs of airports of anything that looks like police or military equipment or property – especially in the Comoros, unless you want to make a mercenary's day.

Finally, if you are worried about X-ray security machines at airports ruining your film, despite assurances that they won't, simply remove your camera and film stock from your luggage and take it through separately for inspection.

## BOOKS

You'll find books in English are very rare in Madagascar and Comoros so if you intend reading a lot, bring a few paperbacks with you; you may be able to swap them later with other travellers. In preparation for shoestring travelling, as opposed to package tripping, read *The Tropical Traveller* (Pan, 1982) by John Hatt.

The only example of the rare coelacanth fish you'll see will be stuffed, but there are shoals of other little wonders to make up for this. It's best if you refer directly to either *A Field Guide to the Coral Reef Fish of the Indian and West Pacific Oceans* (Collins, London, 1977) by R H Carcasson or *A Guide to Common Reef Fish of the Western Indian Ocean* (Macmillan, London, 1987) by K R Bock.

## WHAT TO BRING
### Clothes

Keep clothing light and in cotton wherever possible; this applies especially to socks if you intend to do lots of tramping.

Anything so formal as a suit is unnecessary, but it's good to have a smart pair of trousers and shirt or dress or skirt for dinners out; don't forget good shoes too. Such an outfit can also help at customs and immigration, when entering or leaving a country. If nothing else, it makes you feel more respectable and authoritative (and thus respected) if trouble arises, than you would feel in shorts, T-shirt and thongs (flip-flops).

Make sure you have protection from the sun. Bring a hat and an appropriate-strength sun cream. Take it easy to begin with when you go about exposing yourself to the fiery elements. It's so easy to get badly burnt, even when it's overcast, because you won't realise how strong the sun is until it's too late.

At the other extreme, a light wrap-up plastic cape or mac will stop a downpour from ruining the odd day or week. It's a must during the wet season. Also, remember to take precautions to keep your camera equipment and personal gear dry. Pack everything in plastic bags before you leave home.

At night it cools down a bit on the coast, but not enough to need woolly blankets and thick jumpers. It's a different story if you are up in the hills – the Karthala Volcano on Grande Comore for example, or on the plateau in Antananarivo or Antsirabe in Madagascar. You will definitely need warm clothing during the nights and it will soon become obvious why certain Malagasy have a penchant for blankets.

Take good, solid footwear for trekking.

## Emergency Kit

If you're to be roughing it away from the overt tourist hotels and living in Malagasy hotels or Comorian guest houses, you should bring a torch (with spare batteries), toilet paper, a small mirror (shiny metal without glass is best), a Swiss Army knife (or the like), a first aid kit, a sewing kit (with safety pins), sticky tape, and a small padlock (for locking rooms or luggage). That doesn't add up to much extra weight. If you're looking to save on the kilos, keep your towels thin.

## ACTIVITIES
### Diving

Madagascar and the Comoros have some reasonable diving locations that are known and perhaps many better ones waiting to be discovered. But there are few schools that can provide an introduction to scuba diving.

Your ability, health and qualifications should be checked before any operator sells you courses or takes you out on an introductory dive. This is done through a check in the swimming pool or lagoon. All beginners must be able to swim at least 200 metres before proceeding.

Some hotels in Madagascar's tourist areas provide diving equipment and 'instructors', but unless you are an experienced diver or they provide recognised qualifications, you may be taking a great risk with both instruction and equipment.

## LANGUAGE

French is an official language in Madagascar and the Comoros. Malagasy and Comorian words are given in the language sections of the respective Facts about the Country chapters. The following lists contain useful French words.

## Accommodation

| | |
|---|---|
| price, tariff | *prix, tarif* |
| included | *compris* |
| not included | *non compris* |
| per day | *par jour* |
| week | *semaine* |
| month | *mois* |
| bedroom | *chambre* |
| air-conditioned | *climatisé* |
| single room | *chambre simple* |
| double room | *chambre double* |
| double bed | *grand lit* |
| extra bed | *lit supplémentaire* |
| twin beds | *lits jumeaux* |
| half board | *demie-pension* |
| full board | *pension complète* |
| meal | *repas* |
| breakfast | *petit déjeuner* |
| lunch | *déjeuner* |
| dinner | *dîner* |
| bathroom | *salle de bain* |
| shower | *douche* |
| toilet | *WC* (pronounced 'doobl vay say') |
| hot water | *eau chaude* |
| towels | *serviettes* |
| washbasin | *lavabo* |
| deposit | *dépôt de garantie, caution* |
| kitchen | *cuisine* |
| dining room | *salle à manger* |
| swimming pool | *piscine* |
| terrace, balcony | *terasse* |
| facilities | *facilités* |
| with | *avec* |
| without | *sans* |
| on request | *sur demande* |

## Food

I hope I'm not teaching granny to suck *oeufs* here or making a *repas* out of something simple, but you'll find that menus are mostly in French with local variations in some cases. Here is a list of French and local words which often turn up on menus.

## Seafood

| | |
|---|---|
| seafood | *fruits de mer* |
| fish | *poisson* |

trout — *truite*
tuna — *thon*
lobster — *langouste, homard*
octopus — *ourites*
prawns, shrimps — *crevettes*
squid — *calmar*

## Meat
meat (generic) — *viande*
beef — *boeuf*
chicken — *poulet*
duck — *canard*
goat — *boucan, cabri*
ham — *jambon*
hare, rabbit — *civet, lapin*
mutton — *mouton*
pork — *porc*

## Vegetables
vegetables — *légumes*
beans — *haricots*
cassava — *manioc*
chips — *pommes frites*
onions — *oignons*
potato — *patate, pomme de terre*

## Fruit
fruit — *fruit*
apple — *pomme*
banana — *banane*
coconut — *noix de coco*
custard apple — *corossol*
lemon — *citron*
mango — *mangue*
passionfruit — *grenadelle*
pineapple — *ananas*
star fruit — *carambol*

## Desserts
cake — *gâteau*

cheese — *fromage*
ice cream — *glace*
jam — *confiture*
pastries — *pâtisseries*
sugar — *sucre*

## Drinks
drinks — *boissons*
milk — *lait*
fruit juice — *jus de fruit*
tea — *thé*
coffee — *café*
beer — *biére*
wine — *vin*
lemonade — *limonade*

## Condiments
chilli — *piments*
curry — *carri*
ginger — *gingembre*
salt — *sel*
pepper — *poivre*
salad dressing — *huile de table*
sweet and sour — *aigre-doux*

## Miscellaneous
bread — *pain*
butter — *beurre*
eggs — *oeufs*
noodles — *mines*
rice — *riz*
glass — *verre*
plate — *assiette*
cup — *tasse*
spoon — *cuiller*
knife — *couteau*
fork — *fourchette*
napkin — *serviette*
bill — *note, addition*
special — *spécial*
vegetarian — *végétarien*

# Getting There

## AIR
The choices are quite simple – or limited.

### From Europe
There are only two services – one from Paris three times a week with Air France or Air Madagascar, to Madagascar and the Comoros (via Marseilles, Jeddah, Djibouti and Nairobi); the other, once a week from Moscow (via Aden) with Aeroflot.

### From USA
There are no direct services from the USA. You must fly from Paris or Nairobi. The alternative is to get to Singapore and fly into the Indian Ocean islands of Mauritius or Réunion. From each it is a relatively short and inexpensive hop to Madagascar or the Comoros.

### From Australia & NZ
The route via Singapore and Réunion/ Mauritius (as explained for the USA) seems most logical. Also worth considering is a Qantas flight to Zimbabwe, taking a connecting flight to Kenya and then flying from Nairobi.

### From Africa
Nairobi is the closest departure point for either the Comoros or Madagascar. Also South African Airways has a weekly flight from Johannesburg to Moroni in Comoros via Lilongwe (Malawi).

There are regular direct services from Mauritius and Réunion (but not Seychelles) to the Comoros and Madagascar.

## BOAT
There are some yachts, mostly from South Africa, which sail to the Comoros. But the objective is the sailing, not the ports of call. There are a few cargo vessels plying the route between Madagascar, the Comoros and Africa or France, but nothing that will take passengers, unless maybe you hang about the docks at Mombasa or Marseilles for a month or two.

MADAGASCAR

# Facts about the Country

It has become cliché to describe a country as 'unique' or 'a land of contrasts'. But so distinctive is Madagascar from its neighbouring islands, the African mainland and indeed anywhere else, that such terms are hard to avoid.

Most of the animals and plants on Madagascar are found nowhere else in the world. The country has been called a 'living museum'. Even the waters off its coasts are home to such living fossils as the coelacanth – a deep sea fish, long presumed extinct – which partially bridges the gap between fish and land animals.

The people, united by a common language and culture, are as racially diverse as in any other country you might imagine, despite a history which extends back only 1500 years. The landscape ranges from lush, tropical rainforest to mountain heathland and arid, thorny scrub. Even the rocks and soil are sufficiently distinctive as to have given geology a whole new term – *lavaka*. This is the Malagasy word for 'holes', and refers to the gaping sores which, as a consequence of erosion, now cover much of the Madagascan landscape.

Perhaps the greatest attraction of this island is that it has remained relatively untarnished by the trappings of tourism. It is not hard to find villages off the beaten track where few, if any, white faces have been seen in living memory. As they wander down the street white visitors to the country will soon become accustomed to hearing cries of *vazaha*, the name used for all white foreigners.

In many parts of Madagascar tourists are still regarded as a curiosity, though all are likely to be treated to traditional Malagasy hospitality. One reason for the few tourists is the small scale, or limited availability, of all services that are necessary to support them. This means everything from tourist organisations and hotels to reasonable roads.

This is slowly changing. The country can now cater for everyone from the luxury tourist who wants to visit the tropical beaches of Nosy Be or stroke the pampered lemurs of Fort Dauphin, to those who have time to experience all the potholes of Madagascar's national road network and discover this unique country for themselves.

Needless to say, this guide concentrates on the bumpy side.

## HISTORY

Despite its proximity to the African mainland, Madagascar apparently remained uninhabited until around 1500 years ago. Even then the first settlers had their origins not on the nearby continent of Africa, but on the distant shores of Indonesia or Malaysia, over 6000 km away.

How these first settlers reached their new home is not clear, although the distribution of Indonesian-style sailing boats along the northern shores of the Indian Ocean suggest the first settlers took a round-about route rather than making the mammoth journey directly. These boats were coastal vessels not ocean-going craft so they may have skirted around the Indian Ocean, possibly trading and settling along the shores of India, Saudi Arabia and Africa before finding Madagascar.

On the other hand the Afro-Asian nature of Malagasy culture, as well as other information now being pieced together by anthropologists, ethnographers and the like, suggest that these Indonesians may well have colonised Madagascar after migrating in a single voyage by way of the coast of East Africa.

The population evolved into 18 tribes (or separate ethnic groups, as some prefer to call them). Asian features are predominant in what became the ruling group of the island, the Merina of the central highlands, as well as in the neighbouring Betsileo tribe. The main coastal tribes, the Sakalava of the west coast and the Betsimisaraka of the central east coast, around Tamatave, are more African in origin.

### European Discovery

The first Europeans, in the form of a Portuguese fleet under the command of Diego Dias, reached the island in 1500. Following this 'discovery', the name of St Lawrence Island was briefly adopted.

The origins of the word Madagascar are still unclear. The existence of the island had been reported by Marco Polo and was known to Arab cartographers long before the Europeans added it to their map. It has been suggested that the name could be a corruption of anything from Mogadishu (a region with which it may have been confused), to the names of various tribes in Madagascar, perhaps with an Arabic suffix.

Whatever its origins, the name Madagascar soon became widely accepted. The centuries which followed its discovery by Europeans saw a number of attempts by the Portuguese, Dutch and British to establish permanent bases on the island. Some of the most successful attempts, however, were by distinctly nongovernmental organisations.

For several decades, from the end of the 17th century onwards, bands of pirates had their main Indian Ocean bases in Madagascar (especially on and around Ile Ste Marie) and made a significant genetic, as well as financial, contribution to the local communities. Trade in slaves and arms also allowed the development of Malagasy kingdoms.

It was the son of an English pirate and a Malagasy woman who was largely responsible for uniting the indigenous tribes of the east coast during the first half of the 18th century. (See the Tamatave section.) This was one of three attempts at empire building recorded in Malagasy history. It was to be followed by the first, and only, attempt to unify the entire country, prior to the French adding Madagascar to their collection of colonies in 1896.

### Merina Rule

In the 1790s, the Merina were unified under King Andrianampoinimerina (that's the shortened version of his name!) and emerged as the dominant tribe. After 1810 his son, Radama I, extended the Merina kingdom and developed relationships with various European powers. Britain signed treaties with Radama I, in 1817 and 1820, recognising Madagascar as an independent state.

British influence and aid was strong well into the 19th century, during which time the Merina court was converted to Christianity. Missions of various denominations, most notably the London Missionary Society, arrived to spread the word. Schools were started and the language

King Adrianampoinimerina

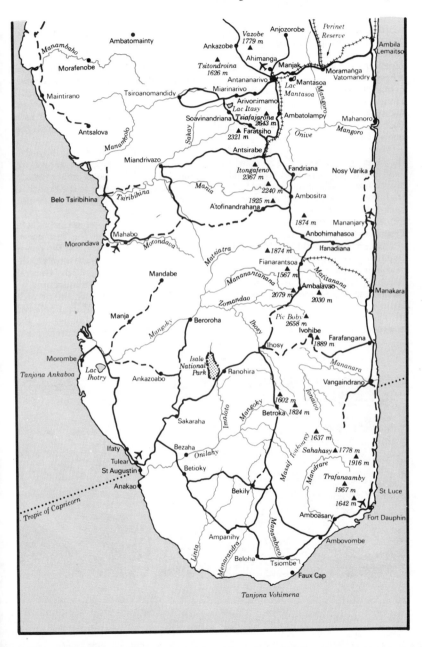

written down. (Most words in the Malagasy language relating to anything educational or literary have an English base. Those to do with food and drink have a French base.)

In 1828, Radama's successor, Ranavalona I (one of his wives), declared the Christian faith illegal. Those missionaries and their flock who did not leave were put to death during a mini reign of terror.

When King Radama II came to the throne in 1862, however, he reversed the dead queen's pagan policies, reopened the kingdom to outsiders and granted foreign trading concessions. The Europeans were back in favour, only this time the influence was weighted on the side of the French and Catholicism.

This caused a rift within the Merina elite. Radama II was murdered after less than a year in power and replaced by his widow Rasoherina. She lasted five years until Ranavalona II was crowned and after the latter's death, in 1883, came Ranavalona III. Throughout this succession of queens, however, the actual power was held by the

prime minister, Rainilaiarivony, who married all three in turn!

Meanwhile British-French rivalry continued on the religious front. The Merina rulers sided with the British despite the fact that, on the political and strategic fronts, the British became less and less interested in Madagascar as a colony, especially after the opening of the Suez Canal in 1869.

In 1890 France and Britain signed a treaty over their respective spheres of influence, which stated that Britain would leave Madagascar to the French in return for French recognition of British control of Zanzibar.

In 1894 the French, whose stronghold was Tamatave port on the east coast, demanded the capitulation of the queen and her government. When it wasn't forthcoming, the French Army under General Duchesne, marched on Antananarivo.

The French didn't launch their attack from Tamatave, as the Merina believed they would, but from Majunga on the opposite coast. When they marched into

A royal, jewel-encrusted Merina belt

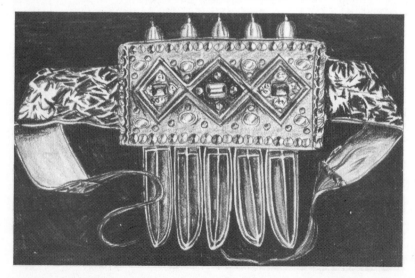

the capital on 30 September 1895, 11,000 men had died of diseases along the way. Although only 4000 soldiers were fit enough to fight, they were able to overcome the Merina defences which had been equally decimated by sickness and starvation. Ironically, what remained of the Merina defences was in the charge of a former British artillery officer, Major John Graves.

## French Rule

Madagascar was declared a French colony in 1896. The French administration began under General Joseph Galliéni, the first governor-general, who abolished slavery on the island. French became the official language as Galliéni tried to destroy the power of the Merina aristocracy by suppressing the Malagasy language and all British influence. In 1897 he managed to abolish the monarchy by exiling Queen Ranavalona III.

Not surprisingly, several nationalist movements evolved among the Merina and Betsileo, resulting in various strikes and demonstrations. (The most revered leader was a Betsileo, Jean Ralaimongo.) The French, however, pushed ahead with transport, construction, education, economic and other developments.

During WW II, the French in Madagascar came under the authority of the Vichy Government of Marshal Pétain. The British captured Diego Suarez (Antseranana), to prevent the Japanese using it as a base. Antananarivo and the other major towns were also captured. These were handed back to the Free French of General de Gaulle in 1943.

Postwar Madagascar saw a nationalist backlash. As many as 80,000 were said to have been killed in a massive uprising in March 1947. When the revolt was eventually put down, its leaders, Joseph Raseta and Joseph Ravoahangy, were exiled.

Political parties were formed in Madagascar in the 1950s, the most notable being the Parti Social Démocrate (PSD – pronounced 'pish dee') of the French National Assembly member, Philibert Tsiranana.

When General de Gaulle returned to power in France in 1958, the Malagasy voted in a referendum to become an autonomous republic within the French 'Community' of overseas nations. Tsiranana was elected the first president in 1960, when Madagascar made the peaceful transition to independence.

## Independence

Madagascar remained very much under French control and influence during the early years of Tsiranana's 12 years in power. Tsiranana was a *côtier* (from the coastal people) and referred to the French as the '19th tribe'. The *colons*, as the French were known, still ran the shop. Although the Merina were the most 'gallicised' of the Malagasy tribes, they were also the main opposition to the French, and their republicanism leaned towards the Soviet camp.

Tsiranana became more and more unpopular as the Malagasy economy went down the tube. He made matters worse by introducing close links with South Africa. In 1970, he had to start importing rice for the first time. Until then, the country had been a major exporter of rice.

Although about 85% of the country's industry was in French hands, France did not interfere when, in September 1972, after massive antigovernment demonstrations Tsiranana resigned and handed over power to his army commander, General Gabriel Ramantsoa.

Ramantsoa turned Madagascar towards the eastern bloc and other communist countries such as China. However in February 1975, after a few coup attempts, the general decided to relinquish the hot seat to Colonel Richard Ratsimandrava.

Ratsimandrava, a Merina, was assassinated in his car within a week of coming to office. The Merina blamed the murder on rebels of a dissident paramilitary group made up of tribes from the coastal region.

Later that year, the foreign minister and navy commander, Didier Ratsiraka, took over the reins and he remains leader to this day.

In the meantime, production of the country's principal exports – vanilla, coffee, cloves and meat – had stagnated and the education system collapsed. There was little, if any, development taking place. The banks, insurance companies and other major businesses were nationalised without compensation and the French exodus continued, taking all technical skills with it. The French also closed the air base in Antananarivo and their large naval base at Diego Suarez.

Few things improved under Ratsiraka, who continued to reverse all of Tsiranana's pro-west policies, cut ties with France and side more with the communist nations in an 'all points' policy. He has a 'red book' of government policies and theories, just like Mao's. Lately, however, Ratsiraka has begun to improve relations with the west and free up the economy.

Now in his 50s, Ratsiraka heads and selects his Supreme Revolutionary Council, which is the main government body. Under Ratsiraka and the Council is the prime minister, a 20 member cabinet and the 135 member Popular National Assembly. The ruling party is AREMA (Advance Guard of the Malagasy Revolution). There are another six parties, all socialist, but they can't really be said to be in opposition.

In March 1989 Ratsiraka was elected to his third seven year term, sparking off a series of riots which left six dead and about 70 injured.

Although Ratsiraka is a military man, you can hardly call his regime a military dictatorship. The government tends to suffer from a lack of decisive action in its policies rather than from any disastrous mistakes caused by wild philosophies or strong-arm tactics. If anything, Madagascar is undergoverned.

## GEOGRAPHY

The island of Madagascar lies south of the

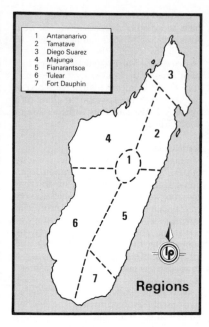

1 Antananarivo
2 Tamatave
3 Diego Suarez
4 Majunga
5 Fianarantsoa
6 Tulear
7 Fort Dauphin

Regions

equator, 400 km east of Mozambique in the Indian Ocean. Separated from the African coast by the Mozambique Channel, it is crossed by the Tropic of Capricorn near Tulear in the south.

Madagascar is 1571 km long, from north-east to south-west, and 571 km wide at its widest point. It sits amid a flotilla of smaller islands and coral atolls, including Nosy Be and Ile Ste Marie. With a surface area of nearly 590,000 square km, Madagascar is the fourth largest island in the world after Greenland, New Guinea and Borneo. It is well over twice the size of the UK.

The island can be divided geographically into three parallel north-south zones: the low plateaus and plains in the west, the high central plateau, and the narrow coastal strip in the east.

Madagascar can boast no really high mountains. Running almost the length of the island, the high plateau ranges in height from 750 metres to 1350 metres and forms the backbone of the country.

The three principal massifs of the high plateau are (from north to south) the Tsaratanana, the Ankaratra and the Andringitra. The volcanic peak of Tsaratanana, at 2876 metres, is the highest point on the island.

To the east of the high plateau's dividing line lie abrupt escarpments and stretches of tropical rainforest which extend towards a narrow coastal plain. An inland waterway, along the virtually straight eastern coast, is formed by an almost continuous chain of lagoons connected by the Pangalanes Canal.

To the west of the high plateau there is a well-marked, though less dramatic, escarpment. It drops away gently, in a succession of hills, through wide lowlands towards the coast. Once extensively forested (as was most of the island), the western zone is now principally a vast open plain supporting Madagascar's most intensive cultivation. It is basically savannah grasslands, with a few remaining stands of deciduous trees. There are some mangroves along the western coastline, which is bordered to the east by sand dunes and to the west by coral reefs and volcanic islands in the Mozambique Channel.

Flying over the country at the end of the dry season, you quickly see how this once green island gained the sobriquet 'Red Island'. Centuries of deforestation have exposed the red, lateritic soil covering much of the country to extensive erosion. Wide, red rivers writhe from their source in the mountains, across the western savannahs to deposit loads of precious topsoil in the oceans, tinting the waters far beyond the coast with a lurid red.

On the coast this topsoil covers relatively recent sedimentary rocks. Further inland, the crystalline bedrock, which extends across two-thirds of the island, was formed over two billion years ago – long before the formation of Madagascar itself.

A vast array of minerals and semiprecious stones can be found across the country in deposits generally too small to be mined intensively, but sufficient to supply the tourist industry demand for colourful solitaire boards and other souvenirs.

Unlike the neighbouring Mascarenes (Mauritius, Réunion and Rodrigues) and the Comoros, Madagascar is not part of a volcanic chain of islands. It owes its formation not to volcanic activity, but to the process of plate tectonics, or continental drift.

About 200 million years ago the earth's original, single landmass known as Pangaea began to break up into the two super-continents of Gondwana and Laurasia. Sometime between then and around 135 million years ago the huge southern land mass of Gondwana began drifting north, losing large sections on the way. Australia and Antarctica, then a single land mass, were left behind and sometime later the chunk that was to become India freed itself and shifted northwards to Asia.

Around 65 million years ago South America finally separated from Africa, heading north-west. Madagascar also broke free of Africa eventually taking the shape of the island now inhabited by the descendants of those people, plants and animals who chanced upon its shores.

## CLIMATE

Madagascar's climate varies greatly from place to place.

Rainfall ranges from more than 3600 mm a year on the east coast escarpments (where the dry season is only a few weeks) to less than 300 mm in the arid south-west region. The east is also subject to cyclones between December and March. Temperatures vary from a maximum of 44°C in coastal areas right down to –15°C in the more elevated parts of the high plateau, where it sometimes snows.

Most of the rest of the country is characterised by a distinct wet and dry season, the length of which depends on altitude and latitude. Generally, the wet season lasts, as on most islands in the Indian Ocean, from October to April, although in the south what little rain there is may fall in only a few months around the turn of the year.

With such variations in climate, it is difficult to nominate the best time to visit Madagascar. Antananarivo is warm and wet for half the year; and dry and cool for the other half. Ile Ste Marie may be more interesting than Nosy Be to visit, but you have a much better chance of good weather on Nosy Be.

## FLORA & FAUNA

Each climatic region in Madagascar is associated with a different type of vegetation – thorny scrub in the southwest, tropical rainforest along the east coast, heathland and moss forests on the central plateau and savannahs throughout much of the western lowlands.

In each of these habitats resides a distinct set of plants and animals, most of which are found nowhere else in the world.

Madagascar's peculiar assortment of plants and animals evolved from the few which happened to cross the 'border' as the island split from Africa in the great Gondwana supercontinent breakup. With nothing to threaten the survival of the early Madagascan creatures there was, in many instances, little need for evolutionary change.

Madagascar has no dangerous beasts: no lions stalk the plains in search of wildebeest or antelope, no tigers or panthers lurk in the forests and no vultures soar in the thermals above. In many ways the plant life is more vicious than the animal life or, as one writer put it, 'in Madagascar, the benign far outweighs the malign'.

Most of these plants and animals were in existence when humans reached the island about 1500 years ago and some had survived by the time the first Europeans arrived. However, when the landscape was radically changed for the agricultural

needs of human settlement, the animals were the first casualties.

Small clearings were made in the tropical eastern forests for crops, while large areas of the drier western forests were burned to provide pasture for cattle. These practices have continued to the present day, and each year, more than a quarter of Madagascar burns in fires lit to clear the land.

The resulting destruction of native forests has not only contributed to the demise of much of the remarkable wildlife, but now threatens to turn the whole country into an eroded wasteland. The government has introduced measures to stop the widespread burning, whether for rice planting or firewood, but these are not strictly enforced.

That major problem apart, the flora of Madagascar, like the fauna, has its own peculiarities. Best-known among the Malagasy plants is the fan shaped ravenala, also called the 'traveller's palm' because it contains a supply of pure water in the base of the leaf stalk. You'll find it on other islands throughout the Indian Ocean and in botanic gardens all over the world. The tree, a cousin of the banana tree, is incorporated on the country's seal and on the Air Madagascar logo.

Mini baobab

Lemur at Select Hotel, Antananarivo

There are more than six distinct species of baobab (the tree with the trunk that is huge in proportion to its branches), whereas only one species exists on the entire African mainland.

Another plant with claims to international recognition is the rosy periwinkle. For years, extracts from the plant have been helping to combat leukaemia.

A thousand varieties of orchids festoon the forests, many serviced by their own exclusive brand of moth, while the thorny forests of the arid south are home to the didierea, which are cactus-like plants with no close relatives anywhere in the world.

Lemurs, which can be found only in Madagascar and on a few nearby islands, including the Comoros, are the best-known native animal. They are prosimians, a rare primitive suborder of primates, and are related to the bushbabies of Africa and the lorises of Asia.

Almost 30 species of lemur are currently

recognised, although that may well change. As recently as 1987 the existence of a new species of bamboo-eating lemur, called *hapalemur aureus*, was confirmed. Other better-known species include miniature mouse lemurs, the smallest existing primates which hunt the forests for insects and fruit in the darkness; the larger, white lemurs, or *sifaka*, which leap from tree to tree; and the black and white, ring tailed lemurs which patrol the forest floor beneath.

This list also includes the remarkable 'ET'-like aye-aye, which has large ears, a pinched face and elongated skeletal fingers. It looks so alien that it is widely feared by many Malagasy. The largest lemur of all, weighing up to 20 kg, is the indri, whose melancholy cry, like that of a baby, haunts the eastern rainforests. (See the section on the Perinet Reserve.)

Alongside the lemurs live a host of other unique animals such as the small, insect-eating tenrecs, which resemble shrews or hedgehogs. There are 21 species of tenrec and many scientists regard them to be the most primitive of all mammals.

The fossa, which is the largest of Madagascar's four species of carnivore, looks more like a small member of the big cat family than the mongoose or civet to which it is more closely related.

Madagascar also has a variety of rodents, including a giant jumping rat; 26 species of bat, of which 13 are endemic; more than 140 species of frogs; several species of tortoise; and 257 reptiles, including chameleons, geckos and boa constrictors.

Larger animals once roamed the forests of Madagascar. These include the giant lemur, which hung around like an overgrown sloth in the trees; the giant tortoise; the pygmy hippo; and the giant, flightless ostrich-like *aepyornis*, which stood more than three metres tall and whose crushed eggshells still carpet remote areas of the south-west.

## ECONOMY

Madagascar is potentially a rich country. It's just that the economic management went haywire after the French managers pulled out and the population doubled.

The country's economy is still based on agriculture, which employs about 85% of the people and provides up to 80% of its export earnings.

Rice is the most important commodity and the indicator of all economic ills. Until 1971 the country exported rice. Now it has to import it to meet the population's needs. The government nationalised the rice farming industry in 1976, but the move failed terribly and the industry was denationalised in 1984.

It is said you can gauge the ebb and flow of Malagasy feelings by the rice supply situation. If there is none, feelings are at rock bottom, panic sets in and people are starving – even though there are plentiful supplies of other products.

Famine, however, is a reality especially in the arid, deep south which suffers long droughts. By the end of 1986, more than 40,000 people were said to have died in a famine in the south-east region. (So it appears the closer to Antananarivo you are, the better off you are likely to be.)

Exports of other crops such as vanilla, sisal, coffee and cloves have also suffered badly, as has the once mighty cattle industry.

The situation is similar to that of Argentina in many respects although, with accompanying erosion problems through deforestation, high population growth and famines, many see the country going the way of Ethiopia.

The government has, in the past few years, tried to attract foreign investment but for many potential firms the incentive conditions are seen as too strict and subject to excessive state control. Several big companies, however, have moved to explore and possibly exploit the country's rich mineral and oil resources.

Madagascar still leans on France, with whom it does most of its trade, while the USA is the country's second largest trading partner. Both countries provide a lot of aid to the Malagasy, while, to a lesser extent, Japan and West Germany are also generous. Assistance from the Soviet Union has principally been on the military front. Apart from the United Nations organisations, there are few voluntary aid bodies in the country. I was told this was because the Madagascar Government suspected such groups of harbouring spies.

## PEOPLE

Do *not* refer to the Malagasy as African. They don't like it.

The inhabitants of Madagascar are known in English as the Malagasy and, in French as the *Malgaches*. You can pronounce it 'malgash', but the most common is 'malagash'.

They are officially divided into 18 'tribes', on the basis of old kingdoms rather than ethnic characteristics.

For a country which shares one basic culture and language, the physical and racial diversity of the Malagasy is quite exceptional. While some groups, such as the Merina of the Antananarivo area, are predominantly Indonesian in appearance and others, such as the Vezo of the south-east coast, clearly have close affinities with black African tribes of East Africa, most people are a mixture both.

A few tribes, notably the Antaimoro (of the east coast, near Manakara), have closer connections with the Arab world. Their use of a form of Arabic script called *sorabe*, and their duty in preserving the Islamic traditions handed down to only a few using the *sorabe*, have given these tribes considerable influence over neighbouring Muslim communities.

The country's rapidly rising population of 11 million (it has doubled in the past 25 years) also includes many Europeans, mainly French of course, as well as Comorians, Indians and Chinese. Many of these are well integrated into the

Malagasy community and, on the face of things, racism seems absent.

Certainly the genuine warmth of the reception most white foreigners receive is sometimes surprising given the island's recent history. They should be careful, though, about wandering alone too far off the beaten track. Some young children will have been told strange tales of white folk or may never have seen them.

In contrast, the reaction to the Indo-Pakistani community, whose members own many of the shops around the coast and most of the jewellery stores on the high plateau, is not so warm. Early in 1987, riots against the Indo-Pakistani community forced many to leave for Réunion or further afield.

Such outbreaks are rare, but if you spend long enough in the country you become aware of an undertone of unease or inequality between the more educated Malagasy of the high plateau and the *côtiers* of the coastal regions. Even within Merina society itself, a subtle colour-orientated discrimination can be found.

This, however, rarely becomes apparent and many travellers more experienced than I have described the Malagasy as some of the most free and easy, friendly folk around. Providing their traditions are treated with respect, their hospitality can be hard to match.

Appreciating those traditions, however, depends on understanding the Malagasy idea of time, and a few other concepts the logic of which we take for granted. The social structure and politics, along with the Malagasy (particularly Merina) architecture, for example, was described by one expat as 'Byzantine. The European mind never quite gets to grip with it', he said. 'Your understanding and their acceptance of it only gets to a certain point.'

## ARTS & CULTURE
### Music

Most contemporary and traditional Malagasy music is based around various dance rhythms: the *salegy* of the

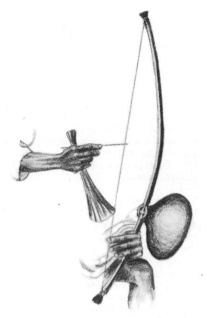

Cordophone

Sakalava tribe; the African *watsa watsa*; the *tsapika* from Fort Dauphin, Tulear and the south; the *basese* from the north and Diego Suarez; the *sigaoma*, similar to black South African popular music; and the Creole *sega* of Mauritius, Réunion and Seychelles.

The basic traditional instruments used are the flute, whistle and *valiha*, a unique and distinctly Malagasy instrument on which the strings are strung around a tubular wooden sounding box. The cordophone, which uses a calabash resonator, is popular and guitars are used in all forms including the *kabosy*, a small Malagasy ukelele-type guitar. Accordions acknowledge the French influence and there's a variety of percussion instruments.

Madagascar boasts many good folk and pop musicians. The best known of the contemporary Malagasy groups are Mahaleo. Other top sounds are Rossy and Les Smockers. The traditional experts are

Rakotozafy for the valiha and Rakotofra for the flute. Each region has its own favourites.

The local record company is Discomad and several shops sell records. Cassettes are less popular. If you return home without any records or want to hear Malagasy music before you leave, Globe Style Records, 48-50 Steele Rd, London NW10 7AZ, UK, has released two recent albums of traditional and contemporary music under the titles *Madagaskirara 1 & 2*. Ocora Records also issues a series of Malagasy music.

### Traditional Dances

You could imagine yourself up among the Andean Indians or peasants when you see Malagasy dancing and hear the music. The formation folk dances I saw all seemed to tell a story. Women threw down scarves and the men picked them up, then the men threw down their hats and the women picked them up.

One of the best places to see Malagasy dancing is at the Rova (King Andrianampoinimerina's palace) in Ambohimanga, about 25 km north of Antananarivo. Otherwise, call Madagasçar Airtours at the Hilton Hotel Arcade to see where there are tourist shows.

### Cinema

Madagascar doesn't really have a film industry but in 1988 Raymond Rajaonarivelo, a Malagasy director who studied cinema in France, made the feature-length *Tabataba* on the south-east coast of the island.

The movie is set in a small village called Maromena, near Manakara, during the bloody 1947 rebellion against French rule. *Tabataba* featured in several film festivals throughout the world including London, Cannes and Sydney. *Tabataba* means 'the spreading of rumours'.

### RELIGION

During the 19th century Madagascar witnessed the comings and goings of missionaries from many denominations who divided the country between them. Protestantism, of the form espoused by the London Missionary Society, was the first variety of Christianity to gain a major foothold, but as French influence increased, so did the popularity of Catholicism. Both are now equally widespread. There are also many Muslim communities especially in the villages of the north.

### Traditional Beliefs

Beyond the major cities and accessible towns neither western religions nor Islam hold much sway. Traditional beliefs and values are far more important. The ancestors, or *razana*, have an all-pervasive influence on everyday life, manifested in a complex system of taboos, or *fady*, and burial rites.

Care must be taken to avoid infringing on local taboos. It may, for instance, be fady to whistle on a particular stretch of beach near one village or to walk near a sacred tree in another. It is fady to eat pork in one village, while there are hundreds of pigs in the neighbouring one. There are thousands of these superstitions. They have a powerful influence especially over the country people, and are not to be taken lightly.

Because it's not always possible to anticipate the fady that applies to any specific place there's not very much the traveller can do to take precautions so as not to offend. Just be very careful and always seek permission before visiting tombs or burial sites.

Normal 'western' behaviour and habits do not appear to upset the townsfolk, which is no surprise after more than 60 years of French rule, and unless you stay with Malagasy people for a lengthy period, you're unlikely to be affected by fady in urban areas.

Elaborate rituals such as the *famadihana*, or 'turning of the dead', practised on the high plateau, and the decoration of memorial sites with symbolic wooden sculptures common in the south and west, are particularly distinctive features of Malagasy life.

The famadihana (second burial) is a Merina custom, although it has been adopted by some other tribes. Every few years when they can afford it, feel it necessary, or want to bury someone in the family tomb who died away from home, a family will throw a party in honour of its ancestors – and invite them to it.

The bodies are exhumed from their tombs, sometimes washed and rewrapped in new shrouds, hugged and talked to or sung to by their descendants, and then returned to their resting places, often accompanied by gifts.

These occasions are more like weddings or Irish wakes than a ghoulish funeral and are certainly not sombre occasions. Visitors may well be asked to honour the family and the razana with their presence, and the fady of important white strangers is also positive. The chances of coming across a famadihana are very remote: they are certainly not advertised in or around Antananarivo.

To see such ceremonies as morbid is to miss the point. The Merina hold their dead dear but not departed. Their ancestors, the razana, are still part of the family and play a greater part in it than they probably did when they were alive. They are at the centre of much of the fady. They are placated, consulted for advice and asked to bestow good fortune.

Even Christian ministers or priests have been known to attend a famadihana, as the families concerned are frequently also practising Christians.

The ritual is becoming more rare these days, however, because of the enormous cost. Many families can't afford to employ a band, an *ombiasy* or holy man, feed scores of guests for a day or two, and sacrifice *zebus* (oxen), all of which are necessary to the famadihana.

Other aspects of Malagasy culture derive from other continents. Belief in *vintana*, or destiny, has its roots in Islamic cosmology, while the religious significance and status of cattle is clearly linked to an African way of life. Huge herds of zebu are kept by the Antandroy and Mahafaly tribes of the arid south, as well as by some of the Sakalava in the west. The total number of zebu in Madagascar has only recently been overtaken by that of humans.

## HOLIDAYS & FESTIVALS
Most of Madagascar's holidays are religious ones.

January
*New Year's Day*
March
*National Day* (29th)
April
*Easter Monday*
May
*Labour Day* (1st)
*Ascension Day* (40th day after Easter)
June
*National Day* (26th)
August
*Assumption* (15th)
November
*All Saints' Day* (1st)
December
*Christmas* (25th)
*Republic Day* (30th)

Festivals are also held for circumcision ceremonies in some tribes between June and September, the famadihana rituals take place between June and October, and the rice harvest is celebrated in February in many areas.

## LANGUAGE
If you haven't already noticed, Malagasy words and names are long. In some cases, they make Welsh words look like hip jargon by comparison.

People's surnames are a mouthful. Most have got more 'rams' in them than a New Zealand sheep farm. I ended up calling everybody by their first names, which are usually biblical ones. Often they will invite you to do so; they're obviously used to tongue-tied foreigners.

English will not get you very far in Madagascar. Besides by a few tour guides, hotel receptionists and a small, but increasing number of students, it is rarely spoken. Having said that, if one admits to speaking English, it is not hard to find folk who are only too willing to try out a few words they picked up at school or elsewhere.

Malagasy and French are the two official languages in Madagascar. French is used in business and for some administrative purposes. It is essential if one is to get by in the capital or in other towns, whether dealing with officials, shop owners or hotel staff. In rural areas, you will find only a few people speak French. More than likely, they worked for or with the *colons* at some time.

Stall holders, even at the main market in Antananarivo, know only enough French to be able to sell their produce. Beyond the major towns a little of the local language can go a long way.

It is not difficult to learn enough Malagasy to communicate with people, especially since there is comparatively little regional variation. It certainly makes travel much more fun – for the Malagasy, if not for you.

Malagasy belongs to the Malayo-Polynesian family of languages but just as Malagasy culture has absorbed aspects of other cultures from around the globe, so too the language has adopted, and adapted, a number of words from Arabic, French and English, to name a few.

French words for the time of day are widely used, if somewhat loosely interpreted. Many words associated with teaching or religion are clearly English in origin, while the Arabic-sounding *salama* is a common greeting on the north-west coast.

For a language which is supposed to have been written down phonetically by the early missionaries, written Malagasy bears remarkably little resemblance to the spoken language. Syllables seem to evaporate when words are uttered and

vowels are rarely pronounced as an English speaker would anticipate.

The letter 'o' for instance, is usually long, while the last syllable is usually silent. Thus *veloma*, which means 'goodbye', sounds more like 'veloom' than 'vel-o-ma'; and *salama* comes out as 'salam'.

For this reason, the dictionaries and textbooks available in Antananarivo are slightly less useful than you might expect, but it is generally worth investing in at least one. (See the Books section in the Facts for the Visitor chapter.)

There are 21 letters in the Malagasy alphabet. The letters c, q, u, w and x do not exist. With words borrowed from English, French or other languages, the c is replaced by an s or k, the q by a k, and the x by ks.

Here's one tip I was given about attempting to pronounce Malagasy names: 'swallow as many syllables as you can and drop the last one'.

Here are some words to practise on:

## Useful Words

| | |
|---|---|
| I | *aho* ('a-hoo') |
| yes | *eny* or *eka* |
| no | *tsia* |
| thank you | *misaotra* |
| excuse me/please | *azafady* |
| good | *tsara* |
| bad | *ratsy* |
| good day (any time) | *salama* |
| how do you do, sir/madam | *manao ahoana, tompoko* ('toop-k') |
| very well, thank you | *tsara dia tsara fa misaotra* |
| welcome | *tonga soa* |
| goodbye | *veloma* |
| come in | *midira* |
| I'm in a hurry | *maika aho* |
| I'm hungry | *noana aho* |
| I'm sleepy | *matoritory aho* |
| I'm hot | *mafana aho* |
| I know | *haiko* |
| It's cold | *mangatsiaka izy izany* |

| | | | |
|---|---|---|---|
| OK, alright | *ekena* | lake | *farihy* |
| today | *androany* | island | *nosy* |
| time | *fotoana* | street | *lalana* |
| tomorrow | *rahampitso* | embassy | *ambasady* |
| yesterday | *omaly* | bridge | *tetezana* |
| easy | *mora* | beach | *morona* |
| father | *ray* ('ra-ee') | sea | *ranomasina* |
| mother | *reny* | waterfall | *riana* |
| friend | *sakaiza* | market | *tsena* |
| kind | *tsara fanahy* | tomb | *fasana* |
| | | forest | *ala* |

## Buying

| | | | |
|---|---|---|---|
| | | chief | *lehibe* |
| how much | *ohatrinona* ('h-wa-treeno') | guide | *mpitarika* |
| to buy | *mividy* | map | *sarin tany* |
| change (money) | *manakalo* | danger | *loza* |
| too expensive | *lafo loatra* | help | *fanampiana* |
| very cheap | *tena mora be* | swim | *milomano* |
| stamp | *tambra* | deep | *lalina* |
| | | driver | *mpamily* |
| | | entry | *fidirana* |

## Travel Terms

| | | | |
|---|---|---|---|
| | | exit | *fivoahana* |
| traveller | *mpandeha* ('pan-day-a') | lost | *very* |
| | | bandit, pirate | *jiolahy* |
| walk | *mandeha* | people | *olona* |
| name | *anarana* | | |
| right | *havanana* | | |

## Accommodation

| | | | |
|---|---|---|---|
| left | *havia* | tariff | *tarify* |
| next to | *akaiky* | room | *efitra* |
| be quick | *fiangana ianao* ('fine-gana-ha-an-ow') | kitchen | *lakozia* |
| | | bed | *fandriana* |
| slow | *votsa* | accommodation | *zavatra ilaina* |
| where? | *aiza* | breakfast | *sakafo maraina* |
| show me | *atoroy ahy* | lunch | *sakafo antoandro* |
| food | *hanina* | more | *mihoatra* |
| I feel sick | *marary ny am bava foko* | dirty | *maloto* ('mal-oo-too') |
| beautiful (re: people) | *tsara tarehy* | rubbish, stupid | *fako* |
| | | cloth, linen | *lamba* |
| beautiful (re: scenery) | *mahafinaritra* | | |
| interesting | *mahasondriana* | | |
| big | *be* | | |
| little | *kely* | | |
| breakdown | *mandrodana* | | |
| station | *gara* | | |

In most cases I have used the traditional names for the major towns in Madagascar rather than the new Malagasy ones. This is because the old names are still commonly and officially used, are less confusing, easier to pronounce and save space!

# Facts for the Visitor

## VISAS

Every visitor to Madagascar needs a visa. They are issued by Malagasy embassies and consulates for a maximum stay of 30 days. Unlike Seychelles, the Comoros or Mauritius, visas are *not* issued at the airport on entry to Madagascar; as some travellers discovered during a very brief stay.

It doesn't matter which Madagascar consulate or embassy issues the visa. The routine is the same – repetitive but usually straightforward. You have to fill in four identical forms and supply four passport photos. It takes two to three days.

Visas cost A$15 in Australia, £20 in the UK, FFr 70 in Réunion, KSh 170 in Kenya, CFr 2500 in the Comoros and only MRs 20 in Mauritius.

If you have to apply by post, take precautions to make sure your passport and visa are safely returned. I suspect that the fortunes of the less stable Malagasy diplomatic missions fluctuate wildly.

The steadfast consulate in Sydney, under consul general Frederic Barnes, recommends you enclose a prepaid self-addressed certified mail envelope with your application.

Malagasy diplomatic address overseas are:

Australia
    Consulate General, 4th Floor, 92 Pitt Street, Sydney, NSW 2000 (tel 221 3007)
UK
    Consulate, 69-70 Mark Lane, London, EC3R 7JA (tel 480 6644,7961) or through embassy in France
USA
    Embassy, 2374 Massachusetts Ave NW, Washington DC 20008 (tel 265 5525)
Canada
    Permanent Representative, Room 903, 1000 West Sherbrooke St, Montreal (tel 285 8317/8)

France
    Embassy, 4 Ave Raphael, 75016 Paris (tel 504 6211)
    1 Blvd Suchet, 75016 Paris (tel 503 3247)
Germany (West)
    Embassy, Rolandstrasse 48, Bad Godesberg, 5300 Bonn (tel 33 1057/8)
Mauritius
    Embassy, Queen Mary Ave, Floreal (tel 6 50 16/7)
Réunion
    Consulate, 51 Rue Juliette Dodu, St Denis (tel 21 66 52)
Kenya
    Consulate, Air Madagascar office, Hilton Hotel Arcade, Nairobi (tel 25286, 26494)


In most countries, the Malagasy consulate is attached to the Air Madagascar office. The consulate in the Comoros is opposite the new market in Moroni, Grande Comore. There are also embassies in Tanzania (Dar es Salaam), Algeria (Algiers), Japan (Tokyo), Italy (Rome), Belgium (Brussels), USSR (Moscow) and China (Beijing).

### Visa Extensions

These can be easy or difficult to get in Madagascar, depending on when, where and to whom you apply. Extensions up to a maximum of two months are granted and can be obtained from either the Ministry of the Interior, Anosy, Antananarivo (the building shaped and known as the 'elephant's foot' near the Hilton Hotel); or the commissariat of the National Police (*Polisy Nasionaly*) in each provincial capital – Tulear (Toliara), Diego Suarez (Antseranana), Fianarantsoa, Tamatave (Toamasina) and Majunga (Mahajanga).

It is possible to get the paperwork done at police headquarters within one day if you can persuade them to hurry (eg 'We're catching a flight to Ile Ste Marie in the morning'). At the Ministry of the Interior, it can take more than a week. And

Top: Carnivorous pitcher plant (DC)
Left: Lemurs at Nosy Komba (RW)
Right: Alley of baobabs, north of Morondava (DC)

Top: Malagasy tomb on the high plateau (DC)
Bottom: Destruction of eastern rainforest (DC)

remember, you cannot change money at the bank if you have no passport.

Applications for extensions have to be accompanied by two forms, two passport photos, your *devise* (currency declaration form), a letter in French explaining why you want to stay longer, FMg 5000 for the extension fee, FMg 200 for a treasury stamp and your passport. It has to be taken to the treasury for stamping. You may also be asked to show airline tickets and proof of funds. After sending it upstairs for approval, the passport officer will then scribble at length on your passport and stamp it 10 times.

A second extension after three months is very difficult to get and will require a good reason for wanting to stay (like the amount of money you have to spend and who you know).

## CUSTOMS

Officially, you are permitted to bring in 500 cigarettes or 25 cigars, one bottle of alcoholic drink, two cameras, one cine-camera, 10 rolls of film and one typewriter. Watch out if you're carrying two typewriters!

## MONEY

Because of the country's economic ills, money – or rather the lack of it – and all its evils is playing a larger role in Malagasy life. As rules and regulations governing its control increase, so does the black market to combat them.

## Currency

In July 1987, the Malagasy franc (FMg) was considerably devalued, and its value tied to that of the American dollar. The best currencies to carry, for ease of exchange and better black market rates, are American dollars, French francs, UK pounds or Deutschmarks. You will find it very difficult, if not impossible, to change Australian, New Zealand or Canadian dollars. The Swiss franc, Japanese yen and Italian lire are acceptable.

| | | |
|---|---|---|
| US$ 1 | = | FMg 1580 |
| FFr 1 | = | FMg 250 |
| UK£1 | = | FMg 2630 |
| DM 1 | = | FMg 820 |

The Malagasy franc = 100 centimes.
Malagasy bank notes are in denominations of 10,000, 5000, 1000 and 500, and coins range from 100 downwards, but not without some confusion.

The silver FMg 100 coin is marked 20 Ariary and the FMg 50 is marked 10 Ariary. One Ariary is worth FMg 5. (Ariary are also referred to, and are the same as, *piastre, drala* and *parata*.) The copper FMg 20 and FMg 10 coins are just what they say, as are the little silver FMg 1 and FMg 2 pieces.

Don't get stuck with large-denomination notes when travelling out of the main towns and cities. The small Malagasy hotels and roadside stalls probably won't be able to change them.

There are strict currency controls on entering and leaving the country. As a visitor you can bring in as much foreign currency as you wish, but on arrival you have to declare all money – down to your last cent. This is recorded on a currency declaration form, or *devise*, which you must present to the bank for stamping when you exchange money. Don't lose it.

This form must be submitted and checked on departure. The amount you exchanged and spent and the amount you have left (and must declare again) should equal the amount you brought in. If not, there may be trouble. You are not allowed to take any Malagasy bank notes out of the country and you cannot exchange them back into foreign currency.

Of course many visitors get around these restrictions by not declaring all of their money on entry and exchanging it later on the black market for up to 30% more. The more you change, the bigger the rate. French francs are most sought after, then US dollars.

Keep in mind, however, that you can't change any excess back into foreign currency and that many things, including top hotels, airfares and 1st class travel, have to be paid in foreign currency anyway. Remember too that you must declare a sufficient amount to live on over the time you intend to stay. If you get caught changing money unofficially the penalties, at best, could be deportation and a heavy fine.

## Luxury Sales

Another way around the currency controls is to bring in and sell much in demand luxury items such as new or second-hand radios, watches, cameras and vehicle spare parts. Fashionable western clothes, including sports shoes and shoulder bags are also popular. There can be quite a tidy profit to be made. Réunion tourists often subsidise their Madagascar holidays with the mark-up on smuggled watches.

The people to approach concerning such transactions or unofficial money matters are the Indian and Pakistani traders. But be careful. Often they will approach you, but there have been instances where the would-be dealer has been a police informer. It's their way of getting money and keeping in with the authorities. It is best to ask another traveller who knows a good contact. Also beware of people who offer to forge your currency declaration form.

## Credit Cards

These are of limited use in Madagascar

unless you want to stay at the Hilton and travel with a tour company. Most restaurants and hotels do not accept them. Cash advances are not obtainable from any bank with any card. The American Express representative for card holders and those who are deprived of their travellers' cheques is at Madagascar Airtours (tel 241 92), Hilton Hotel Arcade, Anosy, Antananarivo. They also have offices in Diego Suarez, Fianarantsoa, Nosy Be and Tulear.

### Banks

The main banks are the Bankin'ny Tantsaha Mpamokatra (BTM), the Banky Fampandrosoana ny Varotra (BFV) and the Bankin'ny Indostria (BNI). They are open Monday to Friday from 8 to 11 am and 2 to 4 pm. There is no bank on Ile Ste Marie. Exchange is relatively painless, but make sure you check the weekly rate if you're in a bank outside the capital. The telexed rate from the head office often contains errors.

There is a branch bank at the airport on the second level, open for international arrivals, but it is sometimes limited in the amount per passenger it can exchange. I was only allowed US$50.

### Emergencies

Getting extra money sent to Madagascar can mean a nightmare wait, while officials sort out bank transfers and currency controls.

### COSTS

Because of the devaluation of the Malagasy franc in 1987, tour operators and the major tourist hotels (those of three-star standard and above) have raised their prices considerably, to bring them into line with international-standard rates. They now require payment in 'acceptable' foreign currency only.

The smaller, cheaper hotels, which rely more on local custom, could not have justified such a high increase or rating, and they remain extremely cheap. You

can still find reasonable places to stay for under FMg 10,000 (about US$6) a night.

The same price hike applies to air travel, but not so much to food or road and rail transport. About FMg 8000 a day will cover meals. Local transport is very cheap too, although air and 1st class rail fares must be paid in foreign currency.

So, you can get by very comfortably in Madagascar on the equivalent of US$100 a week, excluding flights and long-distance fares.

### TIPPING

The French established the custom and the expats continue to tip at all restaurants. The Malagasy, however, won't spit in your face or kick up a fuss if you don't tip.

You will frequently be asked to play God by children begging in the centre of Antananarivo and some other cities. Keep a pocket of small change if you do not wish to feel heartless.

### TOURIST INFORMATION
#### Local Tourist Offices

The principal tour operator in the country is Madagascar Airtours, Hilton Hotel (BP 3874), Anosy, Antananarivo (tel 241 92). With the lack of any public tourist office, it is the best place for tourist information, and many of the staff speak good English.

Madagascar Airtours (usually abbreviated to Mad Airtours) offers various package tours around the island, usually based on a particular interest such as wildlife, trekking, minerals, art and culture or history. You'll stay in the best hotels, prearranged village accommodation or national forest camps. Day tours in and around Antananarivo are also arranged. Prices are high compared to doing it yourself, but reasonable compared to western tour companies.

Mad Airtours used to run Air Madagascar, before it was returned to government hands. They have agencies in Tulear, Fianarantsoa, Diego Suarez and Nosy

Be, and are the American Express representative in the country.

The other main agencies are Transcontinents, 10 Araben ny Fahaleovantena, Antananarivo (tel 223 98) and the Madagascar Tourist Bureau, Immeuble La Pergola, Antananarivo (tel 223 64). The latter is a private, non-government agency. Trans 7 and Tourisma are two more options. However, after the little help I was given, it is difficult to recommend any of these. Stick with Mad Airtours.

The government tourist office was under the central post office, but along with the airport counter, has since closed due to lack of funds – and tourists. If you require particular help with your travelling and spending, or have major problems, you can try writing to the Direction du Tourisme, BP 610, Antananarivo (tel 262 98). Their offices are on the same road as the entrance to the zoo. They have some brochures and maps. The provincial offices of the department are next to useless.

Overseas, Air Madagascar and the Madagascar consulates are two other sources of tourist literature. They are usually in the same office.

### Foreign Embassies & Consulates

The principal embassies and consulates in Antananarivo are:

France
   3 Rue Jean Jaurès (tel 204 09)
Germany (West)
   101 Rue Pasteur Rabeony (tel 328 02)

Holland

(tel 252 25)

UK

Immeuble Ny Havana, 67 Ha (BP 167) (tel 277 49, 273 70)

USA

14-16 Rue Rainitovo, Antsahavola, Ambohidahy (tel 205 96, 212 57)

In cases of emergency outside the capital, contact the French consulates in the provincial capitals – Fianarantsoa (Rue Verdun), Majunga (Rue Edouard VII), Tamatave (Rue de la Convention) and Diego Suarez (Rue Benyowski).

## GENERAL INFORMATION
### Post

The post offices are open Monday to Friday from 8 am to noon and 2 to 6 pm, and on Saturday mornings. At the central post office in Antananarivo, the 1st floor is open for telegrams, international calls and poste restante from Monday to Saturday between 7 am and 7 pm, and on Sundays and public holidays from 8 to 11 am.

The postal service is generally reliable. All my postcards and letters reached their overseas destinations, and letters I sent into the country later were delivered and answered within a reasonable time. Do not, however, send packages or anything valuable.

**Postal Rates** Postal rates are cheap, but be careful when buying Malagasy stamps. I was given seven to make up a FMg 245 fee for a letter. When I stuck them on, there was no room for the address! It's better to buy larger denomination stamps, even if it costs a few FMg more than it needs to. Of course, the lucky dip selection is great for philatelists!

Postcards cost FMg 125 to Europe, FMg 150 to the USA and FMg 200 to Australia or New Zealand. Light-weight letters cost between FMg 150 and FMg 300. There are no aerogrammes, but don't forget to indicate 'Air Mail' on postcards or envelopes, because surface mail takes forever.

### Telephones

The international telephone lines are good, but the internal ones are lousy. From Antananarivo you can phone Paris or Sydney most of the time, but you can rarely get through to Fort Dauphin or Tulear. The best way to get a message to another part of the country is by letter or word of mouth. It is just as bad phoning elsewhere in the country from the provinces. In Fort Dauphin, they say if the radio works, the telephone doesn't and vice versa.

A telephone call within Antananarivo is FMg 105 for unlimited time. From Antananarivo to Tulear it's FMg 1312 for three minutes. There are few public telephones.

Make international telephone calls from the central post office, a private phone or through one of the major hotels. You have to book, but you should get through within the hour. All overseas calls are routed via Paris or Rome.

A call to France is FMg 7050 for the first three minutes and FMg 2350 for each extra minute. To Australia it is FMg 12,205, then FMg 4095; West Germany and the UK are FMg 11,685, then FMg 3895; and the USA is FMg 16,395, then FMg 5465.

### Electricity

The electricity company does an excellent job considering the circumstances. The streets may be dark because they can't afford to do general maintenance and repair, but if you specifically report a fault with your street lamp, they'll come out and fix it. Blackouts are rare.

Voltage varies from 110 to 220 depending on the area. Two-pin round plugs are used.

### Time

Madagascar is three hours ahead of GMT, but the Malagasy concept of time varies from the European one imposed on it. It is circular, rather than progressive, and the Malagasy stand in the centre of the circle. The past is as important as the present or the future.

One writer likened their way of viewing life to the chameleons' ability to independently move its eyes, enabling it to look forward and backwards at the same time.

With the Malagasy, however, the present often misses out. Punctuality, deadlines or urgency are concepts that are just not recognised. If it can't be done today, it'll wait. If you arrange a meeting with a Malagasy, chances are they will be late. That's known as a *rendezvous malgache*. If the *taxi-brousse* (bush taxi) breaks down, they'll patiently wait hours or days for the next one, while you worry and fume.

## Business Hours

Government offices are open Monday to Friday from 8.30 am to 3.30 pm (but try not to arrange anything between noon and 2 pm). The shopping hours are from 8 am to noon and 2 to 6 pm, Monday to Friday. Most of the main shops are closed on Saturdays and Sundays.

Salons de thé are closed two hours for lunch. Restaurants are open lunch times and evenings until late.

Government offices close *by* and *after* a certain time, not on it. To be safe do not leave things to the last minute.

### Laundry

Most established hotels have a laundry service. Your clothes are scrubbed clean by hand, not washed by machine. In Antananarivo, on Araben ny Fahaleovantena next to the Neige Blanche salon de thé, there is the Net à Sec laundry for suits, etc.

## MEDIA

### Newspapers & Magazines

Newspaper and administrative paper in Madagascar has the feel and constitution of paper towel, and toilet paper is very closely related to cardboard.

There are two daily newspapers, published in French and Malagasy. The *Matin* (morning) comes out at noon and the *Midi* (noon) comes out in the morning! Both are government controlled and contain little national or world news. But the *Midi* is held to be the more informative and the better at getting round the restrictions – if you read between the lines. More open and substantial reading is provided by *La Croix* weekend newspaper.

### Radio & Television

For radio news, you can pick up the BBC World Service, but the reception is poor. Voice of America is better.

The State television service, Radio Télévision Malgache, as you might imagine, is in its infancy and not widely watched. Most people do not have TV sets. To its credit, it often shows soccer matches and good, if old, films. The station does not broadcast hours of government propaganda like some African stations and apologises when things go wrong during transmission.

DEMOCRATIC REPUBLIC OF MADAGASCAR

SANITARY CONTROL AT FRONTIERS

IMPORTAN T ADVICE

Keep this notice during you stay in Madagascar
if you are ill during this period, you should
show this notice to a Physian.

Every-who landing in Madagascar should observe a
anti malarial prophylaxy during the stay and
several weeks after.

## HEALTH

### Water

Jirama, the water and electricity company, does an amazing job of providing a good service under difficult conditions. It is praised frequently by expats. The water in Antananarivo and the provincial capitals is generally safe when it leaves the tap, but make sure it is before you drink it. You can buy *Eau Vive* bottled water for between FMg 600 and FMg 1100 in restaurants and for less in stores.

Water in Malagasy is *rano*. The sea is *ranomasina*, which means sacred water.

### Health Precautions

Malaria is a hazard in Madagascar and the local mosquitoes have developed a resistance to chloroquine. It is, however, still recommended to take this prophylactic as well as a course of either Maloprim or Proguanil.

The coastal regions are the most risky places. Fort Dauphin is one of the worst, if not *the* worst, area in the country. I found the mosquitoes murderous on Ile Ste Marie and in the forests at the Montagne d'Ambre National Park, but practically absent around Nosy Be and Diego Suarez.

If you're coming from Africa or other suspect parts of the globe, you will need to have had vaccinations for cholera and yellow fever.

Other diseases associated with African travel, like bilharzia and hepatitis, are also a threat in Madagascar. Hepatitis is spread through contaminated food or water, so watch where you eat and what you drink. The parasite which carries bilharzia is found in fresh water streams, lakes and often dams; so be careful where you swim. Beware of leeches in the forests, and walking about barefoot anywhere is inviting 'chigger' fleas to burrow into your feet and lay eggs.

### Hygiene

The golden age of toilet training seems to have missed Madagascar. Areas of open ground among towns and cities are, in many cases, treated as public conveniences. The Malagasy throw coyness and refinement to the wind when nature calls, so be extra careful if you're walking on the grass, especially in Antananarivo. Men, and occasionally women, urinate openly in the streets, or rather, on the side of streets. They are more discreet with defecation.

The same climate that produces lush tropical climates also promotes a prolific growth of skin fungi and bacteria. Keeping your skin cool and allowing air to circulate is essential. Choose cotton clothing rather than synthetics, and sandals rather than shoes.

In Fort Dauphin, one out of 10 Malagasy I saw had a bandage on their leg! Now it could be that these were sporting injuries, but it's more likely an indication of how quickly cuts and sores go from bad to worse in a tropical climate. Keep open wounds clean, dry and protected.

There is a risk of bed bugs and lice, especially in the poorer areas and rougher hotels. Use a sleeping sheet and maintain personal hygiene.

Having said all this, please don't get the impression that Madagascar is dirtier than any other Asian or African country – it's not.

### 'Mally Belly'

I found that European travellers are prone to a particular Madagascan fever which lays one flat for a couple of days, like a flu virus. It is by no means peculiar to Madagascar, it is rather a travellers' illness. In Madagascar, however, it could be caused by the climate: the high plateau is cold compared to the tropical heat of the coast, and this seems to encourage colds. It also could be simply a change in diet and routine, or maybe the actual food, drink, or a hundred other things. The chances are it's not malaria. Call it Mally Belly if it makes you feel any better! If it doesn't. . .

### Hospitals

The hospitals in Madagascar are poor by western standards and medical supplies and equipment are in short supply. The British Embassy recommends two doctors in Antananarivo: Dr Louis Razafinarivo, a US trained surgeon, at 15 Rue JJ Rabearivelo (tel 268 62); and Dr Michel Alliotte, a French GP, at 18 Làlana Jean Jaurés (tel 201 71).

The dentists the embassy recommends are: Jean Marc Chapuis or Guy Deramaix, at 13 Araben ny Fahaleovantena (tel 208 88); and Claude Peux, at 13 Làlana Maître Léon Réallon (tel 233 96).

You can also contact the US or French embassies or other diplomatic missions for advice and referrals. They will say that no surgery or treatment for serious problems should be undertaken in Madagascar when evacuation is possible.

That would be to Paris or Réunion in the first instance, or Nairobi if there is an earlier flight. Unfortunately, the Réunion medical air service does not have landing rights in Madagascar.

The three main hospitals in Madagascar are:

L'Hôpital Militaire d'Antananarivo (tel 403 41), which receives French Government support and some French doctors on national service. It has x-ray equipment and basic stocks of drugs and medicines.

Clinique des Soeurs Franciscaines (or Missionnaires de Marie) (tel 235 54), is run well by Franciscan nuns. It is clean and has x-ray equipment.

L'Hôpital Général de Befelatanana (tel 223 84) in Antananarivo is the free public hospital with much lower standards of care and hygiene.

The first two hospitals require payment in advance of treatment. I was quoted FMg 6000 per day.

There is no ambulance service outside of the capital and the hospitals or clinics in other cities are much worse off for staff, medicines and equipment. If you become seriously ill or suffer an accident outside of Antananarivo, call the nearest French consulate in the provincial centres. Bear in mind that telephone communications between Antananarivo and the provinces are often impossible and the roads impassable.

### DANGERS & ANNOYANCES

Sharks, currents, taxis-brousses (buses) and falling off bicycles (on Ile Ste Marie) are hazards. It's great to find a lovely isolated beach, but check with locals or other travellers before swimming in the sea. I should also warn you that most scuba diving outings offered in Madagascar are not done under any recognised safety procedures. If you are qualified, check the equipment first. As for road safety – cross your fingers!

If you see the notice *Alika Masiaka*, it means 'Beware of the Dog'!

## Security

Where other Indian Ocean countries have the odd coup or two every so often, Madagascar specialises in riots. Some are racial like the Majunga riots in 1977, when the large Comorian community was set upon. Hundreds were killed and the rest were airlifted back to Comoros.

Then there were the 'Kung Fu' riots in 1985 which left 31 dead. Kung Fu had become a craze after Bruce Lee films reached the country in the 1970s. They spawned many clubs with a predominantly right wing membership. When the president of Madagascar had the clubs outlawed, the Kung Fu brigades took to the street and targeted their anger against the bully boys of the presidential youth movement. The Government eventually set the tanks on the kicking and screaming martial arts followers.

**Police & Army** It's hard to tell which is which and what they do. I call both groups the '40 Shades of Green' because they wear a mix 'n' match variety of camouflage and khaki uniforms. The youths in green uniforms are doing their two years' compulsory national service.

The police and army may not be very effective, but at the same time they are not very bothersome or intrusive and are at least disciplined enough not to throw their weight around. Generally, civil liberties are allowed.

If you do get into trouble, it is better to call your embassy for help and advice, or the French consulate if you are in the provinces.

If you have any trouble with rip-off merchants, threaten to report them to the Direction du Tourisme or the Direction des Eaux et Forêts.

## Theft

The deteriorating economic situation has resulted in an increase in crime during recent years. Much of the latest aggression has been directed wrongly and foolishly at the Indo-Pakistani traders whom the Malagasy resent for their business control. They are the scapegoats for the system because they are the Malagasy's first and only contact with it. The French expatriate population has suffered to a lesser extent, but other white foreigners have never been a target except for petty crime.

Despite the unfortunate and uncharacteristic upsurge in theft and violence, Madagascar is still a much safer place than most of the African countries.

Antananarivo, not surprisingly, is the main problem area in the country. However diplomatic and relief agency workers I talked to said the city was a long way behind Nairobi for crime. Even so, they still warned visitors not to walk around Antananarivo's poorly lit streets at night and advised taking a taxi instead. The tourist authorities echoed this warning.

The recognised danger area in Antananarivo is the *Zoma*, which is the big weekly market in the Analakely district. Although Friday is the main market day there are permanent stalls in the area so care should be exercised at all times when browsing and shopping. The open market atmosphere is a breeding ground for bag and camera snatchers and skilful pickpockets.

The drastic drop in the number of zebu in Madagascar has given rise to gangs of cattle rustlers in the south-west of the country – particularly between Tulear and Fort Dauphin. The bandits are quite versatile and when pickings are lean in the zebu business they occasionally resort to highway robbery.

Cars-brousses are generally safe but it is advised you don't travel by car in remote areas at night, although the Ministry of Tourism says it knows of no visitor who has been robbed or injured by bandits. Check with local people and car-brousse or taxi-be drivers if you're venturing into or across a suspect area. If there is any danger *they* won't go, so take their lead.

## FILM & PHOTOGRAPHY

Bring an adequate supply of film with you, as it is expensive and not widely available in Madagascar. It is more expensive outside Antananarivo.

In the capital, the two main photographic stores are Opticam, next to Aeroflot on Làlana Ratsimilaho, near the GPO, and Express Photo, on the steps leading up to the GPO from the Ako Cinema. I would recommend the latter as the staff are friendly and helpful.

Kodak Gold costs about FMg 7500 for 36 exposures, developing any film costs around FMg 1000, and printing is FMg 350 for a nine by 12 cm print or FMg 450 for a 10 by 15 cm print. Therefore 36 small prints would cost about FMg 12,600. Printing and developing takes one to two days, so it is best to choose which prints you want from the negatives or contact sheet.

Express Photo does passport pics – four colour ones for FMg 1200 or six black & white for FMg 600. Handy to know if you're extending your visa.

Film and photographic equipment fetch good prices, if you get stuck for cash.

## ACCOMMODATION

### Hotels

The busiest time is during the holiday periods – around Easter, Christmas/New Year (15 December to 15 January) and August. Some hotels have a high season tariff, but there are always vacancies.

The Malagasy tourist authorities have a star and a ravenala (travellers' palm) rating system for food and hotel accommodation. They are not strictly applied, but a one star hotel or a one ravenala restaurant is probably better value than one without any stamp of approval. The top establishments have a four star and three ravenala rating.

When you sign into a hotel, you will be asked to fill in a registration form for police. Along with your name, passport number and other expected info, you are asked to provide the names and occupations of your mother and father! This is aimed at the Malagasy, but tourists have to do it too.

You'll have no problem finding a place to stay, of any standard, in Madagascar. There are three luxury hotels – the Hilton and the Colbert in Antananarivo, and the Holiday Inn at Nosy Be. Each provincial capital and Antananarivo has either a couple of new developments or some old 'colonial class' hotels, as well as several medium range hotels which are usually run by French expats.

I have estimated all hotel room and meal rates in Malagasy francs for the sake of continuity. The major tourist hotels, however, will want the bills paid in foreign currency and will probably quote you rates in French francs or US dollars.

These hotels include the three luxury ones just mentioned; the Hôtel de France, the Solimotel and Le Lac in Tana; the Hôtel de Thermes and Diamant in Antsirabe; Chez Papillon and the Sofia in Fianarantsoa: the Zahamotel in Ihosy; Le Neptune, the Joffre and Flamboyants in Tamatave; the Hôtel de France and the Zahamotel in Majunga; the Plaza and Capricorne in Tulear; Mora Mora Village and the Zahamotel at Ifaty; Le Dauphin/Galion, the Miramar and Libanona in Fort Dauphin; Les Cocotiers, Residence d'Ambatoloaka and Palm Beach on Nosy Be; and the Soanambo on Ile Ste Marie.

These hotels are much higher in price (usually set in French francs) because they rely on overseas businesspeople and tourists so they have to provide a reasonable standard of comfort, service and amenities. The difference between them and the more local hotels, however, is not all that great (except in money terms). In other words the ordinary traveller is well catered for.

Prices are more negotiable as you come down in standard. There are some good bargains in the lower medium and bottom range Indo-Pakistani and Malagasy hotels (called *hotelys*), which can be clean and well run. Most small towns and villages have one. If not, someone will usually give up a room or home for you. There are some real holes, but I've seen much worse in Asia. In any event, take a sleeping sheet if you are planning to slum it, plus a torch, a small padlock, toilet paper and mosquito coils or repellent.

## Camping

You can camp anywhere without restrictions, except in the national parks. Few people do, however, unless they're on a long trek, since it is not very safe. Two German travellers I met had their tent and belongings cleaned out on Nosy Be when they were away for the day.

## Military Messes

Another cheap alternative, if hotels are full or absent, are the military messes. They are run more like hostels than hotels, but are clean and relatively modern. There's one in each major town.

## A Reminder

If you go into a remote village or small town without a guide, consider the impact of your visit and all the responsibilities and implications it carries.

Before you will be accepted, you must first satisfy the villagers' curiosity and allay their fears. Seek out and introduce yourself to the local chief or mayor: *Iza no lehiben'ny tanana?* means 'who is the village chief?' You then say *Salama, tompoko* to greet him.

It's most likely that he will then offer food and a bed or house. Villagers often will not accept money as payment or thanks, preferring instead condensed milk, chocolate, cigarettes or something they can't buy from the village shop.

Make sure you have sufficient food to last your proposed stay. Don't expect them to feed you. They will, but it won't be much and they cannot afford to.

An excellent ice-melter, if not ice-breaker, is a letter of introduction, preferably in Malagasy and on official-looking notepaper, explaining who you are and in what you're interested. You could organise this through any friends you may have in one of the capital towns or through a consul or other official contact in your own country.

## FOOD

There's one dominant food in Malagasy cuisine – rice or *vary*. It doesn't accompany anything. Everything accompanies the rice. The average daily meal in Madagascar is a big bowl of rice, with perhaps a small bit of stewed/boiled meat, fish or chicken and some boiled *brêde* (a green vegetable), in water. The water is used to wash down the rest of the mound of rice. It's filling, but relatively tasteless and heavy.

Apart from the rice, if there was to be a national dish of Madagascar it would be *romazava* or *ravitoto*, which are meat stews. But these dishes are not as common as you would expect and are difficult to get in good restaurants, as most of those are Chinese or French. In some areas, baked cat and rotting fish are the local delicacies.

In Malagasy, food is *ny sakafo*, meat is *hena*, fish *trondro*, chicken *akoho*, soup *savony*, vegetables *legioma*, fruit *voankazo*, banana *akondro*, and orange *voasary*. Bread, *ny mofo*, is baked French-style and varies in taste and quality. On the coast, there's a greater variety of seafood and coconuts. In villages, cassava or manioc, which looks like a long, narrow potato with a string in the middle, forms a major part of the diet.

This, of course, can be supplemented with plenty of fruit, mainly oranges and bananas. Of the hundreds of things you can do with a banana, the Malagasy have found one: pour rum on and set it on fire. It's called *banane flambé* and it's the national dessert. Every menu has 'flaming bananas' and often has only 'flaming bananas'. Hope you like it. (The Malagasy also refer to a stud or romeo as a banane flambé!) The lychee season is November to December.

The Malagasy also love yoghurt. Hundreds of street stalls sell it with sugar in small cartons for as little as FMg 50. It's delicious and relatively safe. Other stalls offer a variety of cheap sweet and savoury titbits, ice creams and soups. Try the specimen called *parique*; it's made from peanuts, rice and sugar, wrapped up tightly in banana leaves, cooked and sold in slices.

### Eating Out

Apart from the numerous street stalls in the cities and towns, there are salons de thé. There are several of these cafés on Araben ny Fahaleovantena in Antananarivo which offer pastries, cakes, sausage rolls and ice cream, as well as tea, coffee, soft drinks and milkshakes. They do not do meals, are closed during lunch hours and before tea time, but are great for breakfasts if you can wait until they open at 8 am.

Apart from the Malagasy hotels, the restaurants are either French or Chinese. Most have set menus (*menus du jour*) for around FMg 3500. At the best restaurants a good à la carte meal should cost no more than FMg 7000 per person and set menus are around FMg 6000.

### Self-Catering

Tinned and packaged foods are mostly imported, relatively expensive and in short supply outside Antananarivo. There are a few-well stocked supermarkets in the centre of the capital.

### DRINKS

Milk seems to be available only in the central plateau area around Antananarivo and Fianarantsoa. Elsewhere you will get condensed milk.

Star, not Coca Cola or Pepsi for a change, produces most of the soft drinks, which come in large and small bottles. *Visy Gasy* says it all about soda water. The pink *Caprice Limonady* is known as *Bon Bon Anglais*.

### Alcohol

You have to be careful with home-made alcoholic drinks. If you are visiting villages or Malagasy family or friends, you may well be offered either *toaka gasy, betsabetsa* or *trembo*. You'll have to judge that fine line between being careful and being polite. The toaky gasy is crude rum made from sugar cane (commercially,

distilled rum is *roma*); betsabetsa is a sort of beer, also made from the sugar cane; and trembo is an aptly named toddy made from the coconut.

There are some small hotels which make a milky rum punch from coconuts called *punch coco*, which looks and tastes not unlike Bailey's Irish Cream! You can get a nice drop of it on Ile Ste Marie.

**Beer** The national brew is *Three Horses Beer* brewed by Star at Antsirabe and Antananarivo. It's a perfectly acceptable drop by any standards when it's taken cold. It leaves no ill effects apart from the obvious ones if you drink too much. The big bottle (*grand modèle*) costs around FMg 1000, and the small one (*petit modèle*) is FMg 600. A few years ago Star launched a new light pilsner called *Beeks Brau*, but it hasn't caught on yet. It is often priced cheaper to get rid of stocks.

**Wine** One of the delightful surprises of Madagascar is the fact that they produce very good wine around Fianarantsoa. It was introduced by the Swiss. There is a reasonable variety of wines, but the ones to try are the *Lazan'i Betsileo* red and rosé and the *Beau Vallon* and *Coteauz d'Ambalavao* reds. There is also a grey coloured wine, known as *gris*, which is interesting. Bottles can be bought from shops for around FMg 1500 – half the price charged in restaurants.

## BOOKS & BOOKSHOPS
You really have to do your reading or book buying before you arrive as there are few books of any use available in English in Madagascar.

### General
There is one good, locally published introduction to the country which is written in English and sold in the bigger bookstores in Antananarivo. It's called *A Glance at Madagascar* (Librairie Tout Pour L'École, Antananarivo, 1973). Although no author is credited, I was told

it was written by an English missionary. It costs FMg 1500 and a note inside says all royalties from the book will go to help mentally handicapped children from poor families.

Two other comprehensive books on Madagascar worth looking out for are *The Great Red Island* by Arthur Stratton (Macmillan, London, 1967) and *Madagascar Rediscovered* by Mervyn Brown (Damien Tunnacliffe, London, 1978). The Mauritian historian, Auguste Toussaint, deals with Madagascar in his *History of the Indian Ocean* (Routledge Kegan Paul, London, 1966).

### Travel Guides
I strongly recommend you read Irish travel writer Dervla Murphy's *Muddling Through In Madagascar* (John Murray, London, 1985). Murphy and her teenage daughter spent several months in 1983 backpacking around much of the country, and had the best and worst of experiences. It is a humorous as well as informative read, but some of her account is suspect and should be treated as opinion rather than fact. (Of course, you may not be able to tell which is which until you go there.) I also feel a lot of their misfortunes could have been avoided with a little more care and forethought. The book is also available in paperback in the Century Hutchinson Travellers series.

A much more safe and comfortable view of Madagascar is provided by Colin Simpson in his *Blue Africa* (Horwitz Grahame, Sydney, 1981). Other chapters in the book cover the rest of the Indian Ocean countries and East Africa. All of Simpson's travelling is done courtesy of, and in the company of, tour companies or tourist authorities.

David Attenborough's *Journeys to the Past* (Penguin, London, 1981) contains a section titled *Zoo Quest to Madagascar*. The great nature commentator tells of a visit to the country, shortly after its independence, when he went in search of lemurs, chameleons and extinct bird eggs, among other things. His trip took him, like Murphy, to Perinet Reserve, Lake Ihotry and Ampanihy in the south-west.

These are your choices of guides in English, I'm afraid, unless you can get a copy of the translation of *Madagascar Today* by Sennen Andriamirado (Les Editions Jeune Afrique, Paris, 1977). It has some nice colour plates, but the language and impressions are all rose tinted. The practical information is limited and well out of date, and he says some daft things like 'a map is of no use in Antananarivo'.

The French Hachette *Guide Bleu* is about the best of a bad bunch of French guides. But the Germans have an excellent guide from Wolfgang Därr published by Dumont (Köln, 1985).

### Phrasebooks

There are two cheap English-Malagasy phrasebooks on sale. The better of the two is *Les Guides de Poche de Madagascar*. It has the Malagasy for such useful phrases as 'I have some pimples', as well as a conspicuously large road traffic section. The editors feel there may be occasion to report: 'My car is in the ditch' and 'One person is dead'!

### Bookshops

Perhaps the best-stocked bookshop in Antananarivo is the Librairie de Madagascar, just along from the Hôtel de France on Araben ny Fahaleovantena. There are a number of others in or around this street.

### Libraries

The US Cultural Center, near the bridge tunnel entrance at the top of Làlana Dok Raz Randramazo in Antananarivo, has a large library and magazine section which you can use if you produce your passport or ID card. It is open from 9 am to noon and 2 to 6 pm each day, except Sunday.

Similarly, there is the Centre National de l'Enseignement de la Langue Anglaise (the English Language Learning Centre) (tel 275 54), on Làlana Havana, Antsahabe, Antananarivo. It has an English language library and it is possible to exchange books with students or teachers. The centre sometimes runs English 'nog and natter' evenings if you wish to be social and let Malagasy teachers practise on you.

The German equivalent is the Cercle Germano-Malagasy (Goethe Institute) in the old Lido building on the steps leading up to the GPO off the Araben ny 26 Jona 1960, in Antananarivo. This is also a good place to eat and drink.

The National Library is next to the Hilton Hotel at Anosy in Antananarivo. They are very helpful if you are doing research.

### MAPS

There are plenty of maps available, all based on the work of French colonial cartographers. They vary in style and quality, depending on how much and in what manner the Malagasy have altered them, but are generally quite accurate.

They are all produced by the Foiben Taosarintanin' i Madagasikara (FTM) – the National Institute of Cartography. The main bookshops in Antananarivo carry a reasonable selection and the FTM occasionally sets up mobile shops for map sales. If you can't get the one you want, you can go directly to the FTM on Làlana Dama Ntsoha Razafintsalama, Ambanidia,

Antananarivo (tel 229 35). Each map costs between FMg 1500 and FMg 3000.

There are road maps covering each province; town plans for Antananarivo, Fianarantsoa, Diego Suarez and Tulear; and tourist maps for Nosy Be (and Hell-Ville) and Ile Ste Marie. There are no town plans for Majunga, Tamatave or Fort Dauphin.

For maps in advance of your visit, Bartholomew includes Madagascar on the *Africa, Central and Southern* map. Michelin may offer another alternative.

## THINGS TO BUY

There is a wonderful selection of handcrafts and souvenirs to choose from. Most are available from the Zoma and stalls lining Araben ny Fahaleovantena in Antananarivo. Bargaining is the norm and you can only hope you do not follow a group of well-off package tourists.

Among the items to look out for are those featuring semiprecious stones (solitaire and chess sets), Malagasy musical instruments (particularly the valiha), leather goods (bags, sandals, belts), basketwork, handmade tin and wooden toys, embroidered linen, hats and wood carvings. The 'straw' hats come in all shapes and sizes, including top hats, boaters, sombreros and pillboxes, and some are very elegant. To get the real Betsileo or Merina look you'll need a lamba to keep out the chill on the high plateau. The lamba is the national dress of the Malagasy, a shawl-like garment which goes over the head and shoulders. You might see men wearing what looks like their nightshirt – it's called a *malabary*.

Of the other towns, Ambositra is noted for wood carving, silk and raffia; Ambalavao for silk and wrought iron; Antemoro for paper; Ampanihy for mohair carpets; and Antsirabe for semiprecious stones.

You are not supposed to take products made from crocodile skins or turtle shell out of the country without export authorisation. This can be obtained from the Direction des Eaux et Forêts, near the US Embassy in the centre of Antananarivo, between 8.30 am and 2.30 pm weekdays. You must bring the products, your visa, receipts of purchase and FMg 200 tax. This is not necessary if you buy leather goods for your own use. Many countries, however, will not let you import them.

If you have a special interest in any craft (or art) it might be worth contacting the Ministère de la Culture et de l'Art Révolutionnaire (tel 270 92) in the central Antsahavola district of Antananarivo.

### Luxury Items

You are more likely to be selling than buying these, but if you are after items you are used to getting back home, then try the French Prisunic Department Store near the GPO in Antananarivo. They'll probably have it, but it won't be cheap. A small box of tissues cost FMg 4000.

**Cigarettes** Malagasy cigarettes take after the French ones and are cheap, ranging from FMg 300 to FMg 600 for a packet of 20.

## SPORT & ENTERTAINMENT

The French had little influence on local recreâtion. Even *boules* or *pétanque* haven't caught on. You may see men playing the board game *fanorona*, a Malagasy version of draughts.

Soccer is the main sport. Often unable to afford a ball, children play in the streets with tightly rolled bundles of newspaper tied and shaped by string. They also spend a lot of time running old tyres, hoops and other wheels along the road with a sticks.

For visitors, there is little opportunity to participate in any sport. Diplomatic and affluent sets in Antananarivo can provide access to tennis and swimming. A couple of beach hotels offer subaqua sport, but the equipment and tuition, if any, is suspect. Alternatively there is snorkelling and boat hire. Yacht charters and deep sea fishing are possible, but only on a limited basis. Trekking and 4WD tours are popular in their own right and as a means to an end for nature enthusiasts.

CONCERT D'ADIEU
Dimanche 12 avril à 15
au Centre Culturel ESC
ROSSY + MAHALEO + SMOK

### Films, Theatre & Concerts

Antananarivo and the provincial capitals have cinemas. A seat costs between FMg 150 and FMg 800. Some of the films are worth seeing. The US Cultural Center, Alliance Française and Centre Culturel Albert Camus (CCAC) in Antananarivo also show quality movies regularly.

The CCAC also has an excellent programme of French and local theatre; jazz, rock and classical music; and art exhibitions. Companies, artists and directors from France visit Madagascar. If you are lucky you will come across impromptu Malagasy plays and singing in Antananarivo. They are practising for the occasional shows and contests held at the Municipal Theatre in the Isotry central district of the capital.

Check posters and newspaper advertisements for folk and pop concerts and other shows.

As with all the other islands in the Indian Ocean, the only real method of getting in and out of the country is by air, although a few ships still ply the route between the Comoros and Majunga in Madagascar

## AIR

Only four carriers operate to and from the international airport at Ivato, 16 km from the centre of Antananarivo. The national airline, Air Madagascar, flies weekly to Nairobi, Kenya (via Moroni in the Comoros); directly to the Comoros; to Paris three times a week (via Nairobi, Djibouti, Jeddah and Marseilles); to Réunion six times a week; and to Mauritius three times a week. It shares these routes with Air Mauritius and Air France. The other carrier is Aeroflot, the Soviet airline, which flies once a week to and from Moscow, (via Aden).

A traveller from the UK warned that the Aeroflot flight out of Madagascar is fully booked far in advance and that people had to wait weeks to get a cancellation. So it's best to get a confirmed return when you buy the ticket rather than an open one. You can always cancel and take your chances if you must.

On the Paris route there are a range of return fares, including excursion, youth and student fares, at almost half the cost of a normal economy return. Air France offer a 'special' return fare Paris-Antananarivo for about Fr 7395, but this must be booked in France. A regular excursion fare costs around Fr 10,350.

Air Madagascar match that with a 'YPX' special fare (minimum stay 13 days, maximum 60 and excluding 15 June to 15 September) for FMg 1,697,500 (about US$1000).

Continuing the specials, you can get a Fr 1820 return flight from Réunion to Antananarivo instead of the normal economy return of Fr 3060. If you want to make a side trip to the Comoros, Air Mad have an excursion return (seven days minimum, 30 maximum) for FMg 407,500.

The Antananarivo-Nairobi return excursion is FMg 582,700, with a minimum stay of six days and a maximum of 21.

Always remember to confirm any flight within or out of Madagascar as early as possible and always re-confirm it three days in advance.

In Madagascar you must pay for all domestic and international fares in foreign currency.

Air Mad's head office is at 31 Araben ny Fahaleovantena, in Antananarivo (tel 222 22). They are linked up to the computer booking system and you can confirm all onward flights here. Air Mad's overseas offices are in:

Paris
    7 Ave de l'Opéra, 75001 (tel 260 30 51)
Nairobi
    Hilton Hotel Arcade, 723 (tel 264 94)
Réunion
    2 Rue MacAuliffe, 97461 St Denis (tel 21 05 21)
Mauritius
    Rogers House, 5 Président J F Kennedy, Port Louis (tel 08 35 40)
Zurich
    c/- Atash, 34 Neumuehlequai, 8035 Zurich 35 (tel 362 77 70)
Munich
    c/- Atash, Herzog-Rudolfstrasse 3, 8000 Munich 22 (tel 23 18 01)

For other countries, contact the Madagascar embassy or consulate.

Air France's office is just along from Air Mad's on Araben ny Fahaleovantena in Antananarivo. Aeroflot is on Làlana Ratsimilaho, along from the central post office.

## Arrival

The arrival procedures at Ivato International Airport are the worst advertisement for the Malagasy people and country. It can put you in a hostile state of mind before you begin travelling and ruin happy memories when you leave. This is due to a series of immigration, health, customs and monetary checks thrust upon a flood of tired and unsuspecting visitors. It is a bureaucratic assault course.

First, you must fill out a health form and get it stamped. You won't get to the next stage unless it is stamped. At the immigration counter, you will be asked to fill in a money declaration form. You must show what you have declared and they will count it before authorising your currency declaration form. This is followed by a body and bag search. Once through that hurdle there are further passport, ticket and currency declaration form checks by police. Then it's down to collect your baggage, which is usually lying in a heap by this time. Of course, customs officials then have to check your bags.

There is a bank open for international arrivals, and a 'welcome desk' run by the hotels and tour companies. The tourist department does not have an information counter.

## Airport Transport

There is no airport bus service to or from Antananarivo but several taxi touts will wrestle and scream for your business. A taxi into the city centre costs around FMg 10,000.

There are two other possibilities. If you are lucky, you may be able to get a lift with the Air Route Services minibus which transports the airport staff. If there is room and you are not likely to start a rush by other tourists or travellers, the driver will take you, for a FMg 2000 'tip', to the railway station in the city centre.

The public Antananarivo to Ivato taxi-brousse service runs from about 6 am to 7 pm, but you must walk one km from the airport to Ivato village to catch it. As you leave the main gate to the airport, turn left and walk alongside an army barracks. The trip into the city takes 30 minutes or more, depending on the number of stops and costs only FMg 180.

The taxi-brousse (bus) terminus in Antananarivo is on Araben ny Fahaleovantena, just outside the Hôtel Terminus. This is a much better alternative when going to the airport from the capital.

There may be long queues, but the taxis-brousses run continuously and the turnover is quick. Obviously there will be difficulties if you have heavy luggage.

## BOAT

Madagascar is not a popular stopover or destination for cruise ships and yachts. If you have the contacts, patience, money and determination, you may pick up a passage out of South Africa, Mayotte (Comoros), Réunion or Mauritius, between April and November. But getting one from Madagascar is unlikely.

Your best bet is a small sugar or rice cargo boat from Majunga to the Comoros. For advice, contact Ramzana Aly, Armement Tawakal, BP 60, Majunga (tel 227 21). His family runs several ships, mainly to Nosy Be. He speaks good English and is a good source of help and information in general.

## LEAVING MADAGASCAR

Leaving the country from Antananarivo does not appear to be such a time consuming ritual, but it is best to allow plenty of time at the airport before your flight leaves. Unless you are prepared to puff and bluff it out, make sure your remaining money and the amount you changed/spent tallies with the amount on your currency declaration form, that you have the form and that your visa is in order. There are body searches and plain clothes police ready to take you into a room and question you at length.

### Departure Tax

The departure tax is FMg 1500. Remember you cannot reconvert any remaining Malagasy money or take it out of the country.

# Getting Around

Dealing with the Malagasy is half the battle and half the fun of getting around Madagascar which is always an adventure. It's travelling in its purest form; it's testing, trying and terrific! Anything can happen and anything does. The only exception, I hasten to add, is air travel. Air Mad, despite the name, is relatively safe and efficient, as well as relatively cheap.

If you are on a tight budget or limited for time, it is important to plan a travel itinerary. Allow plenty of time for road travel, take climatic factors into account and check whether it is better to take the train or plane. It is a good idea to travel by road, rail and sea one way and return by air, so you don't cover the same ground.

In 1987, the famous Camel 4WD endurance rally was run the length of Madagascar. The Malagasy may have felt honoured and been impressed by the occasion, but the skills involved must have seemed commonplace because every road journey in Madagascar turns into a Camel rally – especially if you go long distance by taxi-brousse. Few such journeys go by without incident, but out of them comes a great sense of camaraderie. The Malagasy are great travel companions.

The main forms of road transport are taxi-brousse and taxi-be. The taxis-brousses are, strictly speaking, the small Peugot covered wagons, but the term is applied more to the larger cars-brousses (bush minibuses). Within the towns and cities, there are bus, taxi and, in some places, *pousse-pousse* (rickshaw) services.

The police occasionally stop vehicles and carry out random checks, but goodness knows what for. There are usually 1001 possible infringements, including overcrowding and 'vehicle held together by string', but they never seem to charge anyone.

## AIR

Air Mad has a surprisingly busy and widespread network linking Antananarivo with 51 other centres, including the provincial capitals of Fianarantsoa, Majunga, Diego Suarez, Tamatave and Tulear, and tourist destinations like Ile Ste Marie and Nosy Be. There are regular flights to Sambava and Maroantsetra in the north-east and Morondava and Morombe in the south-west. Twin Otter planes also cover many smaller towns such as Ihosy (handy for visiting Isalo National Park) at least once a week.

Air Mad like flights to appear fully booked. Most times, they'll tell you to try again, or come back later that day if the flight is the same day. Usually, you'll get a seat. If you have previously booked successfully, always confirm the flight three days in advance. Double check the day before departure, as schedules sometimes change.

The flights are much more reliable and safer than trains or road transport, but they are still affected by bad weather and communications breakdowns. Usually, Air Mad will change the timetable and put on an extra flight, rather than cancel completely.

The transport is mainly Boeing 737 workhorses and Twin Otters. Flight and safety details are given in Malagasy, French and English, but are generally inaudible. No inflight meals or snacks are served. Your luggage is tagged as normal, but when it comes to collection at the provincial airports, you must shout out your number or hold out your baggage ticket for a porter to hand it to you. There's always shoving and jostling, which dies down completely after a few minutes.

Flying was cheap in Madagascar until the devaluation. Fares for residents increased by 15% but they rocketed up for tourists who now must pay for tickets in foreign currency only. You can also pay by credit card.

The following are one-way fares from Antananarivo to: Tamatave – US$59; Diego Suarez – US$160; Fianarantsoa or Ile Ste Marie – US$81; Fort Dauphin, Tulear or Nosy Be – US$148; Majunga, Morondava or Manakara – US$92; Sambava – US$127; Maroantsetra – US$104.

You can still get cheaper excursion fares on the Fort Dauphin, Tulear, Nosy Be and Ile Ste Marie routes if you stay between six and 30 days.

Refer to the Getting There chapter and the provincial capital sections for the addresses of Air Mad offices.

### Air Touristic Pass

Air Mad offers visitors an Air Touristic Pass for a month's unlimited air travel in the country for 2750 French francs, which is about US$500, or the equivalent in another major currency. (If you buy it in France it costs Fr 2500).

You can get the pass from any overseas Air Mad office or embassy/consulate. If you're not sure, before you travel to Madagascar, whether you will want it or not it is best to get a letter of authority from the consul or airline representative to keep the option open. Without that authorisation, you will have difficulty buying the pass in Madagascar.

You need not necessarily miss out on the fun of taxi-brousse adventures by flying around Madagascar on the air pass. You can bus it up to Nosy Be or take a train down Tamatave and fly back, which means you avoid going over the same interesting but uncomfortable ground again. Flights can also get you into areas which are often inaccessible by road. The Air Touristic Pass does not, however, make booking any easier or quicker.

### TAXI-BROUSSE

Taxis-brousses or cars-brousses are large Renault, Mercedes or Peugot minibuses which link every town and city in the country, weather and road conditions permitting. These vehicles are, for the most part, in a dilapidated state.

The fact that they continue to operate long after they should have been consigned to any self-respecting vehicle scrapheap, is both a tribute to Franco-German technology and the ingenuity of Malagasy popular mechanics. Some of these vehicles seem to be held together by wire and the crudest of welding. They frequently break down, though not as often as you might expect. When they do, you'll be surprised how, in many cases, they are often repaired with the assistance of another passing taxi-brousse or truck. The only windscreen wipers and speedometer I ever saw working were in a Bedford truck.

Catching or booking a taxi-brousse is easy enough, but getting inside one is. . .well, let's say challenging. There are some things you should know about the process. First, you must go to the right taxi-brousse station to find out the times that the long-distance ones leave and book a seat. If you are leaving the next day, go the day before. If you are leaving on a shorter day trip in the afternoon, go in the morning.

Antananarivo has several stations or *gares routieres* – one for destinations north, one for those south, etc. The provincial capitals usually have two stations.

Several regional public transport cooperatives, known by their acronyms, FITATERANA, KOPFMMM, SONATRA, etc, may operate the same route and tout for your trade. The fares are the same, but you may fancy the look of one vehicle more than another.

The ideal seat is the one beside the driver in the front, although on occasions it is shared by up to six people. This seat is usually assigned on a first come first served basis, although to get on the bus you do have to reserve your seat and pay for your *karatra* (ticket).

There is every likelihood, however, that you will be granted the front seat if you play the tourist who: (a) is interested in actually seeing the Malagasy countryside and getting the best view of it; (b) is the poor, beleaguered traveller with the bad back, sore feet and travel sickness; (c) has heard of, but not yet experienced, the terrific Malagasy hospitality to visitors; or (d) simply offers to pay a bit more or bring a packet of cigarettes for the driver. Sometimes the front seat is kindly offered to the *vazaha* without all that rigmarole.

Taxis-brousses rarely leave until they are full – especially on shorter journeys where there is no timetable. In most cases, they wait until they are overfull, in fact packed in like sardines. Any Guinness Book of World Records attempt at cramming people into a Mini is child's stuff compared with the Malagasy use of space. It's amazing into what small spaces the human body can squeeze. It's a good way to get very close to the local people.

On top of, and interspersed with, the seething human mass is luggage of various sizes and shapes, animals, vegetables, minerals, bags, crates, rice, chickens, bundles of hats and mats, charcoal, mail and fuel. Your major item of luggage will have to be roped on to the roof as well. Make sure there is nothing valuable or breakable inside and keep checking on it to make sure it is covered properly from the dust or rain.

Allow plenty of time in your plans for taxi-brousse trips. Journeys which should take two hours can take four or five, and a five hour journey can take all day. It all depends on the number of breakdowns and the state of the roads.

You can often wait for an hour past the set departure time until the driver or cooperative boss decides to move. It's extremely infuriating when they wait an hour to get just *one* more passenger. The Malagasy don't mind the wait or the squash, but you might find it a touch claustrophobic. Look on the bright side though – at least when it's packed, you don't rattle and bounce around inside.

There used to be big buses running regularly from Antananarivo to Tulear and back but the road conditions wore them down and the Malagasy were unable to get enough spare parts to repair them. Sturdy Mercedes buses still run between Majunga and Antananarivo, competing with the taxis-brousses and taxis-bes.

## TRAIN

The Malagasy railway system, built and still technically assisted by the French, is efficient but limited to only 850 km of track. The Antananarivo to Tamatave line goes via Moramanga and Ambila Lemaitso; the other north-bound line from Antananarivo goes through Moramanga to Ambatondrazaka; and the south-bound line connects Antananarivo with Antsirabe via Ambatolampy. Further south there's a separate railway line connecting Fianarantsoa and Manakara.

Each journey is worth the time and money, and makes a pleasant change from quick, soulless flying or long, incident-packed road travel.

### Classes & Costs

There is the choice of 1st or 2nd class travel with a 30% to 45% difference in price, and you must pay 1st class fares in foreign currency.

The following are the 1st/2nd class fares from Antananarivo to: Antsirabe – FMg

4250/2750; Tamatave – FMg 11,500/6350; and Ambatondrazaka – FMg 8300/4500. Return tickets are equivalent to 1½ times the single fare. First class travel is comfortable but not plush; 2nd class is more crowded and harder on the bum.

Reservations are advisable, as most trains are heavily booked, especially during holiday periods. There is one train a day each way between Antananarivo and Tamatave, which leaves early in the morning and arrives late in the afternoon. Two trains run each day on the four hour trip between Antananarivo and Antsirabe (three on weekends), leaving early morning and at lunch time. There is one train a day each way between Fianarantsoa and Manakara.

There is no buffet car on the trains, but there are swarms of platform hawkers at each of the stops en route.

The trips, although very scenic, are in many parts as bumpy as the roads! My fellow passengers and I agreed unanimously that it was only a matter of time before a train came off the rails. If you've got the nerve, go to the front of the Antananarivo to Antsirabe locomotive, next to the driver, and marvel at how it doesn't come off the narrow-gauge track when it swings 45° on each side.

Soarano station is in the centre of Antananarivo at the head of Araben ny Fahaleovantena. The national rail company is known as the Réseau National des Chemins de Fer Malgaches (tel 205 21).

The trains also transport vehicles. It costs around FMg 12,000/20,000 (one-way/return) to take your car on any trip, but you must accompany it on a separate first class fare.

### The Micheline

The Micheline is a special 'train' which runs on tyres and is said to be one of only three remaining in the world. Groups can hire it for any journey, short or long, from Antananarivo. It carries 19 people, has a bar and music, and provides a much smoother ride. It costs about FMg 300,000

to take it from Antananarivo to Tamatave, and FMg 140,000 from Antananarivo to Antsirabe. Call 205 21 for more details and bookings. If you are not with a group, you could put your name down for any spare seats going!

### TAXI-BE

Also sometimes referred to as a taxi-familial, a taxi-be is quite simply a 'big taxi'. These Peugot 404 and 504 estate/station wagons are a more expensive, but more comfortable and faster alternative to long-distance travel by taxi-brousse. They are run by the same cooperative, and carry up to 10 passengers. But, like the taxi-brousse, you can sometimes spend agonising hours waiting for one or two passengers to make up the numbers.

### TRUCK

Trucks (camions in French and Malagasy) are a possible alternative to taxis-brousses when the latter cease running or cease to exist for a variety of reasons. You simply ask the truck driver and he'll charge you a similar rate to the taxi-brousse. The trucks can handle road conditions which thwart other, lesser vehicles, but you will be competing with stranded Malagasy for the favours of truck drivers.

Heavy trucks are also responsible for all the broken bridges. You'll often come across a bevy of truckies affecting temporary repairs to a previously temporary repair on a floorless iron bridge, using planks and rearranging loose steel girders and plates.

### BOAT

You might find yourself crossing more water than you anticipated, simply because, in the words of Jimmy Cliff, there are 'many rivers to cross'. On some coastal roads, cars-brousses or taxis-brousses are ferried by raft across river estuaries. Occasionally, the bridges are down or too dangerous to cross, especially during the wet season. You have the choice of getting a boat across and continuing under your own steam, or waiting for repairs.

On other occasions, *pirogues*, dugout canoes, are used by villagers to get you to certain places of interest, such as the Fort du Portugais near Fort Dauphin, and Ile aux Nattes, off Ile Ste Marie.

### Inter-Island Ferries

There is a fishing boat and motor ferry service to Ile Ste Marie from Tamatave and Manompana. Ferries run more frequently between the mainland and Nosy Be on the opposite coast. These are all very vulnerable to weather conditions, as well as mechanical breakdowns. Boat travel is as eventful and just as hazardous (or adventurous) as road travel.

Hotels and private operators on Nosy Be, Ile Ste Marie and around Tulear, hire out boats and run yacht or boat trips for tourists.

### DRIVING

The Malagasy drive on the right hand side of the road and all vehicles are French.

Compared to European drivers, Malagasy drivers are slow and careful in the city and on the open road. That may have something to do with their temperament, but it is more likely due to the state of the roads. Of the 35,000 km of roadway in the country, only 4000 km is tarred, and most of that is in bad repair. In fact it's often little more than a series of holes connected by pieces of tar!

A warning when driving or being driven on wet roads: the holes in the roads fill with water and there's no telling how deep some are unless you get out and test them with a stick. There are many instances of wheels buckling, axles and chassis snapping, and even whole cars dropping into deep holes in the road. I kid you not. The best way to find out about the condition of any road, especially if you intend to drive on it, is to go to the taxi-brousse station running that area.

There are some shocking stretches of highway. For example, the National Route 7 stretching between Fianarantsoa and Ihosy, is so rutted in parts it makes a ploughed field look like a billiard table. In some places, there are four tracks to choose from where a succession of trusty taxis-brousses and trucks have carved out a new route after the previous one became impassable. And this is in the good weather. During the rainy season from November to March, several main roads, in particular the routes from Tulear to Fort Dauphin and Antananarivo to Ambanja or Diego Suarez, are impassable for months.

Most accidents are due to human error, however, rather than dangerous vehicles and roads. The ones I read about were caused by rum drunk drivers, so check the sobriety of your driver before leaving.

### Car Rental

Both cars and 4WD vehicles can be hired but it's a risky business on both sides because of the road conditions. It's definitely worth considering though if you can get a few people together to share the cost.

Drivers must be at least 23 years old and have held a driving licence for one year. A deposit of FMg 200,000, or FMg 400,000 if you are under 25, is required.

Car hire is around FMg 18,000 per day, with an extra FMg 6000 a day for insurance and FMg 250 per km. There are a few hire companies in Antananarivo, notably Aventour (tel 317 61), 55 Route de Majunga, Antanimena, Antananarivo (near La Cascade hotel). Some hotels and Mad Airtours also offer hire arrangements.

You can hire 4WD vehicles at much greater expense – around FMg 50,000 a day.

Petrol stations of the state company Solima are rare in the towns and cities and virtually nonexistent outside them. Petrol costs about FMg 600 a litre in Antananarivo.

### BICYCLE & MOTORCYCLE

There are few motorcycles in Madagascar, and fewer bicycles than you would imagine. There are no hire outlets for either. Some hotels in the holiday areas of Fort Dauphin, Ile Ste Marie and Nosy Be, however, can arrange private hire of a bicycle.

## HITCHING

This is not really a viable alternative in Madagascar, despite the people's generosity. Traffic outside and between the towns and cities is very thin and you are likely only to flag down a taxi-brousse, taxi-be or truck – all of which will be full. If not, you'll have to pay the fare anyway.

## LOCAL TRANSPORT
### Bus

Antananarivo has a good public bus service run by several companies. A FMg 50 fare will take you anywhere. Other provincial capitals and major towns, with the exception of Antsirabe, have few, if any, services. They are not really necessary as taxis-brousses, taxis or pousse-pousses are sufficient.

### Taxi

Mostly Renault 4 buckets, taxis are limited to the towns and cities. There are no meters, you just have to know the going rate. The taxi drivers, by and large, are not a crooked lot. There are not enough tourists to spoil or corrupt them. There are plenty of taxis around the airports, railway stations and taxi-brousse stations. There is a surcharge on fares after dark.

### Pousse-pousse

The 'push-push' is actually a 'pull-pull' rickshaw that comes with various levels of comfort and shade. They are a legacy of the Chinese who were brought in by the French to help build the roads and railways.

Pousse-pousse numbers vary from city to city. There are few left in Antananarivo, because of the good bus system and congested roads; they are rare to non-existent in Fort Dauphin, Diego Suarez and Tulear; but are teeming in Antsirabe.

# MADAGASCAR AIRTOURS

"La qualité aux meilleurs prix!"

Locals pay FMg 200 for a ride, tourists start at FMg 500.

## Stagecoach

There are still a few of these covered wagons clattering along the streets of Antananarivo, giving you an idea of what it was like before the taxi-brousse.

## TOURS

Madagascar Airtours and Transcontinents operate a range of tours in and around Antananarivo. (I wouldn't chance any other operator than Mad Airtours for national or international packages.) They run guided speciality tours, for 10 to 14 days, around the country by bus, mixing comfort and security with adventure.

These tours are titled Trekking & Expedition, Sculptures & Art, Succulents & Orchids, Natural History, Birdwatching, and To Climb the Hills. Prices range from approximately US$500 to US$750 for accommodation, food, guide and transport. The bigger the group, the cheaper it is per person. For info on the tour operators refer to the Facts for the Visitor chapter.

Hotels in Nosy Be, Tulear and Ile Ste Marie offer yacht/boat, snorkelling, walking and sightseeing trips; and there's a new tour operator in Tana offering trekking and 4WD tours (see the Antananarivo chapter).

## Walking - National Parks

Getting around on one's feet is the Malagasy way, but you don't see many tourists hoofing it because of the distances and conditions involved. The best places for tramping about are in the 36 national parks, many of which were established and managed with international assistance in order to protect the country's dwindling forests and unique wildlife. Ironically, only two of the parks are open to the Malagasy public, and some are restricted to scientists, biologists and the like.

**Permits** For several of the reserves, including the most popular ones – Isalo, Montagne d'Ambre and Perinet (Andasibe) – you have to get prior authorisation from the Direction des Eaux et Forêts (DEF). It is best to do this in Antananarivo before beginning your tour as the parks are, in most cases, a long way from the regional DEFs. You could try bluffing or bribing your way in, if desperate, but the forest rangers are generally conscientious and loyal in their duty. It's more than their job's worth.

In Antananarivo, the relevant DEF office is near the agricultural school at Nanisana on the outskirts of Antananarivo. You take an ANTAFITA No 3 bus from the centre of town. It is no use going to the DEF in the centre of the city.

When you apply for a permit, you need to know which national parks you intend to visit. You can't get a 'general rover' pass. If in doubt about one or two, note them down anyway just in case. If you have a 'multiple park' permit, remember to get it back from the warden after he has made his mark.

There is no charge, but don't complicate matters by mentioning any professional or academic interest for your visit. That opens up a different can of worms and different authorities may have to be consulted first. State your reason as touristic only.

# Antananarivo

If there is one word to describe Antananarivo, formerly Tananarive and affectionately known as Tana, it is 'mediaeval'. The tall, narrow houses add most to this impression with their crumbling red brickwork, terracotta-tiled roofs, wooden balconies and shuttered windows. These houses are spread on various levels over the 12 hills of Tana, which are surrounded by rice paddies, and rising from amongst them are the spires of the town's many churches. Crowning all, is the palace of Queen Ranavalona.

I imagine there are ancient hill towns in Italy, Yugoslavia or Albania which look like parts of Tana. It feels occasionally like you're in a time warp, as if, apart from the traffic, the 20th century hasn't had much impact in some areas.

Because of the nation's economic woes, however, the streets of the capital city have become meaner over the past decade. Abject poverty is on open display around the main thoroughfare of Araben ny Fahaleovantena, and reports of increased crime and prostitution are common. In 1987 there were riots, fires and soldiers in the streets.

For these reasons, many visitors are prejudiced against the city on arrival, or shortly after, and want to spend as little time there as possible. That would be a pity. Tana, with its 600,000 or so people is much less dangerous than most other cities in the world. It's just that because of the generally placid and warm nature of the Malagasy, their troubles are magnified.

It might have been simply familiarity breeding content, but I was always happy to be back in Tana after touring other parts of the country. The anonymous author of the locally published *A Glance at Madagascar* proffers this reason:

Tananarive is medically known to have some influence which can have an effect on a person liable to suffer from nervous depression. Various suggestions have been made as to the cause, including magnetism, altitude, ultraviolet rays or the winds which have an effect similar to the *foehn* wind in Austria.

The author doesn't state whether the effect is a positive or negative one, but I assume it is the former. Altitude does have an affect in one undisputed way. The city lies on the central plateau at 1300 metres, so it can be very chilly after the sun goes down.

The population of Tana is 90% Merina, the ruling tribe (whose members don't object to the use of the term 'tribe'), so the city appears much more Asian than African (they do object to the use of 'African'). While we're on name terms, Antananarivo means 'town of a thousand' because it was here, in the early 17th century, that the Merina chief Andrianjaka stationed a garrison of a thousand men.

## Orientation

*Làlana* is Malagasy for street; *arabe* or *araben* is avenue; and *kianja* or *kianjan* is place or square. Street signs are difficult to find and read, however, and most of the streets have been renamed after Malagasy heroes, though the occasional French name survives.

The hub of Tana is Araben ny Fahaleovantena (or the Ave de l'Indépendance if you're using the old French name), with the Soarano railway station and the Hôtel Terminus at one end and the Hôtel Glacier at the other, where it narrows into a single two-way road.

This district is known as Analakely and that's what you ask for, or look for on the fronts of buses when you want to go to the centre of town. The area is thronged with permanent street markets, but once a week it expands considerably when out of

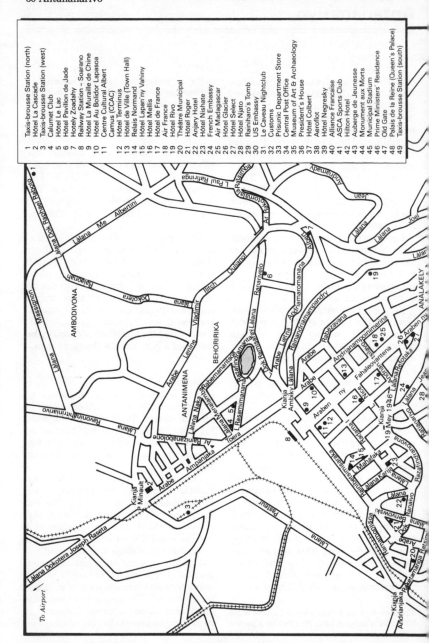

1 Taxis-brousse Station (north)
2 Hotel La Cascade
3 Taxis-brousse Station (west)
4 Calumet Club
5 Hotel Le Lac
6 Hotel Pavillon de Jade
7 Hotely Zoadåhy
8 Railway Station – Soarano
9 Hotel La Muraille de Chine
10 Hotel Au Bolidor Lapasoa
11 Centre Cultural Albert Camus (CCAC)
12 Hotel Terminus
13 Hotel de Ville (Town Hall)
14 Relais Normand
15 Hotel Lapan'ny Vahiny
16 Hotel Mellis
17 Hotel de France
18 Air France
19 Hotel Rivo
20 Théâtre Municipal
21 Hotel Roger
22 Anjary Hotel
23 Hotel Nishate
24 French Embassy
25 Air Madagascar
26 Hotel Glacier
27 Hotel Select
28 Hotel Njato
29 Rainiharo's Tomb
30 US Embassy
31 Le Caveau Nightclub
32 Customs
33 Prisunic Department Store
34 Central Post Office
35 Museum of Art & Archaeology
36 President's House
37 Hotel Colbert
38 Aeroflot
39 Hotel Negresky
40 Alliance Francaise
41 ASCA Sports Club
42 Hilton Hotel
43 Auberge de Jeunesse
44 Monument aux Morts
45 Municipal Stadium
46 Prime Ministers' Residence
47 Old Gate
48 Palais de la Reine (Queen's Palace)
49 Taxis-brousse Station (south)

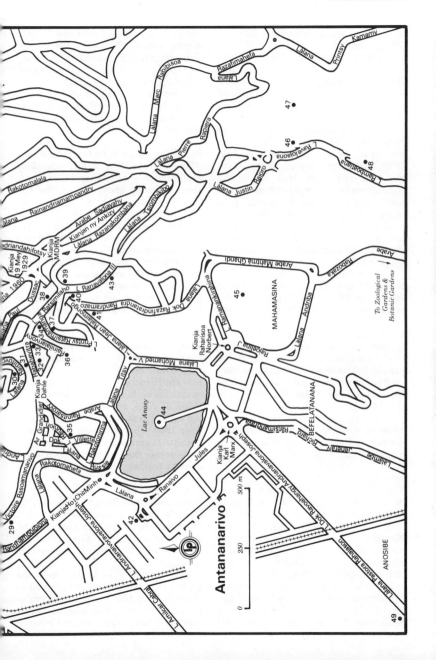

town traders arrive for the great *Zoma*, or 'Friday' market.

*Analakely* means 'the little forest', though what trees there once were have long since been replaced by a forest of off-white umbrellas, balanced precariously on old tyre rims, set up by all the traders over their stalls.

The stalls extend off Araben ny Fahaleovantena and continue along Araben ny 26 Jona 1960 (Ave 26 Juin 1960), up the stone steps on either side. On the west side, they lead up to the administrative and nightclub quarter of town, which includes the central post office, Government House and other ministry headquarters. From here, there are narrow streets leading up past churches and other noble structures to the Queen's palace.

An important rendezvous spot in Tana is the Madagascar Hilton beside Lac Anosy. (A FIMA No 10 bus from the centre near the Hôtel de France will take you there.) If you're walking from town to the Hilton, armed guards will firmly but politely order you to walk on the lake side of the road because the grounds of the presidential house also front onto the lake.

Other government buildings, including the national library and the Ministry of the Interior, are next to the Hilton. Further around the lakeside is the national stadium in the Mahamasina district and the big public hospital at Befelatanana.

### Information
There is no tourist information office in Antananarivo. If you have a tourism problem, contact the Direction du Tourisme (tel 262 98), Làlana Fernand Kasanga, Tsimbazaza (near the zoo entrance). You could try asking for Miss Elyane Rahonntsoa, the head of promotion. She speaks good English.

For other travel information, contact Madagascar Airtours at the Hilton Hotel Arcade. Maps are available from most bookshops. Visitors of the relevant

nationalities may find more specific help or companionship from either the Alliance Française, the Cercle Germano-Malagasy (ex-Goethe Institute) or the English Language Education Centre.

There are more details on embassies, consulates and airline offices, post offices and banks in the Facts for the Visitor chapter.

**Post** There seems to be two central post offices in Tana. One is half way along Araben ny 26 Jona 1960, and the other is almost directly above it, via the two flights of steps up to Kianjan ny Fahaleovantena, near the Hôtel Colbert. They are open during the week from 8 am to noon and 2 to 6 pm, and on Saturdays from 8 am to noon.

At the latter post office, the 1st floor is open for telegrams, international calls and poste restante from Monday to Saturday from 7 am to 7 pm, and on Sundays and public holidays from 8 to 11 am.

**Banks** The main banks are easily found around Kianjan (Place) and Araben ny Fahaleovantena. There is a BTM bank near the Blanche-Neige cafe in the block next to the burnt remains of the town hall (hôtel de ville), and a BNI bank next to the central post office on Araben ny 26 Jona 1960. They are open for business from 8 to 11 am and 2 to 4 pm on weekdays. I believe they close on the afternoon before a public holiday.

### Palais de la Reine
Also known as the *Rova*, in Malagasy, the Queen's Palace is open to the public Tuesday to Saturday from 2 to 5 pm and on Sundays and public holidays from 9 am to noon and 2 to 5 pm. It is closed on Mondays.

Entry to the Rova is free, as is the guided tour, but you are not allowed to photograph or film inside the palace or grounds without prior permission. That is easy to get, but you must come at least the day before to apply. If not, you will be asked at the gate to surrender all cameras and cine or video equipment, which you can collect on the way out.

There is one slight drawback with the main palace *Manampisoa*, which was built in 1867 for Queen Rasoherina. It is closed for restoration – and has been for a number of years. The stonework by Scots missionary architect James Cameron, is, as you would expect from a Scot, solid. But it sheathes an earlier wooden palace, called *Manjakamiadana*, built for the cruel Queen Ranavalona I by a French castaway called Jean Laborde.

The linchpin of the whole building is a 39 metre high ebony tree trunk, now blamed for the structural problems. (Slaves dragged the log from a forest 300 km away. A thousand are said to have died in the process.) The guide will show you the inside by pointing through a window.

Completely accessible is the earlier and much simpler palace and tomb of King Andrianampoinimerina. (That's short for Andrianampoinimerinandriantsimitoviaminandriampanjaka!) He was the man who united the Merina, and the country, at the end of the 18th century and opened Madagascar up to the Europeans, and is the chap with the spear featured on many postcards. His own Rova is actually on a hill at Ambohimanga, 25 km north of the capital (you can see each palace from the other), but his tomb, along with the other kings and queens, is here.

The third building is the museum, but the paintings it contains are being restored and may not be seen again for some time. There are copies of letters from the governors of Mauritius and Réunion and from various Malagasy queens – but they all seem to be in the same hand. There are also gifts from the British kings and queens and Napoleon III, such as a bible, cups, goblets and a sabre.

To get to the Rova from the centre of Tana, catch a ANTAFITA No 21 bus, a taxi, or walk. It is a pleasant stroll up through the narrow, twisting streets past other interesting buildings. You can also climb directly up the crag, perhaps after visiting the zoo, through a labyrinth of paths and steps connecting Malagasy homes.

## Zoo

Le Parc Botanique et Zoologique de Tsimbazaza is a little rundown, but worth a visit if you are not short of time in Tana. It is only open on Thursdays, Sundays and public holidays from 8 to 11 am and 2 to 5 pm. Even then, you may have difficulties. Entry is free, but you are supposed to check in at the gate, get permission and perhaps a guide to make sure you don't run off with one of the few remaining crocodiles!

One problem is finding the right gate, as there are several posted with notices of opening times which are never open. The one you want is the Acadamie Malgache gate at the bottom of Làlana Fernand Kasanga. To get there from the centre of town, take an ANTAFITA No 15 bus.

Most of the cages and enclosures within the park are empty, which will please animal liberationists. However, there are still lemurs, herons, egrets, crocodiles, and Aldabra and Malagasy tortoises, as well as an array of palms and other trees to see. The walks and surroundings are pleasant rather than beautiful.

## Acadamie Malgache Museum

They say Madagascar itself is a living museum, which makes this place sort of redundant. Even so this building within the zoo contains some amazing natural and cultural exhibits. You could easily spend a morning or afternoon there. Unless you come to arrange prior permission, the opening times are the same as for the zoo park.

One of the main exhibits is the vertebrae of a dinosaur which was discovered near Majunga in 1907. There's also a preserved coelacanth, the deep water 'prehistoric' fish thought to be extinct until one was fished out of the Indian Ocean in the 1930s. This rare

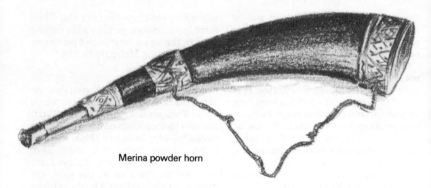

Merina powder horn

specimen was taken from the marine research station in Nosy Be, but when the tank was unveiled for me, the creature lay rotting in about five cm of formalin.

The museum also features the skeletal remains of the extinct giant ostrich-like bird the *aepyornis* and its egg, a short-tailed white hippo and a dugong. Other unusual Malagasy animals stuffed for posterity are the aye-aye, the rare indri lemur, and the hedgehog-like tenrecs.

In another room, there are displays of Malagasy funeral art and tribal village life, including the reconstruction of Mahafaly tombs with their totem carvings. There is also a vivarium with live chameleons, snakes, lizards, small lemurs and tortoises.

## Museum of Art & Archaeology

This museum is more central, but very disappointing. You'll find it opposite Maison de la Réunion on the corner of La Réunion and Làlana Dok Villette, on the hill between Lac Anosy and the grounds of government house.

It's open Tuesday to Sunday from 2.30 to 5.30 pm, but is limited in its selection of exhibits compared to the Academie Malgache. There are some bones and egg pieces from the extinct *aepyornis*, some hippo remains, old photographs of the Queen's Palace and Araben ny Fahaleovantena (when it was all trees), some funeral art carvings, porcelain pots,

an Indian doorway from Nosy Be, and that's about it.

## Zoma & Markets

The Zoma is the big market held every Friday on Araben ny Fahaleovantena. It is actually, however, just an extension of the proliferation of street stalls which operate daily around the centre of Tana.

The Zoma is claimed, by the Malagasy, to be the second biggest open air market in the world. They never tell you which is the first. It is certainly an impressive sight, particularly from the balconies of the Hôtel Select or Hôtel Glacier but, although crowded, the Zoma can hardly be described as bustling.

The Zoma traders, under octagonal white umbrellas, are grouped by the goods they sell. Generally, the best place to buy Malagasy crafts is on the Air France-Air Madagascar side of the avenue and behind the burnt-out shell of the town hall (hôtel de ville). There is a permanent section of stalls there. The CCAC and Hôtel de France side of the street specialises in clothes, and car parts and books are based around the Hôtel Glacier.

It is a sorry reflection of increasing hardship in the city that you find so many people selling what is literally rubbish. These people are not part of the Zoma. You'll find them on any day on any street, but mainly near the railway line. Families

Top: The Zoma, Antananarivo (DC)
Bottom: Lac Tritriva, near Antsirabe (RW)

Top: Girls weaving mats in village Near Tamatave (RW)
Bottom: Early morning on the Pangalanes Canal (DC)

huddle around a few old vegetables laid out in front of them, trying to scrape together a few Malagasy francs.

It is also a display of pride amid desperation. In one small area I found old single shoes, rags, thongs made out of tyre rubber, warped records, pieces of wire and rusty nails being offered for sale. As one Malagasy commented: 'everything has a value'.

There are easier and more lucrative ways to make a quick buck; so there are frequent warnings about looking after your handbag, shoulder bag, wallet, camera, etc when walking in the Zoma. Keep a tight grip on whatever you are carrying at all times. The thieves are noted more for grabbing and snatching than picking and slipping.

### Churches

On the way up to the Queen's Palace you pass the main Catholic cathedral of Andohalo and the Anglican church of Ambohimanoro. The Merinas are mostly Protestant and many are regular church-goers. It is interesting to join a Sunday morning service.

### Other Attractions

On Arabe Victoire Rasoamanarivo stands the tomb of former prime minister Rainiharo.

Just below the Queen's Palace, at the foot of Làlana Raonivalo, is one of the old gates to the Rova. It was closed by rolling a huge boulder in front of it. The boulder now stands permanently to the side. Above is the old residence of the Malagasy prime ministers, which is not open to the public.

Nearby, on the top of the cliff face, is the church of Amboninampamarinana. You can walk up the cliff side to the church from Arabe Rabozaka below, which connects the stadium and the Tsimbazaza zoo gardens.

In the middle of Lac Anosy, on an island connected to the shore by a causeway, stands the Monument aux Morts (Monument of the Dead), a giant war memorial erected by the French.

If you are aimlessly strolling around this area, you may be spotted by the eagle eyes of one Daniel Randimbharijao, an unofficial and semidistinguished tourist guide of advanced years, a chequered past and a slight frame. He might pass for 'dapper' among the Malagasy. He will forcibly befriend you by introducing himself and enquiring after your health in several languages. (His English needs practice.) He will present his card. One side declares him a *directeur* and member of various bodies including the university and the 'society of the friends of the library'. The other promises a 'welcome service assured by Leidan'. (Leidan is an anagram of Daniel.) This entitles him to rattle off potted histories of Tana's royal and recent past and present you with a lucky bag of the less colourful and less precious Malagasy minerals.

His reward? Yes, money gladly received; if not, a cognac and coffee at the Hôtel de France will do just fine. He's hard to shake off. So don't fret if you miss him or he misses you. Madagascar is full of such colourful characters.

### Places to Stay

There is a wide choice of accommodation in the centre of Tana. If you are not happy with one place, you can always shift to another nearby. I moved three times within six days, halving the price and standard each time.

It's only worth the effort of making a telephone booking for the better hotels, but even they are rarely, if ever, fully booked. Most of the lower standard places have no telephone anyway.

All rates are given in FMg, but the Hilton, Colbert and Hôtel de France and Le Lac, at least, must be paid in foreign currency.

### Places to Stay - bottom end

For a cheap and friendly doss, in a nice part of town, try the *Auberge de Jeunesse* at 76 Làlana Ranavalona, south-east of the central post office on the way to the Queen's Palace. It is not affiliated with any organisation, but it is run along the lines of a youth hostel.

The ground floor of the Auberge de Jeunesse is split into seven compartments, including two singles, so it can be noisy and cramped. It caters for sports teams and travellers, charging them FMg 3000 per night for a cubicle or FMg 5000 for half board (breakfast and dinner included). The Auberge is often filled with visiting teams, but there is no phone so you can't call to check. There is no way of locking your belongings in your 'room', but the proprietor claims there have been no cases of theft, and there is someone on the door at all times. You are actually provided with a tourist map of the city, which is more than you get from the hotels.

Another cheapie worth checking is *La Cascade*, near Aven Tour car hire on Arabe Ampanjaka Toera, in the Antanimena district. It is fairly new with seven double rooms at FMg 4000 per night. Or, you can hire a room for FMg 2500 an hour – which most of the Malagasy clients do for you know what. The rooms and furniture are small and plain, but clean and it's popular with backpackers. The *hotely* café below is OK for a beer, but not for eating out.

The *Njato* (tel 280 21) at 6 Làlana Elysée, is well positioned in the middle of the diplomatic quarter. It has seven rooms which cost FMg 4000 a person per night, with a shared shower and toilet. There is also a restaurant/TV room where you can get meals for FMg 1000 to FMg 1500. At the end of the street, there is an annexe with rooms for the same price. But there are no locks for the rooms, the toilets are revolting, room service and linen are nonexistent and it is run (guarded) by youths, who are friendly but disinterested.

The *Hôtel Roger* (tel 309 69), opposite the railway line on Arabe Rainibet-simisaraka, is in a noisy and rough part of town. It has 12 rooms, each with a shower, for FMg 5500 including breakfast.

Nearby, on Làlana Karija, is the *Hôtel Nishate* (tel 268 72), a Muslim-run hotel

with 14 rooms for FMg 6000 or FMg 7000 (with shower).

Two blocks away, on Làlana Radama, is the old *Lapan'ny Vahiny*, a little Malagasy hotel of eight rooms, full of character, but with few modern comforts. Singles/doubles are FMg 3000/4000. There are no showers and you share the toilet. It's a bit dirty, but one German stone collector said he always stayed there when in Tana and had never suffered any ill effects. There is a bar downstairs where you can get simple meals for under FMg 1000.

In the same area, is the Indian-run *Indra* where a room costs FMg 7000. It is beside a disco and can be noisy, but the food is said to be good.

The *Hôtel Glacier* (tel 291 04) is at the corner of Araben ny Fahaleovantena and Làlana Rabefiraisana. It's better known as a restaurant than a hotel, but it has single and double rooms for between FMg 5000 and FMg 10,000 per night. The rooms are old fashioned, which means they either have charm or they're falling apart. Some have excellent balcony views over the main avenue and marketplace. There is little service from staff, which means the rooms are not cleaned. Toilets and showers are poor and often dirty. The hotel features old furnishings and antique portable bidets! You'll love it or hate it.

The *Hôtel Au Bolidor Lapasoa*, on the corner of Làlana Andrianampoinimerina and Làlana Radama, is conveniently placed but little else. Singles/doubles are FMg 4500/5500, and breakfast is an extra FMg 750 per person.

There are several other hotels outside the centre of the city worth trying. Recommended is the *Bridge* (tel 291 20) near the bridge tunnel on Làlana Razafindrakoto (previously 34 Rue Marguerite Barbier). The hotel has a nightclub with live music on Fridays and Saturdays and often caters for wedding parties. The Bridge's restaurant has daily menus for about FMg 4000, and breakfast for FMg 1200. Rooms with a shower and toilet cost FMg 10,000 while rooms witn a shower only are FMg 8000. A single room without a shower is FMg 5000.

The cheapest hotel I found in Tana was the *Hôtel Njiva* (tel 304 19), up the steps opposite the bridge on the corner of Arabe Rakotomalala Ratsimba and Làlana Paul Rafiringa. They have two single rooms for FMg 2000 per night and five double rooms for FMg 3500. The singles are very small and virtually empty, save for the bed, but are easily survivable.

Closer into the city on Làlana Dok Rajaofera is the *Hotely Zaodahy*. It is similar to the Njiva but with nine rooms and it's a few francs dearer.

The *Rivo Hôtel* is around the corner at 74 Làlana Rainandriamampandry. It has only four bedrooms and a single or double costs FMg 3500 per night. It looks very rough and has no locks on the doors.

### Places to Stay - middle

The best situated and most popular hotel with travellers and non-package tourists is the big *Hôtel Terminus* (tel 203 76), directly opposite the central railway station. It's an old hotel, managed by Madame Morvan, and seems to have a few odd, permanent expat guests. Rooms are clean and at least have wash basins. Singles/doubles are FMg 9000/11,000, with a toilet and shower. There is no air-con. Breakfast is an extra FMg 1200 per person.

Directly across the avenue, on the other corner, is the Chinese-run *La Muraille de Chine* (tel 230 13). Rates are similar to the Terminus, but include breakfast and you may now have to pay in foreign currency. Check to see if there is an extra charge for air-con. The hotel has a much better restaurant than the Terminus.

*Hôtel Le Lac* (tel 282 51), north of the central railway station near the small lake in Behoririka, is the four bedroom annexe and restaurant of a 'larger bungalow complex out near Ivato International Airport at Mandrosoa (tel 448 23). It is trying to model itself on the French

*Villages Vacances Familles* holiday villages. The annexe rooms in Tana cost between FMg 7000 and FMg 9000. At Mandrosoa, 14 km from Tana centre, the bungalows cost between FMg 14,000 and FMg 17,000 a night. You can play tennis, ping-pong, boules and something called 'baby foot'; and you can eat Chinese, French or Malagasy meals.

The *Anjary Hôtel* (tel 244 09), on Làlana Dokotera Ranaivo near the end of Làlana Radama on the seedier side of the centre, has rooms from FMg 8000 to FMg 10,000, with breakfast an extra FMg 1000.

Closer to Araben ny Fahaleovantena, at 3 Làlana Nice, is the *Hôtel Mellis* (tel 234 25). It has nine family rooms for FMg 11,500, 28 double rooms for FMg 10,000 and four single rooms for FMg 8500. Breakfast is an extra FMg 1250.

In the upper part of town, around the central post office and government buildings, is the *Hôtel Negresky* (tel 286 77). It's at the end of Làlana Ratsimilaho, along from Aeroflot. Rates for the six rooms range from FMg 10,000 to FMg 12,000. Breakfast is an extra FMg 1500.

The *Pavillon de Jade* (tel 202 73), at 20 Làlana Ranarivelo to the north of the centre, is a Chinese-run hotel and restaurant. It has nine rooms, each with a toilet and shower. Singles/doubles are FMg 12,000/13,000 per night.

The *Hôtel Select* (tel 210 01), at 54 Araben ny 26 Jona 1960, is far from 'select', but it is clean and friendly. Singles/doubles cost FMg 15,000 with a shower and bath. Breakfast is FMg 1500. The rooms are big and haven't changed much since the 1950s. There is no air-con. Try and get a room on the 6th floor with a balcony overlooking the avenue; the view is marvellous. There's a tethered lemur on the dining room terrace.

The *Hôtel de France* (tel 213 04), on Araben ny Fahaleovantena, is really classed in the top bracket by the tour operators, but for my money it is not in the exclusive class of the Colbert or Hilton. Single or double air-con rooms are around

FMg 49,000 per night, although you'll get a reduction if you're on a package tour. The restaurant has a good reputation. Breakfast costs FMg 4000 and the set menu is about FMg 7000.

Another favourite with tour operators is the *Solimotel* (tel 250 40), near the railway line and southern taxi-brousse station in Anosibe. Singles/doubles at this new 'petrol motel' are FMg 18,500/20,500 per night with air-con. Breakfast is an extra FMg 4000.

### Places to Stay - top end

There are only two hotels in this category. The *Hilton Hotel* (tel 260 60) is where you will find the foreign correspondents if there is anything of international news value happening in the country. It is the tallest building in the country and has 190 rooms. Singles/doubles start around FMg 119,500/150,500 (about US$75/95) per night. Group and package rates are cheaper.

The Hilton's continental-style breakfast costs FMg 7350 and an American-style one is FMg 9800. Meals are about FMg 15,000. If you call into their *Restaurant Orchidée* for a coffee (with milk) to read your mail or write your postcards, that'll cost you FMg 1500. The hotel's arcade has foreign exchange facilities, souvenir shops, clothes shops and the Madagascar Airtours office. There is also a nightclub, small casino and a swimming pool.

The Hilton's rival, the *Hôtel Colbert* (tel 202 02), on Làlana Printsy Ratsimamanga (opposite the central post office), is a throwback to French imperialism at its best – or worst, whichever way you look at it. It is smaller, plusher and cheaper than the Hilton, and my choice of the two if I could afford it. Air-con rooms start at about FMg 83,000, with studios at FMg 110,000. Breakfast costs FMg 4000 and meals are Fmg 11,000.

### Places to Eat

Antananarivo is not known as a gourmet's paradise, despite more than half a century of French rule. There are few places of *haute cuisine*, in fact most cater for the lower order of taste buds. The choice, however, is wide and the quality generally good and safe. The only case of food poisoning I heard of happened after a meal at the Hilton!

Many restaurants have set daily menus (*menus du jour*) from which to choose. These are much cheaper than ordering à la carte dishes, but the prices do increase on Sundays and public holidays (See the Food and Drinks sections in Facts for the Visitor.)

**Street Stalls** These are everywhere around the busy parts of the centre. During the day, they sell yoghurt, ice cream, meat brochettes and unidentified objects fried in batter. At night you can get potato and celery broth for FMg 50 a bowl. Bring your own salt though. There is also meat and rice, if you want to take more of a risk.

**Malagasy Hotelys** You'll find them outside the centre of town. In those which do not have tablecloths, you can get a Malagasy meal of rice with meat and boiled vegetable (usually cabbage) for under FMg 1000!

**Salons de Thé** There are several salons on Araben ny Fahaleovantena and Araben ny 26 Jona 1960. Coffee costs FMg 500, as do sausage rolls, cakes and other sweets and savouries. Some places specialise in ice cream concoctions which cost up to FMg 1500. The best salons are the *Honey* and *Blanche Neige* both on the Air Mad/ Air France side of the street. The Blanche Neige was a famous street café during the French colonial period. Across the road is the smaller *Friendship Garden*, and in the arcade leading to the Supermarché is *Le Pingouin*.

**Chinese** About 80% of the medium range restaurants are Chinese, and they are all good value. The best is the *Grand Orient* near the railway station on Kianja

Ambiky. You get a good meal for about FMg 5000 in very pleasant and relaxing surroundings. The service is top class and you are not made to feel hurried. The wine is well priced too. At night, a musical duo plays French and Malagasy songs. It is much more romantic than just another Chinese meal.

*La Grande Ile*, 8 Làlana Paul Dussac (the street on the upper level behind the post office on Araben ny 26 Jona 1960), also serves good food, but without the romance. It is more of a family restaurant.

*La Muraille de Chine* down the street, also has good Chinese cuisine, but the beer is expensive.

The *Relais Normand* (Really Norman!), on Arabe Rainibetsimisaraka, also has a good name, but when it rains there are floods on the street outside and the waiters have to carry the patrons into the restaurant and boat them back to their cars!

Next to the Auberge de Jeunesse is a nice Chinese café-restaurant called the *Bon Accueil*, which has meals for around FMg 1000.

**Indian** Indian restaurants are rare. The *Shalimar*, around the corner from the Relais Normand on Làlana Mahafaka, is a modern restaurant and salon de thé with curries for FMg 2000. There is also the *Indra*, near the Hôtel Njato.

**Italian** The Hôtel de France has a *Pizzeria*.

**Muslim** Opposite the Anjary Hotel is a Muslim café called the *Kismet*. Try their ravitoto.

**French** The two top eating spots in Tana are said to be the *Hôtel Colbert* and *La Rotonde*. The latter is run by a Mauritian and is a favourite with the Tana business set and *bons vivants*. Is not expensive by western standards, however, if you stick to the set menu which costs about FMg 7000.

The Colbert's dishes range from FMg 6000 up. They include such wonders as tripe in apple brandy sauce, *paillarde de zebu*, and *nymphes* which are frogs' legs. The Hôtel de France and Hôtel Glacier also have good restaurants, as do a number of the better hotels.

## Entertainment & Recreation

The Centre Culturel Albert Camus, near the Hôtel Terminus on Araben ny Fahaleovantena, is the main cultural centre in Tana. It screens feature films and videos daily, has regular concert and theatre performances, and presents local and international art exhibitions. Call in for a free monthly programme. CCAC costs FMg 10,000 a year to join, but visitors can pay separately for specific events. Tickets for folk or pop concerts in other locations are also sold there.

The US Cultural Center also shows free video movies and American TV programmes during the week.

You can see regular Malagasy theatre and dance performances at the old colonial Théâtre Municipal in the Isotry district. Check the bill posters for dates and times.

There are a few cinemas, including the Ako, further up from the Hôtel Select and post office on Araben ny 26 Jona 1960. Seats cost between FMg 150 and Fmg 800. On the way out to the north taxi-brousse station, before the bridge on Làlana Ranarivelo, is the Cinema Soa.

There are limited opportunities for more active pursuits. The Association Culturelle et Sportif d'Ambohidahy (ASCA), on Làlana Jean Ralaimongo leading down to Lac Anosy, is the most central. It is open to non-members for swimming, tennis or table tennis.

The club also has a café which is frequented by French expats, the diplomatic community and the Malagasy elite. However, one diplomat said it was very cliquey and served worse coffee than British Rail!

## Nightlife

**Discos & Nightclubs** It's not quite Paris, but Tana has a surprisingly lively nightlife. Araben ny Fahaleovantena is Tana's Champs Elysée and it never seems to go to sleep. There are lots of stalls selling food and you'll often come across musicians performing in the streets.

The *brasseries* and terrace cafés of the Hôtel de France and the Hôtel Terminus are filled until late with French expats, Malagasy business people, tourists and, increasingly, prostitutes. The girls are not pushy or hard bitten, though many have turned to the oldest profession to avoid starvation. The poverty in Tana is all too visible around these cafés in the faces of emaciated, begging children. The hotels Glacier and Colbert also have a busy café set, but are less disturbing.

There is a wide choice of discos and dance halls, the merits of which were outlined to me, surprisingly, by a rather quiet and sober diplomat. Most places are discos, but some have live bands or orchestras, which play a mixture of Malagasy, western rock/folk and prewar French dance music.

It costs around FMg 3000 to get in, which includes one beer. According to the dancing diplomat the *Calumet Club*, near the Soarano station, and *Le Caveau*, on Arabe Grandidier Rabahevitra, are the best. *Le Papillon*, at the Madagascar Hilton, is the most prestigious, and has live music. The *Kaleidoscope*, near the Hôtel Colbert, attracts the 'teenyboppers', and opposite the Hôtel de France on Araben ny Fahaleovantena is the *Boite 7/7*. Then there's the shadier *Cellier* nightclub, near the hotels Lapan'ny Vahiny and Nishate, south-east of Araben ny Fahaleovantena.

Alternatively, the US diplomatic corps runs a TGIF (Thank God It's Friday) knees-up at the Marine House in Invadry (tel 212 57 or 209 56), starting with a 'happy hour'. They usually welcome visitors, but ring to check for times and an invitation.

## Getting There & Around

**Bus** Most buses to anywhere in the city begin and end on Araben ny Fahaleovantena and Araben ny 26 Jona 1960 in the centre of town. They are usually very full.

Five companies, or cooperatives, operate the routes – FIBATA, FIMA, MALAKIA, KOMAFI and ANTAFITA. They only stop at bus stops and there's no need to clap, whistle or ring bells when you want to get off because they stop at every one. Beware of pickpockets in the crush, although the threat is nowhere as great as buses in say Bangkok or Jakarta. The standard fare for any distance is FMg 50. Each bus has a conductor.

**Taxi-brousse** Taxis-brousses serve the towns and villages around Tana, and the rest of the country. The district taxis-brousses also come into town.

There are four taxi-brousse and taxi-be stations, or *gares routières*, serving the north, south, east and west of Madagascar. The two main ones are the north gare routière at Ambodivona (for Tamatave, Majunga and Diego Suarez), and the south gare routière at Anosibe (for Antsirabe, Fianarantsoa etc). The latter is about 1½ km south-west of Lac Anosy on Làlana Pastora Rahajason.

To get to the north gare routière, take a MALAKIA No 4 bus from the centre of town. For the south bus station, take a FIMA No 10 bus. For the west station, behind Soarano railway station, you can walk or catch a KOMAFI No 23 or No 8 bus. And for the east station, way out at Ampasampito, you want an ANTAFITA No 1 or No 2 bus.

Taxis-brousses for Ivato village, one km from the airport, leave every 15 minutes from outside the Hôtel Terminus near the railway station.

**Taxi** There are plenty of taxis in Tana, but stick to the Citroen 2CVs or Renault 4s as they're cheaper than other sedans. Avoid the ones hanging around outside the hotels Hilton, Colbert and France because they will charge inflated prices for tourists. Those which gather outside the ruins of the town hall on Araben ny Fahaleovantena are also quite greedy. Fares range from FMg 1000 to FMg 1500 anywhere in town during the daytime, with an extra FMg 800 after dark.

## AMBOHIMANGA

This is probably the most popular day trip out of the capital. It's only 25 km north of Tana but provides a dramatic contrast to city surroundings. Red earth and eucalyptus trees should make Australian travellers feels at home. En route, you pass several small hamlets and you may feel you have stepped into a people-less Breughal painting. There are tombs of Malagasy ancestors to be seen, but they are mostly large undecorated cement blocks.

Ambohimanga means 'Blue Hill'.

### The Rova

The palace of King Andrianampoinimerina (1788-1810) at Ambohimanga is very spartan compared to the Queen's Palace in Tana, but still worth a visit. The Rova is surrounded by high walls against attack. King A's body is not here though; it was laid to rest in the palace in Tana.

His home, the *Bevato*, is like a big black wooden shed with a high, sloping roof and bunk beds. His majesty's bed is up near the ceiling, and the beds belonging to his 12 wives are down on the floor. Spears, shields and eating utensils cover the walls.

The royal bath is in the grounds along with the solarium, tomb and sacrificial stone. Virgin girls used to carry the water from the nearby sacred lake of Ampparihy to fill the bath. Next to the Bevato are the meeting house and visiting apartments of the monarchs who succeeded him. Ambohimanga became the weekend retreat for the three Ranavalona queens.

In the village itself, about one km down the hill from the Rova, is one of seven gateways to the palace grounds. To one side is a giant flat round stone ready to slide across with the help of 40 slaves! Next to it is a pagoda-style monstrosity of a private house.

The Rova is open to the public every day, except Monday, from 8 to 11 am and 2 to 5 pm. Guided tours, in French, are compulsory but free.

### Places to Stay & Eat

About five km from Ambohimanga, en route from Tana, is the *Auberge du Soleil Levant* (tel 426 12) – yes, the house of the rising sun! It is isolated, but worth calling by, if only to taste the bibasy fruit off their trees. It is a very simple, rustic and friendly place. There is electricity, but no running water (that comes from the well). Rates range from FMg 4000 to FMg 7500 a night for a single or double. The Auberge has a separate restaurant.

Next to the Rova itself, is the *Restaurant Rova*. It has a terrific view across the countryside to Tana, and the owner, Madame Fleurette, has been known to sing to guests. If not, there may be a dress rehearsal or display of Malagasy dancing by villagers, with music.

### Getting There & Away

Take a taxi-brousse from the northern gare routière in Tana. The taxi-brousse takes you right to its terminus in Ambohimanga village. You must then walk about one km up the hill to the Rova. A one-way ticket is FMg 300. Transcontinents and Madagascar Airtours run a half day bus tour. If you join a big party it would cost about FMg 6000 per person.

## LAC ITASY

This volcanic lake at Ampefy village, and the nearby Mandraka Dam, are 140 km south-west of Tana along Route National 1. To get there take a taxi-brousse from the southern gare routière at Anosibe in Tana.

You can stay at the *Kavitaha* (tel 4) or at the *Bungalows Administratifs*, which you must book first in Tana at the Logistic Service, 10 Rue de Nice.

## LAC MANTASOA
This large artificial lake is 65 km east of Tana on the road to Tamatave. On its shores, the French castaway Jean Laborde built a foundry to supply her royal awfulness Queen Ranavalona I with guns and other nasty implements.

There are opportunities for fishing, swimming and sailing, and you can stay and eat at the 27 room *L'Ermitage* hotel (tel 05).

### Getting There & Away
Take the early morning Tana to Tamatave train as far as Manjakandriana, from where you hitch or take a taxi the remaining 15 km down to the lake. The one way 1st/2nd class fare is FMg 1230/675.

Alternatively, you can take a taxi-brousse from Tana's northern gare routière at a cost of around FMg 500 one-way. The trouble with this is that the last returning taxi-brousse can be as early as 11 am. A day tour by Transcontinents would cost FMg 15,000 per person, without meals. Madagascar Airtours are much dearer.

## AMBATOLAMPY
The forest station of Manjakatompo and the hills of the Ankaratra Massif, 80 km south-west of the capital, are interesting areas for hiking.

To get there take the Tana to Antsirabe train (FMg 1680/925 for 1st/2nd class) and alight at Ambatolampy, or take a taxi-brousse from Tana's southern gare routière. You then walk or take a taxi-brousse to the forest station via Ankeniheny village.

This route takes you past Lac Froid and to the foot of the 2643 metre high Tsiafajavona ('place of standing mists'). Don't forget to get a permit first from the Direction des Eaux et Forêts in Tana.

The place to eat or stay here is the *Rendezvous des Pêcheurs* in Ambatolampy.

## IVATO
Ivato is Antananarivo's international airport, named after the nearby village which is 15 km from the city. If you have flown back from, say, Ile Ste Marie and have another flight to catch the next morning but you don't fancy trailing in and out of Tana by taxi, there are some modest hotel alternatives in and around Ivato village. One of the better ones is perhaps *Le Bon Coin*. About one km from Ivato, on the road into Tana, is the *Auberge Cheval Blanc*.

See the Airport Transport section section of the Madagascar Getting There chapter for details of getting to and from the airport.

## ANTSIRABE
This Merina town, with a population of 90,000, is 169 km south of the capital in Tananarive province. It was 'developed' around the hot springs by the French in the 1920s, as a health retreat from the rigours of Tana and the feverish coast.

They built the grand Hôtel des Thermes, the churches, shops and the post office. They also built the railway from Tana, its station at the other end of a wide boulevard and made a small lake in the centre for all to overlook. This Malagasy Vichy was like a small version of Tana.

The Malagasy have kept the thermal baths and surrounding amenities in use without changing much. The town also boasts the Star Brewery (producer of Three Horses Beer), a cotton mill and a tobacco factory.

Antsirabe is well worth a few days away from Tana or on the road to Fiana or Tulear – but be warned, it gets quite cold during the winter months.

### Thermal Baths
These have changed little since being built earlier this century. They are worth having a look at, but it's best to try a private thermal bath when you're exhausted, like after a walk to Lac Tritriva.

Immersion in the mineral-rich water from the hot springs is said to assist in

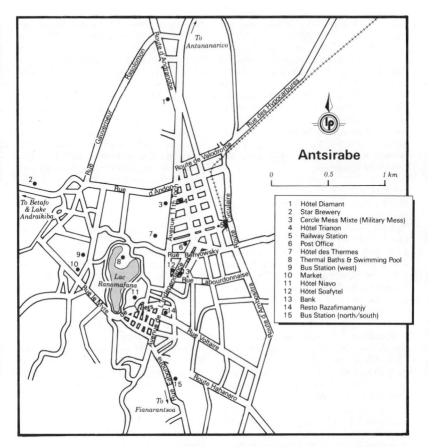

**Antsirabe**

| 0 | 0.5 | 1 km |

1 Hôtel Diamant
2 Star Brewery
3 Cercle Mess Mixte (Military Mess)
4 Hôtel Trianon
5 Railway Station
6 Post Office
7 Hôtel des Thermes
8 Thermal Baths & Swimming Pool
9 Bus Station (west)
10 Market
11 Hôtel Niavo
12 Hôtel Soafytel
13 Bank
14 Resto Razafimamanjy
15 Bus Station (north/south)

curing rheumatism, liver and gall bladder problems. The lake was created mainly for ornamental purposes, but it also helps prevent the escape of thermal gases. The baths are closed on Thursday and Friday afternoons, except for physiotherapy and other special treatments, and all day on Sundays. Entry is FMg 100 to the pool or for a 20 minute private bath. You have to bring a towel.

A new swimming pool was built recently and must be one of the few, if not the only, municipal indoor pools in the country. The Malagasy are healthy patrons of this one. The pool is open from 7 to 11.30 am and 2 to 5.30 pm Monday to Wednesday, and Saturdays from 7 to 11 am.

### Lac Andraikiba
This large lake is seven km west of Antsirabe on the road to Betafo. It was a favourite retreat of Queen Ranavalona II in the 19th century. The French turned it into a holiday aquatic centre. The lake is said to be haunted by the ghost of a girl who drowned, when pregnant, in a race with another girl for the hand in marriage

of a Merina dignitary. Villagers say she can be seen at dawn sitting on a rock.

To get to the lake, take one of the new buses going to Betafo from the market bus station. It costs FMg 100 and the buses run every hour. You can walk from the main road, about one km, to the lakeside. The Club Nautique lakeside chalet is usually deserted during the week but on weekends there may be a chance of water skiing. There is a high-diving board and swimming area. You can get drinks at the bar in the clubhouse.

### Lac Tritriva

Much more interesting and a bigger challenge (even to pronounce) is Lac Tritriva, about 12 km into the hills past Lac Andraikiba to the south. You may get a lift from a passing taxi-brousse or local car. If not, the three hour walk through several small villages is rewarding. You'll be greeted by fear, amusement, derision and warmth. There is a good track up to the edge of the crater lake, which can be done by taxi during dry weather.

The deep lake can be beautiful or forbidding, depending on the weather. I found it an eerie place, even when the sun was shining, and when a thunderstorm broke it was frightening. The crater is very quiet and very deep. The lake is mostly surrounded by a sheer cliff wall, but there is a path leading down through the pine trees to the water's edge. You can dive straight in if you have the courage. Sadly, much of the forest around it is being hacked down for timber.

This lake also has its legends. One is that it is cursed by two lovers who leapt from the cliff edge in a suicide pact when they were refused permission to marry. There is supposed to be a plaque on the cliff's edge commemorating the failed attempt of a vazaha who defied the curse and tried to swim across the lake. I couldn't find it.

### Places to Stay

The *Hôtel des Thermes* (tel 487 61)

dominates Antsirabe like a royal palace, with gardens to boot. This colonial edifice is empty much of the time. It may be expensive to stay in, compared to other options, but it is worth visiting for a look-see or a meal. It also has a swimming pool and tennis courts which nonresidents can use for a fee (FMg 750 per hour for tennis and FMg 1250 for a swim). Standard rooms are FMg 20,000 per night, with apartments and suites at around twice that cost. The set menus, served in high style, cost FMg 5000 during the week and FMg 7000 on weekends. Breakfast is FMg 1500.

If you can't spoil yourself, then there are several good alternatives. The cheapest is the *Hôtel Niavo* (tel 484 67), up a laneway off Rue le Myre de Villers. Some of the bedrooms have great views across the lake to the thermal baths and church. Rates range from FMg 3500 for rooms without cold showers to FMg 5000 with them. All are decorated with Disney portraits. The Indian-run hotel has a good restaurant, bar and TV room. On the menu is 'hamburger à cheval'!

The *Cercle Mess Mixte* is the Malagasy Army's living quarters. You'll find these in many towns and they're always a fall-back for accommodation if you are really stuck. Antsirabe used to be a main troop base for the French, and that may be why this hostel has a prominent position in town along the avenue from the Hôtel des Thermes. Standard rooms are FMg 4000 or FMg 4500 with a shower. There are better rooms and private studios, if you want to go senior officer class. You don't have to get up at reveille, but you must check out before 9 am.

The Hôtel Baobab, at the fork of Ave de l'Indépendance and Rue Georges V, did not have a very good name. It was dirty and poorly managed. However, it has now changed hands and become the *Hôtel Soafytel*. (*Soa* in Malagasy means 'nice' and *fy* is 'delicious'.) The young management is enthusiastic and full of good intentions, promising French trained

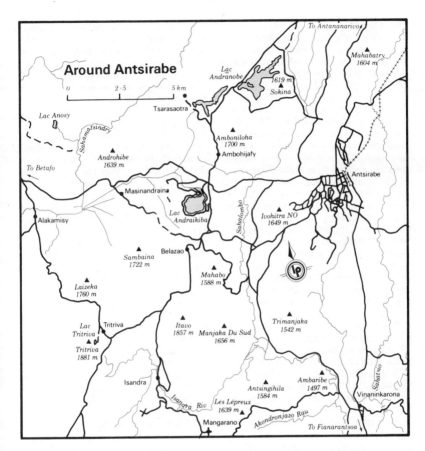

**Around Antsirabe**

chefs. There are 21 refurbished rooms ranging from FMg 5000 for a single or double with a basin, to FMg 8000 with a toilet and hot water. The building is leased from the Tulear province authorities.

The *Hôtel Diamant* (tel 488 40), in the northern part of town on the road to Tana, has 48 rooms and good food.

Finally, there is the *Hôtel Trianon* (tel 488 81). This hotel is opposite the Cercle Mess Mixte and is owned and managed by an old French expat named Monsieur Maurel. He arrived in Madagascar in 1941 as a member of the gendarmes. Now his

passion is collecting and selling semi-precious stones and Malagasy artefacts, and he has a large collection of minerals on display. Pictures of General de Gaulle cover the wall of his office. Several of the young French travellers, not surprisingly, find themselves at odds with this former *colon* and his attitudes to Madagascar and France today. Other nationalities, however, may find him an interesting character. The hotel only has four large bedrooms at FMg 5000 a night for a single or double. Breakfast is FMg 1500 and meals are FMg 4000.

## Places to Eat

The hotels offer the main choice – the *Niavo* is cheap. Otherwise, there is the *Razafimamanjy* in the centre of town on the Ave de l'Indépendance and nearby, the Vietnamese *Le Fleuve Parfumé*.

## Getting There & Away

Taxis-brousses and taxis-bes run daily from Fianarantsoa and Tana (southern gare routière) to Antsirabe. Taxis-brousses run less frequently from Morondava. A taxi-brousse trip to or from Fiana leaves early in the morning, takes seven hours and costs FMg 3500. A taxi-be costs FMg 4500. A taxi-brousse to Antsirabe from Tana costs FMg 1500.

If you're going from Tana to Antsirabe, or points between, it is best to take the train for comfort, speed and scenery. It leaves Tana twice a day during the week, at 5.20 am and 1.30 pm, and takes four hours. It leaves Antsirabe to return to Tana at 4.50 am and 1 pm. On weekends and holidays there are three trains.

The track is narrow-gauge and provides an amazing roller coaster ride, stopping at 12 stations including Ambatolampy. It costs FMg 4000/2200 for 1st/2nd class, although they both smell awful because of the toilets. The track passes rice paddies and tombs, and if you take the afternoon train from Tana in the winter months, you can see great sunsets.

When you arrive at Antsirabe, prepare to be mobbed by pousse-pousse drivers. They will fight between themselves to get you and your baggage into a rickshaw. It's a way of getting the price down, and you feel that if you wait long enough they'll pay you to go in their cart!

## Getting Around

The pousse-pousse reigns in Antsirabe, a legacy of the Chinese coolie labour imported to work on the Tana to Antsirabe railway. They are more plentiful and more decorative here than in any other Malagasy town. The rickshaws became known as pousse-pousses, not because they scoot around like cats, but because when going up hills the pullers would shout to others to get behind the cart and 'push-push'. Locals pay Fmg 300 for a ride, but tourists can expect to pay at least FMg 500. Often, one driver will attach himself to you for the duration of your stay, waiting outside your hotel in the morning and restaurant in the evening.

Antsirabe also has a spanking new bus fleet, courtesy of Japanese aid, which serves the surrounding towns and villages. The drivers and conductors wear uniform overalls. They leave from the bus station next to the Sabotsy market, west of the lake. Fares are very cheap. Taxis also congregate at the market.

# Tamatave (Toamasina) Province

Tamatave is called the Coast of Rosewood or Coast of Greenery, among other less passive names such as the Cyclone Coast and Pirate Coast. The region includes the main town, Tamatave, the rice producing plain of Maroantsetra, the Nosy Mangabe nature reserve, the rainforests around Perinet (Andasibe), the giant Pangalanes Canal and the former pirate havens of the Bay of Antongil and Ile Ste Marie. The latter is the principal attraction for visitors.

It is said there are two seasons for Tamatave province - the wet season and the season when it rains. Every few decades it suffers a very bad blow. Tamatave town was flattened by a cyclone in 1927 and another one caused a great deal of damage on Ile Ste Marie in March 1986.

All this rain makes the Tamatave region the lushest in the country. It has large areas of rainforest, where 90% of the trees are endemic, and a rich variety of palms and pandanus on the coast. Cloves, vanilla, coffee and fruit are produced for export.

The people of the densely populated coastal strip are mostly Betsimisaraka. Formed about 250 years ago this is the newest tribe in Madagascar.

The coast around Tamatave may have many fine beaches, but it is dangerous for bathing because of sharks and currents. Beaches at Mahambo, Foulpointe and Fenoarivo are said to be safe, but double check conditions somehow before using them.

There is a relatively good road from Tana to Tamatave, but unless you have the chance of a lift, it is best to go by train on the very scenic ride through the hills, forests and waterfalls. The Tana to Tamatave line goes directly east, following the road for much of the way, until it hits the sea. Then it does a sharp left and follows the coast and Pangalanes Canal up to Tamatave. (I was told that Air Mad planes follow the same route!) See the Tamatave Getting There & Away section for more details.

## Pirate History

At the end of the 17th century and beginning of the 18th, the east coast of Madagascar around Ile Ste Marie became the world's pirate headquarters. The rich pickings in the Caribbean had become thinner, and policing by the English and French navies heavier. The island was an ideal base from which to set out and ambush the many traders sailing around the Cape of Good Hope to and from India and the Far East.

Many of the pirate leaders, their men and slaves, set up home - or in some cases little kingdoms - in Madagascar. Among them were John Avery, William Kidd, Thomas Tew, John Plantain, Olivier Levasseur (La Buse), and Captain Misson. They married women from local tribes and the offspring, the mulattos, were known as *zana-malata*.

An English pirate, John Avery, set up base about 1695 in the Bay of Antongil. Maroantsetra now lies at the head of the bay. One of the ships he raided was that of an Indian grand mogul on his way to Mecca. On board with the booty was the daughter of an oriental sovereign, whom Avery took as his bride.

He made treaties with neighbouring kings and proclaimed himself a fellow ruler. It is not known how or when Avery's time ended. Some say he returned to England under a different name to live out his days.

However, it was Ratsimilaho, the son of another English pirate, believed to be Thomas Tew, who was to have the greatest impact on the area.

Ratsimilaho was leader of the zana-malata and became founder and chief of the Betsimisaraka tribe. When he died, his daughter Bety took over. She fell in love with a Frenchman and handed over sovereignty of Ile Ste Marie to France in 1750.

Into the story now came the amazing Hungarian-born Baron Benyowski. An officer in the Austrian army, Baron Benyowski was captured by Russians while fighting in Poland. To cut a long, but fascinating story short, he arrived in Madagascar in 1773 and founded a community called Louisville, again in the Bay of Antongil.

Benyowski's power grew through treaties and force, and he went a step further than Avery by declaring himself Emperor of Madagascar. But when he sailed to France to negotiate with the king, his kingdom collapsed. He returned in 1785 to get it back, but was killed at Foulpointe. There is no trace of Louisville now or any grave for Benyowski.

## PERINET RESERVE

If you have time en route from Tana to Tamatave, this forest reserve and former logging centre is worth a stopover for the chance of seeing the rare indri lemur and other wonders of Malagasy flora and fauna.

In the lounge section of the Hôtel de la Gare's dining room, there is a small collection of books, including Dervla Murphy's *Muddling Through in Madagascar* (see Books & Bookshops in Facts for the Visitor), in which she dedicates several pages to Perinet. Her name is in the visitors' book along with other scientists and writers.

Perinet, the hotel and the forest reserve feature prominently in another book – *Zoo Quest to Madagascar* by David Attenborough, who was here looking for the indri lemur.

### National Reserve

The trains arrive in Perinet between 10.30 and 11 am each day. You should arrange a guide as soon as possible, especially if you

Zebu tomb carvings; symbols of wealth & prestige

only intend to stay the night. A visit to the forest reserve also requires a permit, which you must obtain from the Direction des Eaux et Forêts in Tana beforehand. (If you do not have a permit, you might be able to get in under someone else's permit.)

It is unlikely you will spot any chameleons or lemurs without a guide. You also may get lost. To get to the park and warden's house, you walk about half a km down the main road to Tamatave.

The *chef de la réserve* is called Joseph. That is also the name of his young son, who often acts as an unofficial guide. His French is good, but he has no English. He will not seek payment, but deserves a suitable 'donation'.

It took Attenborough over three days to get a glimpse of the indri lemur, although he often heard their baby-like wailing.

Joseph Jnr will know where to look for the indri and how to shout for them. He will also seek out chameleons, the mouse-like lemurs, orchids and carp. If you miss any or all of those, there are many beautiful butterflies to compensate your efforts. You'll need insect repellent and bring a good torch because your best chances are at night. Look out for leeches too, if it is very wet.

The nature walks can be supplemented by a tour of the village, a graphite mine and small sawmills. The graphite refining process is simple but fascinating – and very dirty.

About eight km along the road to Tamatave is the hill of Maromiza, which provides a great viewpoint for the whole region.

### Places to Stay

As soon as you step off the train, you fall into the *Hôtel de la Gare* buffet, bar and dining room. The hotel almost justifies a visit in itself. It was built in 1938 after the fashion of an alpine lodge, is clean and has lots of character. Single/double rooms with washbasins are FMg 10,000/12,000 per night. There are hot showers in the toilets. Meals cost between FMg 3000 and FMg 6000.

### AMBILA LEMAITSO

This is where the railway line from Tana arrives at the coast. The area, alongside the Pangalanes Canal, is popular with holidaying Malagasy.

The *Hôtel Relais Malaky* is right on the beach. Four km further on there is *Les Everglades* seaside bungalow complex (tel Ambila 01). This modest resort offers trips by trimaran and motor boat along the canal, 4WD vehicle tours into the forest, windsurfing and water skiing. The brochure claims: *Très rares moustiques* and *Pas de bilharziose* – mosquitoes are few and there is no bilharzia! The promotional motto is: 'Les Everglades – for ever glad!'

# Tamatave (Toamasina)

Many visitors to Tamatave (population 70,000), find it a big disappointment, especially if they have been talking to the Malagasy. As well as being the country's largest port, it is also the favourite holiday destination. Tamatave is to Tana what Brighton is to London or Nice to Paris, perhaps still living on its reputation as a lively colonial town. It is officially called Toamasina in Malagasy and was named after a Spaniard called San Tomas.

For the overseas visitor, however, there is very little to do or see around the town. Most free-roaming travellers only stop for a day or two on the way up the coast, or en route to or from Ile Ste Marie.

Parts of Tamatave smell constantly of cloves. There are worse things it could smell of. They are grown in the region and exported to India as food spices and to Indonesia for their cigarettes. The Chinese are the main general traders around town.

The town planners have graced Tamatave with wide avenues and boulevards. The place seems very quiet and empty much of the time, with mostly just pousse-pousses running up and down the streets. Blvd Joffre is the main street. There is a beach, but don't swim unless you want to play with the sharks, which are attracted by the abattoir around the corner.

### Information

**Post** The main post office is on Araben ny Fahaleavantena, opposite the old town hall. It is open from 8 am to noon and 2 to 6 pm weekdays, and from 8 am to noon on Saturdays.

**Banks** The banks are also on Araben ny Fahaleavantena, one on the corner with Blvd Joffre and the other opposite the Air Mad office. They are open from 8 to 11 am and 2 to 4 pm on weekdays only.

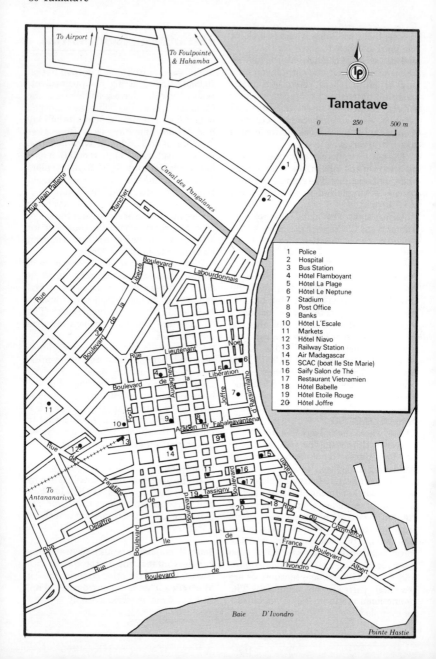

Tamatave

0    250    500 m

| 1  | Police |
| 2  | Hospital |
| 3  | Bus Station |
| 4  | Hôtel Flamboyant |
| 5  | Hôtel La Plage |
| 6  | Hôtel Le Neptune |
| 7  | Stadium |
| 8  | Post Office |
| 9  | Banks |
| 10 | Hôtel L'Escale |
| 11 | Markets |
| 12 | Hôtel Niavo |
| 13 | Railway Station |
| 14 | Air Madagascar |
| 15 | SCAC (boat Ile Ste Marie) |
| 16 | Saify Salon de Thé |
| 17 | Restaurant Vietnamien |
| 18 | Hôtel Babelle |
| 19 | Hôtel Etoile Rouge |
| 20 | Hôtel Joffre |

## Ile aux Prunes

This small island is a one hour boat ride north-east of the port. It is surrounded by a coral reef and is recommended as a mini marine park for snorkelling and fishing. For tours and the safety aspect, enquire at Hôtel Le Neptune or the Club Nautique on Blvd Ratsimilaho in Tamatave.

## Jardin d'Essai Ivoloina

This park on the banks of the River Ivoloina, 13 km north of Tamatave, is one way of seeing all the flora and fauna of the east coast in one shot. There are also lemurs and tortoises to view. A taxi from town is FMg 12,000 return; or you can catch taxis-brousses bound to and from Fenoarivo.

## Places to Stay – bottom end

On Blvd Ponthiau, bordering the railway track as it leads into the station, are four cheap Indian-run hotels in a row, each with seven to 12 rooms. The best of these is the *Niavo* (tel 333 14), which is related to hotels of the same name in Antsirabe and Ambatondrazaka. A room with a shower costs FMg 6000 or FMg 5000 without one.

The *Soamiafara, Vakinankaratra* and *Venance Fils* are much of a oneness; they all have very basic rooms for around FMg 3500 for a single or double per night, with communal toilets and showers. You can get reasonable meals at the Vakinankaratra for around FMg 1000.

Down towards the docks, behind the Hôtel Joffre on Rue du Commerce, is the *Babelle* hotel. It has seven rooms at around FMg 6500 for a single or double.

## Places to Stay – middle

The best alternatives to the good hotels, without taking risks in the cheap selection around the station, are the *Hôtel La Plage* and the *Etoile Rouge*.

The Hôtel La Plage (tel 320 90), opposite the stadium on the Blvd de la Libération, is a ramshackle sort of place and every room seems to be different in size, content and outlook. Some are good,

some are bad. Prostitutes tend to ply the hotel bar and terrace at night. Single/ double rooms range from FMg 7000/9000 per night, with communal toilets and showers.

The Etoile Rouge (tel 322 90) on Rue Delattre de Tassigny has only six rooms, but is a smart, well-run establishment. Rates are FMg 9000 for a room with a shower, FMg 13,000 for an upstairs room and FMg 15,000 for an air-con room.

*Hôtel L'Escale* is not in a good position – beside the station – to justify rates of FMg 10,000, FMg 12,000 and FMg 14,000 for rooms. Breakfast is FMg 2000.

## Places to Stay – top end

The latest up-market project is the *Hôtel Le Neptune* (tel 322 26), 35 Araben d'Ratsimilaho. This seafront hotel boasts a casino, nightclub, swimming pool and 20 air-con single/double rooms for around FMg 29,000 per night.

The *Hôtel Flamboyant* (tel 323 50) on Blvd de la Libération is similar in size, but is cheaper and less touristy. Rooms here are singles/doubles FMg 17,000/18,000, without breakfast.

These two hotels have taken over the lead from the colonial *Hôtel Joffre* (tel 323 90) on Blvd Joffre. The Joffre has more character and you can watch Tamatave life pass you by from its terrace café. Singles/doubles here are FMg 15,000/19,000 and some of the rooms have air-con.

## Places to Eat

Unlike Tulear and Fort Dauphin, Tamatave is not really noted for seafood.

Only the hotels offer European food. Otherwise, most of the places in Tamatave are plain, Asian and cheap. There are three nice restaurants close to the Hôtel Joffre. The *Restaurant Chinois* on Blvd Joffre has a wide selection of oriental dishes ranging from FMg 1500 to FMg 3000. Around the corner, on Rue A Goulette, is the *Restaurant Vietnamien*, whose dishes are virtually indistinguishable from the Chinese selection. You can eat heartily for FMg 3000. The speciality is something called *bumbao*. (Say 'bimbo' and they'll trigger.) Behind the Hôtel Joffre is the highly recommended *Fortuna*.

More Chinese fare is available from the *Cubby Hole*, further along Blvd Joffre, and the *Riaka* on Blvd Ratsimilaho.

On the salon de thé level there's the *Adam & Eve* snack bar opposite the Hôtel Joffre, and the *Saify* between Rue Billard and Rue Bertho on Boulevard Joffre. A continental breakfast of coffee, bread, butter and jam costs about FMg 1200 at the Saify.

It might also be worth checking out the *Restaurant Zanatany*, 13 Rue Delattre de Tassigny.

### Nightlife
Tamatave lets its hair down mostly at the *Queen's Club* disco on the corner of Blvd Joffre and Blvd Libération, *La Chouette* disco at 33 Rue du Commerce and at *Hôtel Le Neptune* nightclub. There is a cinema opposite the Hôtel Joffre.

### Getting There & Away
**Air** You can Air Mad it from Tana to Tamatave for about US$59. The airport is five km to the north of town, via Rue de l'Ivoloina. The Air Mad office is open each weekday from 7 to 11 am and 2 to 4 pm. (Check weekend hours – probably Saturday mornings only). Planes fly separate services from Tamatave to and from Ile Ste Marie, Maroantsetra, Sambava, Mananara (via Mandritsara) and inland to Ambatondrazaka, near the great lake Alaotra.

**Taxi-Brousse** The taxi-brousse station on the north side of town serves all points north to Maroantsetra and south to Mahanoro – roads, rivers, weather, bridges and spare parts permitting.

The journey takes four hours and costs FMg 2000 by taxi-brousse. You must change taxi-brousse at Soanierana-Ivongo to get to Manompana, up to three hours away, for FMg 1800. This secondary road

is virtually a dirt track and the route crosses three rivers by barge. Prepare for delays.

**Train** The train leaves Tana at 6 am every day and arrives in Tamatave at 5 pm, after 36 stops. The main stop is for 30 minutes at Perinet, the half-way point, where the train from Tamatave crosses with the train from Tana.

The single 1st/2nd class rail fare is around FMg 11,600/6300. You can break the journey at any point, but remember to rebook a seat, especially if travelling 1st class. There is no buffet on the train, but there are fruit and snack sellers running up and down the length of the platform at each stop.

The train station in Tamatave is near the centre of town and a taxi to any hotel costs FMg 600. The daily train from Tamatave to Antananarivo, and all points between, leaves at 5.30 am and arrives in Tana at 4.30 pm.

**Boat** The SCAC marine transport company runs a weekly passenger-cargo ferry called the *Rapiko* from Tamatave via Ile Ste Marie and Mananara to Maroantsetra and back the same way. It leaves Tamatave on Tuesday night and arrives in Ile Ste Marie (Ambodifotatra) at 6 am the next morning. It then departs Ile Ste Marie at 11 am and arrives in Mananara at 6 pm. On Thursday morning at 1 am, it leaves for Maroantsetra and arrives 6 am. It starts the return leg at 10 am on Friday and, after calling in again at Mananara and Ile Ste Marie, is back in Tamatave early on Sunday morning. The days may change, but the times should stay the same.

The *Rapiko* takes 75 passengers and there is no need to book. You pay when you board. Check which pier it leaves from. A one-way fare from Tamatave to Ile Ste Marie is around FMg 10,500. Tamatave to Mananara is FMg 14,500 and to Maroantsetra it is about 17,000. Call ahead at

SCAC's office on Rue de Barrière between Rue Billard and Rue Grandidier.

You can also get to Ile Ste Marie by catching or 'chartering' a fishing pirogue from Manompana, almost 200 km north of Tamatave.

**Driving** There are petrol stations in Tamatave, beside the rail and bus stations and across from the Hôtel Plage. The road from Tamatave north along the coast to Soanierana-Ivongo is reasonably smooth.

The 'road' from Manompana up to Mananara and Maroantsetra is very rough and best tackled with a 4WD vehicle.

### Getting Around
Pousse-pousse rides cost between FMg 300 and FMg 600 per trip, anywhere. They'll ask for FMg 1000 or FMg 2000 because no doubt the odd foreign twit with more wallet than brain pays that.

### FOULPOINTE (MAHAVELONA)
Foulpointe is 58 km north of Tamatave. Accommodation is available at the ingeniously named Hôtel Motel (tel 05), which has 16 bungalows and a restaurant, and offers swimming, fishing and underwater activities. Nearby are the ruins of an old Mahavelona fort.

### MAHAMBO
There is, according to travel author Dervla Murphy, a 'strange beauty' to the Mahambo region because of the wonderful vegetation. The village is 10 km from Fenoarivo and 90 km from Tamatave. The only place to stay is Le Récif (tel 345 25), a beach-bungalow motel and restaurant run by Franz Cowar.

### FENOARIVO (FENERIVE)
This is the unofficial capital of the Betsimisaraka tribe because it was here that the founder, Ratsimilaho, proclaimed himself king. At Nosy Kely there is the ancient zana-malata cemetery and also the ruins of a pirates' fort a few km from

the town. You have only the Malagasy hotels Doany and Mandrosa to choose from here.

### SOANIERANA-IVONGO
If you have to spend the night here between taxis-brousses, there are the Antsiraka and Tsiriry hotels.

### MANOMPANA
You catch pirogues here for Ile Ste Marie. Because they leave very early in the morning, you may wish to stay at the Manompana Hotel, where you can enquire about the boats. It is extremely basic with no electricity or running water, but is relatively clean and well cared for. You shower by pouring buckets of water from a trough over your head. The toilet is a hole in the ground. Rooms contain only a bed and cost a mere FMg 1500 a night. Meals are the same price. The manager will give you a candle and mosquito coil. Beer is available at the local store.

About 200 metres from the hotel, at the northern end of the village, is the Palace Bar. A sign at the hotel promises: 'The best place for you. You may watch the sea while sitting in the Palace.' Say no more.

Swimming is not advisable at Manompana. Someone said it was OK up to 1½ metres – then watch out!

### MANANARA
Mananara is 84 km of adventurous driving from Manompana. If you get there, stay at Chez Roger.

### MAROANTSETRA
Another 112 km north from Mananara is Maroantsetra. Most of the few visitors who come here do so by air. Madagascar Airtours organises trekking expeditions from this town across to Antalha on the north-east coast.

From Maroantsetra you can take a

leisurely four hour walk to Navana Beach or maybe a boat trip to Andranofotsy and the Nosy Mangabe Nature Reserve.

Places to stay are the *Antongil* and *Coco Beach*.

## Shipwrecked

Every traveller I've met in Madagascar has a tale to tell about getting from A to B, or from Ampapampalumpy or something to Betsicameltrot and whatnot. (Pronouncing the names of places and people is a challenge in itself!)

Most of these 'incredible journeys' are by the infamous taxis-brousses, the tough little jampacked buses which run for many days and miles between and around the major centres. There is rarely a journey without an incident of some sort, often to do with the state of the vehicle or the roads. My most memorable trip, however, was a waterlogged one.

In this day and age of jet travel and American Express, the last thing I expected was to be shipwrecked. It's true I went in search of desert islands on the cheap, but did it have to be in authentic Crusoe-style?

Ile Ste Marie, off the east coast of Madagascar, was once a pirate haven. Little has changed and most of the buccaneers are still there – in the graveyard. Tourists and travellers go to the island now for the same reason the pirates did.

Most tourists fly across, but I decided to be adventurous. Together with Pascale from Paris and Pierre from Brittany, I taxi-broussed it north along the coast from Tamatave until a sunken ferry prevented our passage across the fourth river, en route to the departure point for Ile Ste Marie.

Instead, we hailed a passing pirogue, diverted it for a few hundred Malagasy francs (or a dollar) to the other side of the river, and walked the eight remaining km to the village. We spent a $2 night in a hotel which managed to be cosy without running water and electricity.

The Ile Ste Marie ferry turned out to be a big, but primitive, double-masted fishing boat. There was no engine and no deck. The sails were scraps of canvas and cloth stitched together. There were no ropes, just creepers. Jeepers!

But she was strong and steady as she sailed slowly out of the calm bay at Manompana at 3 am under a clear sky and full moon.

Pierre and Pascal tinkled and plucked away at unusual Malagasy musical instruments they had bought. It was peaceful, romantic.

Our skipper and his two crew explained in halting French that it could take anything between four and 10 hours to cover the 25 km across to the isle, depending on the wind. The trip was to take us 11 hours, during which time the weather would change dramatically.

It began with a rain squall. We were all concerned with keeping ourselves and our bags dry. Thankfully the wind and our speed had picked up. The showers passed and the open sea was revealed.

The second squall brought stronger winds and rain. We thought we had its measure – but then the rudder's kingpin snapped. The skipper lunged himself over the side of the boat, with one of the crew holding his feet, and grabbed the rudder so we wouldn't lose it completely.

After he had hastily dropped the sails, the other crewman started hammering off bits of the boat to find a nail which would substitute as a rudder pin. Pierre and I left Pascal to protect the luggage, while we picked up the long oars and started paddling furiously to keep us from drifting out to sea.

After 15 minutes of gondoliering our gonads off, the rudder was back in operation and the sails went up. Pierre, Pascal and I sighed and joked about what might have been. But the smile never returned to the skipper's face. Shortly it would change to terror.

The rain continued. Pascal collected fresh water – just in case. I started thinking about the impossibility of any rescue, the likely survival period of five people with one bottle of warm beer and no food, and what little in the way of land there was between Madagascar and Australia.

Then the rudder went again. Same action stations. But this time, the seas were higher, the wind and rain even stronger, and it took longer to complete the makeshift repair. Pascal stopped collecting water and started bailing it out.

Despite our oaring, we had drifted considerably off course. We now aimed for the nearest land which turned out to be the north of the island instead of the south, our original destination. I could see the outline of a sandy shore through the driving rain, getting closer. Old Lord Nelson at the helm was going to beach the thing. Everything – clothes, bags – was wet by this time.

The rudder must have slipped again, because instead of heading for the beach we were heading for the rocks. The oars which had been used for paddling against the current were now used for fending off the rocks and keeping the hull from getting holed. But it was a losing battle as the boat was tossed about by the waves. The rudder snapped completely off. We slipped about the deck that wasn't there. The long oars bent and pole vaulted us into the air. One of the crewmen jumped before he was thrown overboard and narrowly missed being crushed between rock and hull. He was soon joined by the other crewman. Both were cut by coral.

I didn't have time to be frightened. It all seemed unreal. I felt some sympathy for the skipper, watching his livelihood breaking slowly into pieces and going down the gurgler, but forgot that when I realised we could go the same way.

Somehow – by our own or divine guidance – the battered boat found its way between the rocks into the bay, and ran aground about 300 metres from the shore. It wallowed back and forth for a while, listed to one side and stuck. That was the side we would disembark, our sodden bags over our shoulders, and wade ashore.

I looked back on the vessel. It could have been a scene straight out of Robinson Crusoe or Treasure Island. The pirates must have been laughing in their graves. We celebrated by cracking open my warm bottle of beer in one of the primitive huts of a nearby village.

The locals, who fed us fruit and cassava, told us we were lucky to have made it.

# Ile Ste Marie (Nosy Boraha)

This island is taking over from Nosy Be as the prime tourist destination in Madagascar. Neither island is, or has been, a 'resort' swarming with tourists and all the trappings, but Ile Ste Marie as yet lacks any blatant tourist development such as the Holiday Inn on Nosy Be.

It is generally more peaceful, historic and pretty than its western competitor, as well as much less expensive. It is surrounded by good beaches and coral reefs.

The 57 km long, thin granite island, lying eight km off the coast, was originally a pirate haven. It later came under the control of 'princess' Bety of the Betsimisaraka, a tribe formed from the mulatto pirate descendants. She in turn ceded control to the French after falling for a Frenchman called La Bigorne. (The love story has since been turned into a novel and filmed.) The French East India Company later took charge of the island.

Cloves were introduced, in 1823, as was vanilla later in the century. For most of this century, until independence in 1960, the island was used by the French as a penal colony for Malagasy liberationists and insurgents.

Under the independence agreement, the inhabitants of Ile Ste Marie are allowed to choose between French and Malagasy nationality. Most chose to be Malagasy, although they retain French names. The people of Ile Ste Marie are now considered the 19th tribe of Madagascar, in place of the French.

Ambodifotatra is the island capital and the only small town. There are many tiny villages and many mosquitoes.

## Information
If you have any troubles or specific requests regarding money, places to see and stay, getting around, etc there's a new Syndicat d'Initiative tourist body formed by the hoteliers on the island. It is more of a business development club than tourist information and welcome service, but you never know. Contact Jean-Claude Robert, manager at the Soanambo Hôtel.

There are no banks.

### Ile aux Nattes
Make the effort to get to this little island off the southern tip of Ile Ste Marie and visit the Napoleon family.

Napoleon was the village chief of the isle's 600 Malagasy inhabitants and had set up a modest but very warm restaurant and accommodation for visitors. Sadly,

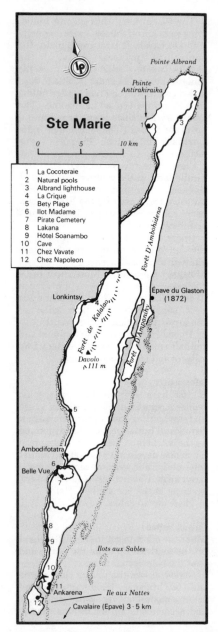

## Ile Ste Marie

| | |
|---|---|
| 1 | La Cocoteraie |
| 2 | Natural pools |
| 3 | Albrand lighthouse |
| 4 | La Crique |
| 5 | Bety Plage |
| 6 | Ilot Madame |
| 7 | Pirate Cemetery |
| 8 | Lakana |
| 9 | Hôtel Soanambo |
| 10 | Cave |
| 11 | Chez Vavate |
| 12 | Chez Napoleon |

Napoleon died in 1986 at age 77, but the business has been taken over by his daughter Jacqueline and son-in-law, Charles Todivelou. Tourists have been coming for 20 years and the family still tries hard to please.

The speciality of their home cooking is chicken in coconut juice. You have to order an hour in advance, but it is worth waiting for. They also make their own punch coco. A glass costs FMg 1000 and a bottle is FMg 4000.

While you wait for the chicken, you'll get a guided tour around the island, and be offered potentially lethal home-brewed betsabetsa beer and home-distilled toaka gasy rum. You may also be treated to an impromptu music performance by Napoleon's grandchildren, using their own home-made instruments – including a replica of a modern drum set! The island's mission and school were destroyed by the 1986 cyclone.

The Napoleon family also have five 'bungalows' on the beach to rent for FMg 4500 per night. They are tiny, basically sheltered beds, but the family's visitor's book testifies to many idyllic nights and weeks spent there. To get there, you must go down on to the beach beside the runway and wave. A pirogue will come and collect you. The boat ride costs FMg 500 one way.

### Pirate Cemetery

This is an obvious and conveniently placed attraction for visitors. For that reason several islanders have tried to make easy money by declaring themselves official guides and guardians of the pirates' graveyard.

You may wish to take advantage of such offers and pay accordingly for a pirogue, guide and caretaker, but there are no official fees. If you have any trouble with forceful and unsubstantiated demands for money, say you are doing a report or the like for the Direction du Tourisme or the Direction des Eaux et Forêts and politely ask for their name and address.

Get ready to write it down. It's amazing how many of these tourism 'pirates' disappear back into the forest.

The Pirate Cemetery is appropriately wildly overgrown and the inscriptions on many of the gravestones illegible. There are no infamous names, given that few if any of the big-name buccaneers died a peaceful death at 'home' on Ile Ste Marie. One stone with the skull and crossbones carved on it reads: 'Joseph Pierre 1788 – par son ami Hulin. Passans priez pour lui'. On top of the Ile aux Forbans, lying opposite the cemetery in the bay, are the ruins of an ancient gateway. Its significance is not known. Perhaps it was a landmark and lookout post for the pirates.

### L'Ilot Madame

This small island lies at the entrance to the bay of Ambodifotatra and is connected to the town and Belle Vue on the south side by two causeways. The island was the fortified administration centre of the French East India Company until it became the local government offices. The waters surrounding it are popular with turtles and tropical fish.

### Ambodiatafana Natural Pools

This is a glorious spot on the north-east tip of the island. There is a series of hollow basins in the coastal rocks which the sea fills at high tide. They make marvellous natural swimming pools. To get there, walk across the main track from Ambatorao on the west coast, for seven km. This takes you via the Albrand lighthouse on top of the hill, from where you can see across to Maroantsetra at the head of the Bay of Antongil. At Christmas, there is an all-night festival at Ambodiatafana.

### Ankarena Beach & Cave

On the south-east tip of the island, there is a fine stretch of peaceful reef-protected beach and a deep cave at the foot of cliffs. Not surprisingly, the cave has given rise to several pirate legends, mainly about treasure. I don't know about jewels, but it is home to hundreds of bats. To get to Ankarena, go over the hill from the airport, via the Hôtel Chez Vavate. Madame Vavate is very helpful.

### Ambodifotatra

The island's capital contains about 2000 inhabitants, an ancient fort and Madagascar's oldest church, built in 1857. The granite fort, dating from 1753, is quite impressive, but it is a military camp and access is forbidden. Be careful taking photos.

### Places to Stay & Eat

Ile Ste Marie has seven beach-bungalow resorts which vary in standard and cost. There are no 'palm beach' package hotels, or even any with a second storey. But unfortunately for budget travellers, the newer bungalow holiday villages are beginning to push up prices in the quest for the 'big tourists'.

The smaller and better value bungalow complexes have limited space and are frequently full for a day or two (during Malagasy holidays and weekends). It is hard to check on vacancies or book in advance because most are not on the phone. If stuck, head for the two Malagasy hotels in Ambodifotatra.

There are no restaurants separate from the hotels, although there are places in Ambodifotatra which will cook up a meal on request.

**Beach Bungalows** *La Cocoteraie*, which belongs to the Robert family, is the most isolated of the Ile Ste Marie hotels. One Swiss traveller declared it the best place to stay in Madagascar. It is run by Madame Louis Robert, whose son Jean-Claude is manager of the Hôtel Soanambo. There are 10 thatched bungalows and a restaurant on the Pointe des Cocotiers, about 35 km from Ambodifotatra. There is a three km long beach with good sand and no sea urchins. One correspondent reported the seafood as exceptional. You can *manger comme le roi en France –*

Church on Ile Ste Marie; the oldest in Madagascar

'eat like the king of France', he said. Meals cost FMg 6500 and breakfast is FMg 2000. One-bedroom bungalows range from single/double FMg 7000/9000 per night, and two-bedroom bungalows from FMg 9000/11,000.

*La Crique* is about 20 km from Ambodifotatra, near the village of Lonkintsy. There is a tarred road from Ambodifotatra up to one km from La Crique. It then becomes a very rough track continuing north. La Crique is run by the Family Blondel and has 10 bungalows with one/two rooms for FMg 11,000/13,500 per night. Breakfast is FMg 2500 and a set lunch or dinner is FMg 5600. La Crique offers various pastimes. Boat excursions up to La Cocoteraie or day trips by road to Ile aux Nattes are FMg 25,000. You can rent a pirogue for FMg 750 per hour or snorkelling equipment for FMg 1500 per half day. La Crique has a sheltered bay and small beach. It's a good place for families.

If La Crique is full, or you prefer the chance of a 'bungalow' in a Malagasy village, the hotel will put you in touch with someone at Lonkintsy village. The rate is negotiable, around FMg 2000 a night, but there are no showers or other facilities.

The *Lakana*, next to the Hôtel Soanambo and the Club Nautique about five km from the airport, is a series of wooden bungalows with corrugated iron roofs. Singles/doubles cost FMg 16,000/22,000 per night half board. Breakfast is FMg 1600 and a meal for nonresidents is FMg 4500. Bike hire is expensive at FMg 1200 an hour or FMg 5500 per half day. The Lakana organises a walking day tour to the east coast of the island, the Pirate Cemetery and the Ile aux Nattes. They also provide equipment for diving trips. You can hire a full tank for FMg 14,000 and a boat with an outboard for FMg 24,000 per half day, FMg 35,000 full day.

The *Hôtel Soanambo* has a telephone (tel 40). It is a new development with whitewashed stone units and thatched roofs, 3½ km from the airport and 12 km from town. The hotel charges FMg 1500 for a transfer to the airport and FMg 4000 to Ambodifotatra. Singles are FMg 28,000 per night and doubles are FMg 36,500. Extra beds are FMg 14,500. Breakfast is FMg 4,500 and set meals are FMg 12,500.

The Soanambo has a swimming pool and tennis court. You can rent bikes for FMg 9000 per day or FMg 5000 per half day. The hotel also runs the nearby Club Nautique, a base for diving, yachting, windsurfing and boat hire. Diving is FMg 11,000 per full tank and FMg 9000 for an introductory dive. Windsurfers are FMg 5000 per hour or FMg 8000 with an instructor. Laser yachts are FMg 8000 per hour or FMg 14,000 with an instructor. Pirogue hire, with a boatman, is FMg 5000 per hour. All prices are approximate.

*Chez Vavate*, about 1½ km up the hill from the airport on the south tip of the island, is a great place to stay. Madame Vavate has been here for more than three decades. She has a varied assortment of six bungalows surrounding the main

house. Some have been renovated after being damaged by the cyclone and new ones are planned. Rates are FMg 7500 for one or two people. The place has a farmyard or homestead feel to it, and is very relaxing. Ile aux Nattes is close at hand and Ankarena is virtually Vavate's beach. Breakfast is FMg 2000 and set meals are FMg 4000. Madame Vavate's coco punch is lovely. She runs diving trips for around FMg 12,000. If you are not diving, you can sometimes go for the boat ride for a fraction of the cost.

If there is no jeep or porter from Chez Vavate to meet the incoming flights, you can hire a freelance porter from among the local crowd.

**Town Hotels** There are two hotels, side by side, in Ambodifotatra. The *Tsimialonjafy*, which has five rooms, is the best. The linen is clean and the beds have mosquito nets. The toilet, down at the bottom of the yard, is a wooden cubicle with a hole in the floor dropping into the sea. The tide is the flush. Singles/doubles are FMg 2400/3500 per night. They also have reasonable Malagasy meals, including good yoghurt.

The *Falafa* is easier to pronounce, but that's about the only advantage. The four rooms are not as clean, but more expensive. Singles/doubles are FMg 2800/4500. There is also a FMg 1000 per day government tax, which for some reason the owner prefers not to include in the price. The toilet is the same as that of its neighbour. Breakfast costs FMg 1500 and a three course meal is about FMg 4000. Fruit juices are the speciality of the house for FMg 700. There is also a laundry service.

Bikes can be hired privately through these hotels for around FMg 4000 a day, much cheaper than from the beach bungalow hotels.

**Getting There & Away**
**Air** There are five return flights a week to Ile Ste Marie from Antananarivo. Four are

via Tamatave and one is direct. A one-way fare from Tana is US$81; from Tamatave it's US$36. There are special excursion fares (six day minimum stay, one month maximum) on the Tana to Ile Ste Marie flights.

The flight, by Twin Otter from Tana, takes an hour. The airport on Ile Ste Marie is a concrete shed and a runway on the southern tip of the island. You must go there to book and confirm return flights. Alternatively you can try calling the Air Mad agent, 'Tranombarotra Roso', (tel 5).

Because of the rough roads on the island, transport between the airport and Ambodifotatra, a distance of 17 km, is by truck for FMg 1300. The truck leaves Belle Vue, at the southern end of the causeway across from Ambodifotatra, about an hour before the Tana flight is due to arrive. Some hotels do transfers to and from the airport by boat, but that costs around FMg 18,000.

**Boat** There is a weekly ferry service from Tamatave, Mananara and Maroantsetra to Ile Ste Marie, run by the SCAC marine company in Tamatave. (See Tamatave section.)

Much more frequent, but more precarious, is the fishing boat service from Manompana. Most of the Malagasy use this method because it is much cheaper – FMg 2000. The trip can take anywhere

from two to eight hours, depending on sea and wind conditions. The boats leave early in the morning, around 3 or 4 am. If one is not scheduled you may be able to charter one for about FMg 10,000. The large sailing pirogues are primitive and nil on comfort and protection. It can be a pleasant sail or an absolute nightmare. (See the Tamatave chapter.)

### Getting Around

There are few cars on Ile Ste Marie and few decent stretches of road on which to drive them. The hotels and island administration have Landrovers or the like for their chores and pick-ups. There are no taxis.

The best way to get around quickly as a visitor is by bike. Most of the hotels can arrange private hire for around FMg 4000 a day. Be careful cycling and watch out for ruts and slippery mud on the roads. Two girls fell off their bikes and injured themselves (one badly) in separate incidents while I was on the island for a few days.

If you have time, there are some good walks across the centre of the island and to some of the villages. The islanders' pirogues are also available for rides across to the Ile aux Forbans or the Ile aux Nattes. Some of the hotels also hire out pirogues and run island tours. (See the Places to Stay section).

# Diego Suarez (Antsiranana) Province

The north of Madagascar is climatically one of the better balanced parts of the country. It is not as wet as the east coast and not as dry as the south. It is also more cosmopolitan, although the ruling tribe in the region is the Antakarana (People of the Rocks).

The area of interest for the visitor lies down the north-west side of the province from Diego Suarez to Nosy Be. The eastern population belt around Sambava (the 'vanilla coast') is isolated and has few known attractions, though I'm sure it would yield some fascinating discoveries to those adventurous enough to visit on spec.

One such place would be the Ankara plateau near Ambilobe. This is an area of sunken forests and a huge cave system. There is said to be almost 100 km of charted caves here, including some of the biggest caverns in the world. The plateau is not a national park, but contains plenty of wildlife – though this is dwindling. The blind cave fish are unique to these caves.

It's probably difficult for travellers to visit this area except on an organised expedition basis.

The town of Antalaha is the centre of the country's vanilla industry.

The Malagasy have named the province the 'coast of undiscovered (or virgin) islands' for the tourist trade. But there are not many islands to be discovered, and it would be a shame to miss the mainland features, such as the Montagne d'Ambre National Park, Diego Suarez town and the sacred lake at Anivorano, in a mad, hedonistic dash out to Nosy Be.

### Getting There & Away

There are flights almost daily from Tana to Diego Suarez (US$148) and Nosy Be (US$150) and four flights a week from Tana to Sambava with one via Tamatave

and Maroantsetra and one via Diego Suarez.

Road travel from Tana is restricted to the winter months between April and November, due to the poor conditions of some 'highways'. Even when they are passable, the trip from Tana to Nosy Be or Diego Suarez takes several days by taxi-brousse. Sambava and the surrounding towns on the east coast are virtually cut off by road from Diego Suarez and the west. There is a track from Ambilobe on the west side to Vohemar on the east, but unless you've got a Sherman tank, forget it. So if you don't fly there, you have to trek it.

Ferries run daily from Antsahampano (near Ambanja) to Nosy Be, and ships run occasionally from Majunga to Nosy Be.

# Diego Suarez

Diego Suarez has one of the finest natural harbours in the Indian Ocean and was, until 1973, a French naval base. There is little port activity now. The bay is often compared to Rio de Janeiro, but the town bears no comparison whatsoever to the Brazilian city. Diego (as it is known to non-purists) has a population of around 50,000, most of whom don't seem to come out until after dark. This may be because Diego Suarez is a crusty, sunbaked town with few trees or other shady places.

There is a large Muslim community and a small group of French expats. Many westerners working on aid or diplomatic assignments in Tana usually stop in Diego for a few days on the way to or from Nosy Be. There are few beggars and prostitutes compared to Tana or Tamatave.

Whether you like Diego Suarez or not may depend on who you meet up with and what you do. The town itself can appear

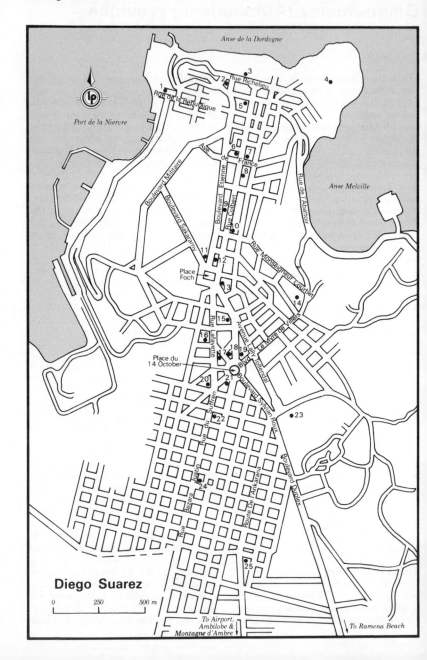

*Anse de la Dordogne*

*Port de la Nievre*

Rue de la République

Boulevard Militaire

Boulevard Sakaramy

Ave. de Étienne

Boulevard Étienne

Rue Richelieu

Rue de France

Rue Colbert

Rue de l'Abattoir

Rue Monseigneur Courtien

*Anse Melville*

Place Foch

Avenue Jully Vollendal

Rue Le Myre de Villers

Rue Lafayette

Place du 14 October

Boulevard Sylvian Roux

Rue du Colbert

Rue Bezara

Rue Justin

Route De l'Ankarâna

Boulevard Duplex

# Diego Suarez

0    250    500 m

*To Airport, Ambilobe & Montagne d'Ambre*    *To Ramena Beach*

| 1 | Customs |
|---|---|
| 2 | Hôtel de la Poste |
| 3 | Bank BFV |
| 4 | Hospital |
| 5 | Bank BTM |
| 6 | Pharmacy |
| 7 | Bank BNI |
| 8 | Hôtel Valiha |
| 9 | Hôtel Fian-Tsilaka |
| 10 | Nouvel Hôtel |
| 11 | Post Office |
| 12 | Restaurant Hortensia |
| 13 | Restaurant Libertalia |
| 14 | Direction des Eaux et Forêts |
| 15 | Restaurant Extrême-Orient |
| 16 | Tourist Hôtel |
| 17 | Tropical Nightclub |
| 18 | Hôtels La Racasse/Orchidée |
| 19 | Air Madagascar |
| 20 | Restaurant Au Lotus |
| 21 | Cinema Ritz |
| 22 | Nina Glace Salon de Thé |
| 23 | Stade Municipal |
| 24 | Hôtel Pavillon du Nord |
| 25 | Bus Station |

Father Caraccioli, and decided to apply the socialist principles of Jean-Jacques Rousseau from scratch – away from France and the much slower route to revolution. After a period of troubleshooting and fund raising around the Comoros, they set up their Utopia in Diego Suarez around the Baie des Français.

They began building with the help of 300 Comorians, who were a gift from the Queen of Anjouan, as well as assorted African slaves and British, French, Dutch and Portuguese sailors. A parliament was formed, a printing press was started, crops were planted, stock was reared, and some sort of integration with local or captive women was attempted. Even a new international language was established. The pirates were Misson and Caraccioli's emissaries, importers and immigration service.

All seemed to be going well until the Malagasy tribes surrounding the 'International Republic of Libertalia' descended en masse from the hills and massacred the Liberi population. Caraccioli was killed, but Misson either escaped to sea or was already at sea when the attack occurred. His eventual fate remains a mystery.

## Montagne d'Ambre National Park

You need a permit from the Direction des Eaux et Forêts to visit the park. There is a DEF office in Diego, out near the abattoir on Blvd Myre de Villers. To get to the park take a taxi or taxi-brousse out to Ambohitra (Joffreville), 32 km south of town. A taxi-brousse costs about FMg 800. You may be able to hire a taxi for the day at around FMg 25,000, or negotiate tour rates with Mad Airtours. The road to Joffreville has a good surface, but thereafter it falls apart and becomes a track.

Once through the entrance gate, the heart of the park and the end of the track is a further seven km away. It halts at the ruins of the warden's house and gardens, which went to seed long ago. From here you can follow a number of botanical paths back to the park entrance. But first, a few hundred metres beyond the ruined house, is a small waterfall (*petite cascade*).

The area is good for walking, with a

barren, lifeless and, in some cases, hostile to the casual visitor. Travellers I spoke with either loved the place or hated it.

## Libertalia

Diego Suarez was named after Madagascar's alleged European discoverer Diego Diaz, the Portuguese navigator who dropped by in 1500. For 35 years during the 17th century, however, it may have been known as the pirate republic of Libertalia.

The story of Libertalia borders on legend, akin to Atlantis, and because there is no physical evidence of this first communist-cosmopolitan state, some historians have reduced it to the level of fantasy.

The pirate republic, the story goes, was founded by a French adventurer called Captain Misson (his first name has eluded the records). Like his notorious counterpart, Olivier 'La Buse' Levasseur, Misson was a well-educated man. But his motives were more humanitarian and revolutionary than selfish and anarchic. This seagoing Robin Hood freed slaves and avoided bloodshed where possible.

He teamed up with a Dominican priest,

great variety of plants and trees to see. Chameleons, birds, butterflies and other insects are plentiful, but there are no lemurs at hand. Deep within the park, up around the 1475 metre high mountain, there are several lakes for the more adventurous trekkers to aim at. If picking leisurely trails, follow the *jardin botanique* and *grande cascade* signs. The path down to the big waterfall is steep and slippery in places, but easily manageable with care for anyone in good health. You can dip in the waterfall, which is about five km from the entrance gate.

You can stay, eat and drink at the *Hôtel Joffre* in Ambohitra. It's a dusty, dirty and dilapidated place with only four rooms. They blamed the 1986 cyclone for the damage. Rooms cost FMg 3000 a night. A better and just as cheap choice is the Malagasy army's Centre de Repos Militaire.

### Ramena Beach

This safe and attractive beach is 15 km away by road on the other side of the Baie des Français, to the east of Diego Suarez. There are no tourist developments or hotels there, just some ramshackle Malagasy bungalows. Catch a taxi-brousse for Ramena or Anoronjia.

### Antanavo Sacred Lake

The tribes around this area worship the crocodiles in the lake as the reincarnations of their ancestors. Every so often, there is a big ceremony with much dancing, beating of drums and heaps of zebu meat to attract all the crocs on shore. Minor feeding rituals or offerings take place each Saturday. The reptiles are attracted to shore by hand clapping. (You can read more about this ritual in David Attenborough's *Journeys to the Past*.)

To get there, take a taxi-brousse to the town of Anivorano Avaratra (Anivorano Nord), 75 km south on the main road from Diego Suarez. It costs about FMg 1200 for a one-way fare. Then you must walk or hitch the four km down to the lake.

### Places to Stay

There are several good, cheap hotels in Diego Suarez and no new tourist hotels with which to compete and spark a rate increase.

The *Hôtel Tourist*, on Rue Bougainville, is run by Muslims. The 15 rooms are each very plain but relatively clean at FMg 5000 a night. A breakfast of coffee and a croissant is FMg 1000. There is no telephone.

Nearer the port on Blvd Etienne is the *Fian-Tsilaka* (tel 223 48). It offers a variety of rooms ranging from FMg 6500 per night for a single or double to FMg 13,000 with air-con and a shower. There is also an excellent, cheap restaurant which serves up good seafood.

The *Hôtel Orchidée* (tel 210 65) on Rue Surcouf, is excellent value for money. But it has only six rooms, two with air-con, the others with fans, and is often full. Singles/doubles are FMg 8000/10,000 per night and breakfast is an extra FMg 1750. Air-con is an extra FMg 2000. The manager, Jean de Dieu, is a good contact for 'what's on' about town. He can arrange hire of a Renault 4 for around FMg 16,000 a day. The hotel restaurant is 200 metres up the road.

The Orchidée's neighbour and main rival is the *Hôtel La Racasse* (tel 223 64). It has eight air-con rooms and eight rooms with fans. Singles/doubles cost FMg 9000/10,000. Breakfast is FMg 1500.

Similar in standard (average) but better value is the *Paradis du Nord* (tel 214 05). Single or double rooms with air-con, toilet and shower are FMg 10,000. There is also a studio for FMg 12,500 per night. Breakfast is FMg 1500. The manager here is keen to please and impress, and can offer car hire at FMg 20,000 a day with the first 50 km free. There is also a disco on Friday, Saturday and Sunday nights and the chance of guided tours depending on demand.

The *Hôtel Valiha* (tel 215 31) on Rue Colbert has good air-con rooms, but is more noted for its food than its hospitality.

QUAND ON FAIT LA GUEULE
C'EST 80 MUSCLES DU VISAGE
QUI TRAVAILLENT
QUAND ON SOURIT
10 SEULEMENT
ALORS POURQUOI SE FATIGUER ?

Salon de Thé "NINAGLACE" B. P. 256 — Tel 227-04 201 Antsiranana (Madagascar)

WHEN YOU SCOWL
YOUR FACE USES 80 MUSCLES
BUT IN SMILING ONLY 10
SO WHY TIRE YOURSELF ?

Poster from Nina Glace Salon de Thé

I found it a very unfriendly place. The staff were more concerned with restaurant clients than room guests. Single/double rooms cost FMg 13,000/14,000.

Up the street from the Valiha is the refurbished *Hôtel Nouvel*. Rooms cost around FMg 10,000.

The 'best' hotel in town is the colonial *Hôtel de la Poste* (tel 220 44) down by the port at the head of Rue Joffre. The 37 aircon rooms here cost single/double FMg 17,000/18,000. Breakfast is FMg 2000 and set meals are FMg 5000.

**Places to Eat**

For good places to eat out, try the *Valiha* and *Hôtel de la Poste* restaurants. The *Fian-Tsilaka* is recommended for lunch. Good independent restaurants are thin on the ground. The *Restaurant Libertalia* at the top of Rue Colbert in Place Foch was formerly the Restaurant Vietnam or Watcha-Watcha (named after the dance music of the same name). It is not distinctly Vietnamese, but the meals are substantial and cheap. A big meal for two costs around FMg 8000. Few people would know Libertalia was the name of the 18th century pirate republic of which Diego Suarez was the centre. They think it's only the name of a restaurant!

Other restaurants in the same style and price range are the *Restaurant au Lotus*, at the top of Rue Lafayette, and the *Restaurant Extrême-Orient*, opposite Rue Château d'Eau between Place Foch and Place du 14 Octobre.

For snacks and good natural fruit juices try the salon de thé *Nina Glace* on Rue de Suffren, south of the Place du 14 Octobre. It is run by a jolly Indian gentleman who will enquire about your origins and hand out used Malagasy stamps as souvenirs. His menu notes in French: 'If you haven't seen Ramena, Joffreville and Nina Glace, you haven't seen Diego.' Fruit juices are FMg 450.

*Tanjona Bobaomby*

*Tanjona Vohilava*

Ilomotro

*Nosy Antaly Be*
*Nosy Suarez*
*Nosy Diego*

Ampanolahimirafy    Ramena    Anoronjia

*Nosy Hara*    Ampasindava

Diego
Suarez
Mangoaka    Namakia

Antsahampano

Mananara
Melivato    Antongombato    *Nosy Tendro*
Ironona

Ambahibory    Ampondrahazo

Sakaramy    Ambolobozokely

*Tanjona Anorontany*

Andranofanjava    Sahasifotra    Mahavanona

Ambohitra

Anjavinihavana    Andrafiabe

Antamotamo    *Nosy Lowry*

*Montagne D'Ambre*    Ambatojoly
*1475 m*
Bobakilandy    Sadjoavato    Irodo

*Farihy*    Antsakoakely    *Irodo*
Ampombiatambo    *Fantany*

Antserasera
Ampandrana
Anivorano Avaratra    *Farihy Antanavo*

Amparihy

Bobasakoa

Matsaborimanga    Anbondromifehy

*Andrevo*

*Caves*

Andranofotsy    Ambararata    Maromokotra
*Mananjeba*

Antsaravibe    *Lokia*

*Mahavavy*    Marivorahona

Antsohimbondrona    Betsiaka    **Around Diego Suarez**

Mantaly    Isesy
0    10    20 km

Ambodibonara    Ambakirano
Ambilobe
*To Ambanja*    Ambadimadiro

Top: Boats moored on Nosy Be beach (RW)
Bottom: Saklava women wearing lambas, Nosy Be (DC)

Top: The late Napoleon's family, Ile Aux Nattes (RW)
Bottom: Returning home by pirogue, Nosy Komba (DC)

## Nightlife

Diego Suarez has a clutter of Friday and Saturday night 'hot spots'. The *Flash* disco opposite the Hôtel Valiha is currently enjoying popularity. Otherwise, try the *Hôtel Paradis du Nord*, on Ave Villaret Joyeuse; the *Tropical* on the street behind the Hôtel La Racasse; or the *5/5* beside the Restaurant Libertalia. The *Hôtel Nouvel* is also a popular night spot.

## Getting There & Around

The US$150 flight from Tana takes an hour. Diego's airport is six km from the centre of town. A taxi into town costs FMg 2500, or you can walk a few metres out onto the main road and hail a passing taxi-brousse for FMg 200. Air Mad (tel 214 75) shares an office in town with Madagascar Airtours, opposite the Hôtel La Racasse, on Ave Surcouf.

The taxi-brousse station is opposite the cemetery on Route de l'Ankanara. If you're going by road to Nosy Be, rather than flying, you can get a taxi-brousse from here for Ambanja. The road is good to Anivorana Avaratra, then terrible to Ambilobe, then OK to Ambanja.

There is no bike hire in or around Diego, but a couple of hotels and Mad Airtours offer cars for hire (see Places to Stay section).

There is a two person agency of Mad Airtours (at the Air Mad office) which organises day tours to the Montagne d'Ambre National Park and around Diego Suarez. The Trans 7 travel agency is of no use.

## SAMBAVA & ANTALAHA

These vanilla producing centres on the north-east coast are difficult to reach because of the state of the roads from Diego Suarez. The countryside en route is not very interesting.

Perhaps they are best coupled with a visit to Maroantsetra and a forest trek across national reserve, the Beagada Massif, and through the Radama pass, to Antalaha. The trek can take up to a week, staying at villages along the way. When you reach the village of Ampataka, there is a taxi-brousse service into Antalaha. The best place to stay in town is in the *Ocean Hotel* bungalows. Or, head south along the coast a short distance to Ampanoavana. There is a good beach here, as well as lemurs and butterflies.

Sambava is 90 km north along the coast. En route you pass through the forest reserve of Marojezy, about 60 km south of Sambava. In Sambava, there is the *Motel Carrefour*.

## AMBANJA

If travelling by road from Diego Suarez or Antananarivo to Nosy Be, you may have to spend a night or two in Ambanja, the nearest town to the ferry port for the island. The trip from Tana by taxi-brousse takes three days and costs FMg 30,000. The taxis-brousses sometimes travel in pairs, depending on demand. However, they usually can run only between May and November, until the rains come and block the last stretch of road between Antsohihy and Ambanja.

The 240 km trip from Diego Suarez can take up to nine hours, including a one hour meal stop at Ambilobe. Fare is FMg 5000. The taxis-brousses leave at 5 and 7.30 am. If you arrive in Ambanja early enough in the afternoon, you can try to catch a ferry from Antsahampano port to Nosy Be. The port is 15 km from Ambanja, but the turn off is five km north of the town.

If you decide to spend the night, Ambanja is not a bad place in which to do it. The town is situated on the River Samirano and there are some fine walks around the bridge at the southern end of town and the estuary area.

## Places to Stay

Don't try and book into the Hôtel de Ville, like I did in an anxious and exhausted moment after a long journey, – it's the town hall! Rather spartan comfort is to be had at the *Hôtel Hawaii*. It has changed hands and been renovated. Rooms come in three standards. Air-con rooms are FMg 10,000, rooms with a shower are FMg 8000 and plain rooms are FMg 6000. Breakfast is pricey at FMg 1750.

Much cheaper is the KOFMAD transport society's *Nouvel Hôtel*, next to the soccer pitch. It is basically a place for long-distance drivers to kip (in small hutch-like rooms) for FMg 3000 a night. They have a friendly bar and simple restaurant.

Other hotels are the *Patricia* and *Poisson d'Or*, and there are several small restaurants and disco-bars at the bridge end of town.

## ANTSAHAMPANO

This is the port from which people head for Nosy Be. You can catch a small Peugot 504 taxi-brousse from Ambanja for FMg 500. The boats for Nosy Be leave around 10 am depending on the tides. The motor boat takes three hours and costs FMg 800. There are also car ferries most days when they're not broken down. Timetables are erratic. Check with Hassanaly in Hell-Ville, Nosy Be (tel 610 18).

You can also stay at the *Burning Spear Hotely*. But the bedrooms are very rough, as you would expect for FMg 2000 a night.

# Nosy Be

Nosy Be is Madagascar's tourist trump card; its 'tropical island paradise' to lure overseas visitors. But with tough competition from the Seychelles and Mauritius, and Madagascar's economic ills, it has never really taken off. There are a few expensive internationally owned hotels, but not enough to have hordes of semi-naked package groups wandering aimlessly about the island. They tend to stay on site.

For the traveller then, Nosy Be and its surrounding islands are not the tourist traps one would expect. At the same time, neither are they really what Madagascar is about. Most visitors go to Nosy Be or Ile Ste Marie for an idle week by the beach, but it would be a pity and a waste to spend most of one's time on either island. Swimming is generally safer around Nosy Be.

Nosy Be (also spelled Nossi Bé) is Malagasy for 'Big Island', and indeed it is the biggest island lying off Madagascar. Like its Comorian neighbours to the west, Nosy Be is a centre for the production of perfume essence from the ylang-ylang tree. Sugar cane, coffee, vanilla and pepper are also produced, but to a lesser extent.

The main town on the island is Hell-Ville (Andoany) and surrounding Nosy Be are several smaller islands, near and far, which are hailed as nature and marine reserves.

## AROUND THE ISLAND
### Hell-Ville

Despite its name, the island capital and port is quite a pleasant place to stay or visit. Like Hell-Bourg in Réunion, it was named after Admiral de Hell, a governor of that island.

Little seems to have changed in Hell-Ville since the French vacated the country – or since they occupied it for that matter. Cannons overlook the port, and the walls leading up from the pier are inlaid with the initials 'HV'. There are some fascinating old colonial buildings, including the jail on the Cours de Hell part of Rue Passot. Hell-Ville has a large Comorian community, whose members let their hair down and celebrate for days and nights on end at the end of the fasting month of Ramadan.

### Mt Passot

This is a great spot to watch sunsets and take in the view over Nosy Be. The hotels run minibus tours up to the summit, via Andrikibo. Mt Passot is surrounded by sacred lakes. It is 30 km from Hell-Ville.

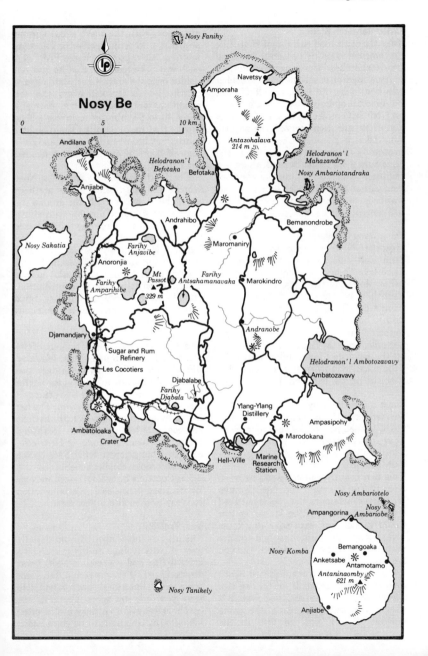

# Nosy Be

0          5          10 km

Nosy Fanihy

Navetsy
Amporaha

Antazohalava
214 m

Helodranon' l
Befotaka
Befotaka

Helodranon' l
Mahazandry

Nosy Ambariotandraka

Andrahibo

Bemanondrobe

Andilana

Anjiabe

Nosy Sakatia

Maromaniry

Farihy
Anjavibe
Anoronjia

Mt
Passot

Farihy
Antsahamanavaka

Marokindro

Farihy
Amparihibe

329 m

Andranobe

Djamandjary

Sugar and Rum
Refinery

Les Cocotiers

Helodranon' l Ambotozavavy

Ambatozavavy

Djabalabe

Farihy
Djabala

Ambatoloaka

Crater

Ylang-Ylang
Distillery

Ampasipohy

Marodokana

Hell-Ville

Marine
Research
Station

Nosy Ambariotelo

Ampangorina

Nosy
Ambariobe

Nosy Komba

Bemangoaka

Anketsabe

Antamotamo

Antaninaomby
621 m

Nosy Tanikely

Anjiabe

## CNRO Research Station

Take the coast road east out of Hell-Ville for three km to get to the Centre National de Recherches Océanographiques, a marine research base. Under the French it was known by the acronym OSTROM, but now it is operated by the Malagasy as an UNESCO project. There was to be an aquarium and a preserved coelacanth. Alas this rare specimen has gone to the zoo museum in Antananarivo and the aquarium is no more. Instead, there is a marine museum full of more commonplace fish, either stuffed or in solution. The station is open from 6 am to 2 pm, Monday to Friday.

## Ylang-Ylang Distillery

Near the CNRO project, on the same road from Hell-Ville, is a small ylang-ylang distillery. There are plantations of the yellow-flowering trees just as you leave Hell-Ville by the road to the airport (Route de l'Est). They are stunted and pruned back like vine bushes. If you want to smell or have a souvenir of the perfume, try the Ylang-Ylang Boutique on the Blvd de l'Indépendance in Hell-Ville. They sell tiny bottles of it, as well as T-shirts, prints, hats and the like.

## Sugar & Rum Refinery

The refinery at Djamandjary, on the west coast, is open part of the year to visitors. You can buy bottles of locally distilled rum.

## Nosy Komba

This is a beautiful little island between Nosy Be and the mainland. Nosy Komba is a reserve for lemurs, but you do not need a permit to visit. All the hotels, as you would expect, run expensive day tours here, but you can visit cheaply if you are prepared to stay for a day or two. And you are well advised to.

Day trips run by the hotels cost about FMg 25,000 per person. If you try and hire a local pirogue for the day, the boatman is likely to charge you nearly the same amount. But if you go late in the afternoon, with the right wind, current and tide, and return early the following morning, then he will charge FMg 2000 each way. The reason is that he goes out fishing or to the market early and returns in the late afternoon when the sea conditions are best. The trip normally takes 30 to 60 minutes each way. If he breaks that routine during the day for a tourist trip, he loses a day's work and gives himself hours of extra paddling against the current.

The 'port' or landing point for Nosy Komba is Ampangorina, at the northern tip of the island. If you bathe around the beaches here, watch out for sea urchins. You don't have to venture very far to see the black-brown lemurs and ruffed lemurs. Head inland a few hundred metres to the fringe of the forest and you'll come to them. Someone will ask you for a FMg 500 entrance fee or contribution. I don't know if it's official, but they'll give you a ticket. You can hand-feed bananas to the lemurs.

**Places to Stay & Eat** There is a choice of two places to stay in Ampangorina. *Madame Madio* runs the local bar (no fridge), two rooms in a bungalow and one at the bar for FMg 2500 a night. She will also arrange a pirogue back to Nosy Be for you. The bar has a resident cockatoo which drinks Coke and beer. The lemurs are 10 metres away. Nearer the beach is *Madame Henriette*. She has a bungalow to let at FMg 3500 a night and cooks excellent meals.

Les Cocotiers bungalow resort on Nosy Be can also organise basic accommodation on Nosy Komba at a higher rate.

## Nosy Tanikely

This tiny island is about 10 km directly west of Nosy Komba and is said to be a great diving and snorkelling spot. I was disappointed by the coral and fish I saw down under, but a local expert is bound to show you to better spots. Certainly the beach is beautiful, although it's often inhabited by Holiday Inn and Palm Beach

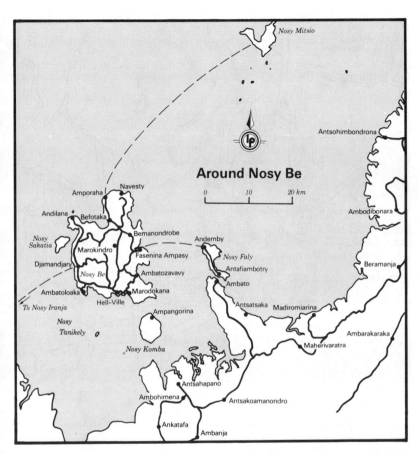

**Around Nosy Be**

tourists getting back to nature and wining and dining on a poor turtle. There's a lighthouse on top of the island's knoll.

### Nosy Sakatia, Nosy Mitsio & Nosy Iranja

There doesn't seem to be much to see or do on Nosy Sakatia, just off the west coast of Nosy Be, compared to Komba and Tanikely. However, you can get trips (via private charter or tours organised by the Palm Beach Hotel, etc) to Nosy Mitsio and Nosy Iranja. Both are at least a two day trip by boat and the rates are around FMg 200,000 per day between six or more

people. Iranja is four hours by boat to the south and is said to be a good diving area. It has a lighthouse and a fishing village. Mitsio is about 70 km to the north in an area noted for big-game fishing and diving.

### Beaches

The good beaches on Nosy Be are on the west side of the island. The good hotels, as usual, have their pick of the best beaches, but there is nothing to stop you wandering along and sharing them. The bay beaches start at the fishing village of Ambatoloaka,

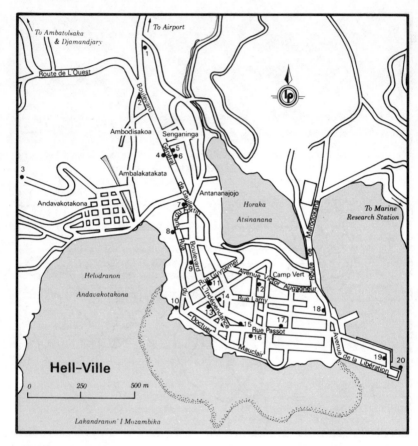

10 km from Hell-Ville, and there are three in a row as you go north.

### Port du Cratère
Take the road to Ambatoloaka and veer off to Andampy to get to this natural, deepwater crater port at the end of the sugar rail line.

### Places to Stay & Eat
The luxury beach hotels split their tariffs into high and low season. High season is at Easter, from 16 July to 31 August and from 16 December to 15 January.

**Hell-Ville** The locally owned and run *Hôtel de la Mer* (tel 613 53) is beautifully placed overlooking the sea on Blvd du Docteur Manceau or Rue du Docteur Mauclair, depending on which map you use! They have a variety of ground level and annexe rooms ranging from FMg 6500 to FMg 10,000, and one studio at FMg 13,000. The best rooms have balcony views and are big and clean, with a toilet and a shower. The restaurant is also well placed, and the food is reasonable in quality and price. There is a disco-bar downstairs.

For a more intimate abode, there are

| | |
|---|---|
| 1 | Chez Kiki |
| 2 | Garage, car hire |
| 3 | Hospital |
| 4 | Cinema Roxy |
| 5 | L'Arlequin Restaurant |
| 6 | Chez Looky |
| 7 | Market |
| 8 | King's City Restaurant |
| 9 | Chez Nana |
| 10 | Hôtel de la Mer |
| 11 | Air Madagascar |
| 12 | Theatre |
| 13 | Chan Fah |
| 14 | Pharmacy |
| 15 | Post Office |
| 16 | Police |
| 17 | Bank BNI |
| 18 | Le Vieux Port Dance Hall |
| 19 | Customs |
| 20 | Boats to Antsahapano |

two rooms to let at the Nosy Be Epicerie, known as *Chez Kiki*, opposite the Jirama pump station on Route de l'Est (the road to the airport). The rate is FMg 5000 per night, but you have to put up with the noise of the power station across the road. Or there is the *Saloon* in town, a Malagasy bar with five rooms, each at FMg 5000 per night.

The restaurants in Hell-Ville are friendly and informal. The *King's City*, north along the street from the Hôtel de la Mer, has a good Chinese menu with dishes from FMg 2000 and a chatty *patronne*. It also runs a disco. Similar in menu and price is *L'Arlequin*, opposite the cinema on Blvd Général de Gaulle. It has a terrace balcony overlooking the street. Nearby, on the same side of the street, is the Indian *Chez Looky* which sells good fruit juices, milk shakes and ice creams as well as Indian meals.

Another nice little restaurant is *Chez Nana* opposite the Ylang-Ylang Boutique on the Blvd de l'Indépendance. You can get seafood dishes here for about FMg 2000.

**Ambatoloaka** Two extremes here. At the bottom end are three bungalow-huts

which cost FMg 9000 per day for a small one and FMg 18,000 for a large one. They can be rented from Chan Fah, who runs the *magasin d'alimentation* (food store), opposite the Merveille de L'Ile craftshop, on the Blvd de l'Indépendance in Hell-Ville. But the huts are in poor condition, dirty and hopelessly overpriced, with a hole for a toilet. Chan Fah probably thinks you are getting a bargain at half the price of Monsieur Franco next door.

At the top end is the *Résidence d'Ambatoloaka* (tel 613 68), built in limestone and thatched so as not to stick out like a sore thumb. It is owned by an Italian, Paulo Franco. The rates, on a half board basis, must be paid in foreign currency equivalent to FMg 40,500 per person for a double, and FMg 55,000 for a single in the low season. That climbs to FMg 49,000/73,000 in the high season. An extra person would add about FMg 39,000 to the total. If you go there for meals alone, you'll pay around FMg 3500 for breakfast and around FMg 12,000 for dinner. The Résidence changes money, hosts discos and runs fishing, diving and pleasure cruises to islands far and near. It also hires out windsurfers, snorkelling gear and Hoby catamarans for between FMg 3000 and FMg 8000 per hour.

Opposite the bungalow-huts, is the restaurant *Angeline* which serves excellent seafood meals for around FMg 5000. The *Tonga Soa* restaurant does meals for FMg 6000 for two and often has live music.

**Ambatoloaka Beach** You can camp here (and perhaps at other beaches) but it is not advised. Anything you leave in your tent is likely to be stolen.

**Palm Beach** The next bay along from Ambatoloaka is the site of the *Palm Beach Hotel* (tel 612 84), a German-operated bungalow resort with 60 rooms, a pool and tennis court. They have a 1001 different rates for rooms/bungalows, singles/doubles, high/low seasons, breakfast, half board, or full board and so on, but you can reckon on between FMg 40,000 and FMg 55,000 per person per night, to be paid in foreign currency on a half-board basis.

Like any of these resorts, a happy time at Palm Beach depends on who you are with. Otherwise, it is quiet and impersonal and a little fraught, as Malagasy staff try and live up to the demands of German organisation. They run trips around the island and to other islands. The hotel's representative in Germany is Individual Tours, Postfach 1529, D-7012 Fellbach, West Germany (tel Stuttgart 57 11 66).

**Djamandjary** *Les Cocotiers* (tel 612 84) is another Italian-owned beach complex in the next bay near the refinery town of Djamandjary (or Dzamandzar). There are 20 bungalows priced at the same rates as the Résidence d'Ambatoloaka. The complex is very similar to Palm Beach and the Résidence d'Ambatoloaka as are its hire and excursion rates. For cruises they use a fast motor launch called the *Ankarea*. For current rates and brochures, or bookings, you can write Largo Dell'Olgiata 15, Isola 2713, 00123 Rome, Italy (tel (6) 378 9733).

**Andilana Beach** Few travellers venture as far out as Andilana Beach, 27 km from Hell-Ville and the airport, to find out what the *Holiday Inn* (tel 611 76) is like. It has a casino, nightclub, nautical club, tennis courts and 120 rooms for singles/ doubles FMg 54,000/60,000 per night in the low season! These rates are reduced if you are in a package holiday group. Breakfast is FMg 5000 and other meals are about FMg 12,000.

### Nightlife
Apart from the casino at the Holiday Inn and hotel discos, there are weekly dances at *Le Vieux Port* hall by the harbour. These are great nights with a live band doing modern Malagasy 'pop sega' favourites. Entry is FMg 750 and there is a bar. It's the best place to meet the locals.

The *King's City* and *Hôtel de la Mer* also run discos.

There is a cinema and an old municipal theatre in Hell-Ville both on Blvd Général de Gaulle. The cinema has some watchable features (in French) and seats are FMg 500. Impromptu band and song contests are held at the theatre, which is beside the market at the southern end of the boulevard.

### Getting There & Around
Getting around Nosy Be and out to other islands is comparatively expensive. It seems the Holiday Inn and Palm Beach hotels set the rate and the local taxi drivers and boatmen apply it whenever dealing with tourists.

There is no bike or moped hire, apart from at the Palm Beach Hotel.

**Air** The air fare from Tana to Nosy Be is US$148 or the equivalent in another major foreign currency. There are excursion fares (six day minimum stay, one month maximum) available from Air Mad. The one-way Nosy Be to Majunga fare is US$81.

The Nosy Be airport is 12 km from Hell-Ville on the east side of the island. There are five flights a week between Nosy Be and Antananarivo and Diego Suarez. The Air Mad office is on the corner of Blvd de l'Indépendance and Rue Guynemer.

Mad Airtours has an agency at the Holiday Inn Hotel, Andilana (tel 611 76). They organise airport transfers to all the hotels for FMg 6000 and various excursions around the island.

**Taxi** Unless you hire a car, taxis are the only way of getting around. They seem to have rates for Malagasy and rates for tourists. They charge FMg 3000 to go 10 km from Hell-Ville to the Palm Beach Hotel. Try and share with other visitors where possible. (Check at the hotel to see if others are going to airport, etc.)

The garage at the top of the Blvd Général de Gaulle, in Hell-Ville, has Renault 4 buckets for hire at around FMg

25,000 per day, including insurance and tax. Petrol is extra. However, you have to leave a FMg 80,000 deposit. Given all that, this is one place in Madagascar where hitchhiking is worth a go.

A taxi into town from the airport is FMg 3000. There are a few taxis-brousses for FMg 350.

**Boat** Small passenger boats and car ferries operate between Hell-Ville and Antsahampano (see Ambanja section) and there are occasional cargo boats between Hell-Ville and Majunga. The little cargo chuggers can take two days to a week to make the trip. (See Majunga section.) There is still some sea trade with the Comoros, but not as much as there used to be.

The main hotel resorts on Nosy Be run trips to the islands for about FMg 25,000 per person per day (see Places to Stay section). For private boat hire, go to the coastal village of Ambatoloaka, nine km from Hell-Ville, en route to the Palm Beach Hotel. There, Louloukha has a 17 metre ketch and a 10 metre motorboat for chartering to Nosy Komba and Nosy Tanikely for diving (FMg 10,000 for a full tank) and sightseeing. But as he also charters to the Holiday Inn, the rates are similar. You can charter the whole boat for around FMg 55,000 per day.

Cheaper and less majestic is Amady Baheja's service, also at Ambatoloaka. He has a pirogue with space for four passengers and a small amount of baggage, which can also visit Nosy Komba, Nosy Tanikely and Nosy Sakatia for FMg 14,000 per person per day. He also organises overnight tent camps and meals, if you go for two days or more.

# Majunga (Mahajanga) Province

The west coastal region from Majunga down to Tulear is home to the Sakalava tribe and is the least populated area in the country. With rivers scattered among wide alluvial plains, it is also the main cattle-raising region. The climate is dry for up to eight months of the year, between April and December, and the average temperature is higher than on the east coast.

Few travellers venture out into the western region, mainly because of the lack of roads. Only Majunga and its environs are easily accessible – if any journey in Madagascar can be termed easy.

## MAJUNGA (MAHAJANGA)

Majunga, or Mahajanga as it is now officially known, stands at the mouth of the Betsiboka River. With its long, wide waterside promenades, it reminded me of Bombay in some respects. It has that end-of-the-world feeling, with the centre of town in a seemingly permanent siesta state during the hot, dusty dry months. Despite its crumbling charm, it does a nice line in open sewers.

There are a number of good, safe beaches nearby, but no resort amenities. In and around town there are several reasonable hotels, mostly run by the large Indo-Pakistani community. There is not a great deal of specific interest around Majunga, apart from the river and seaside, unless you are into religious buildings. There are a great many churches and 20 mosques! Le Rova, by the way, is not the palace as in Tana, but the hospital.

### Information

Apart from Ramzana Aly (see the Getting There & Away section) you can find contacts at the Alliance Française, next to Air Mad. The French consulate is around the corner.

On Ave Gallieni, at the foot of the Ave de Mahabibo, is the Librairie de Madagascar bookshop. They have maps, but not of Majunga itself. They have one of the Majunga region, but it's 90% sea!

**Post** The post office is on Rue du Colonel Barre, north of Ave de Mahabibo. It is open from 8 am to noon and 2 to 6 pm Monday to Friday, and from 8 am to noon on Saturday.

**Banks** There's a BNI across from the Hôtel de France on Rue du Maréchal Joffre, and a BTM on the corner of Rue Georges and the Ave de la Libération.

### Baobab Tree

Majunga is called the 'town of flowers'. You won't see many of them, but you can't miss this grand old tree at the bottom of the Ave de France. It is said to be 700 years old.

### Jardin d'Amour

Maybe the flowers were here once upon a time, but they are no more. As for amour...! The Jardin is mostly just a lookout point at Pointe du Caiman, from where you can see across the wide, red river to Katsepy. The nearby swimming pool, as with all town swimming pools in Madagascar, is empty. They were built by and for the French. The Malagasy are not interested in swimming.

### Amborovy Beach

This is the main holiday beach, six km from the centre of town and close to the airport. To get there, take the No 1 bus from the Air Mad office in town (see the Getting Around section). There is a 'modern' *Zahamotel* (tel 23 24) with 30 air-con rooms at around FMg 13,000/14,000 a single/double without breakfast.

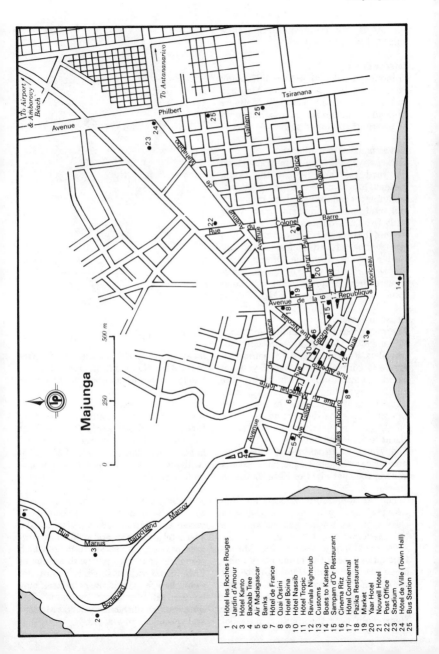

Majunga

1  Hôtel les Roches Rouges
2  Jardin d'Amour
3  Hôtel Kanto
4  Baobab Tree
5  Air Madagascar
6  Banks
7  Hôtel de France
8  Quai Orsini
9  Hôtel Boina
10 Hôtel Nassib
11 Hôtel Tropic
12 Ravinala Nightclub
13 Customs
14 Boats to Katsepy
15 Sampam d'Or Restaurant
16 Cinema Ritz
17 Hôtel Continental
18 Parika Restaurant
19 Market
20 Yaar Hotel
21 Nouvell Hotel
22 Post Office
23 Stadium
24 Hôtel de Ville (Town Hall)
25 Bus Station

For eats, try the restaurant *La Soucoupe Volante* beside the airport.

### Katsepy Beach
Pronounced like 'ketchup', Katsepy Beach lies across the bay from Majunga and can be reached by car ferry. Madame Chabaud rents out bungalows, but you'd be better off staying in town.

### Antkarafantsika Forest Reserve
This reserve is 154 km from Majunga on the road to Tana, across the Boina Plateau. It is home to a variety of lemurs, including the red sifaka, fulvus, mongoose and woolly lemurs, and to many species of birds. In fact, if you are a birdwatcher, this is one of the best areas in the country. Stop at the village of Andranofasika. You will need a permit from the Direction des Eaux et Forêts in Tana or Majunga. Taxis-brousses from Majunga leave at around 8 am and the fare is about FMg 2250.

### Places to Stay
There is a good overall standard and range of hotels in Majunga, especially for travellers. Phoning is usually an unnecessary and difficult task, but if you are having extra trouble with any of the numbers try adding a two to the beginning if it's a four digit number, or taking the two off if it's a five digit number.

### Places to Stay – bottom end
The *Hôtel Continental* on the main street, Rue de la République, has 11 rooms at FMg 4000 per night or FMg 8000 with air-con.

The Muslim *Hôtel Nassib* on Rue Georges is good value at FMg 5000 for a clean room with a fan and shower. The toilet is communal, but clean.

Overlooking the river, on Rue Marius Barriquand, near the promontory lighthouse, is the small *Hôtel Kanto* and restaurant. There are five rooms, without bathrooms or showers, for FMg 5000.

The familiar-looking YH sign, on Rue Henri Palu near the market, does not mean 'Youth Hostel' in this case. It refers to the *Yaar Hotel*, a Malagasy hotel that has 18 rooms with showers. Nightly rates are around FMg 6000.

Behind the Nassib on the corner of Rue Albert and Rue Flacourt are two other Indo-Pakistani hotels – the *Boina* (tel 224 69) and the *Tropic*. Both look safe, and have rooms ranging from FMg 4000 (without a shower) to FMg 9000 (a double with a shower). The Boina also has a separate restaurant.

Around the point at the end of Rue Marius Barriquand is the hotel and restaurant *Les Roches Rouges* (tel 221 61). The hotel also has several small bungalow-huts near the bay at Petite Plage which cost FMg 15,000 a night with air-con or FMg 13,000 without it. Since you cannot swim there, a room in the hotel itself may be preferable; it costs the same. The restaurant has dishes for around FMg 3500 and specialises in seafood.

## Places to Stay - middle

The best two hotels in town are the *Hôtel de France* and the *Nouvel Hôtel*. The Hôtel de France (tel 226 07) on Rue du Maréchal Joffre, is the colonial one with air-con rooms at FMg 18,000 and FMg 19,000. Breakfast is FMg 2000. The Nouvel Hôtel (tel 226 07), 13 Rue Henri Palu, is quite modern with 19 rooms for FMg 9500 per night with a fan and FMg 12,000 with air-con.

You would need to catch a taxi to find the *Hôtel Sofia Satrana* (tel 229 69) in the Miarinarivo quarter. Turn up Blvd Marcoz, opposite the hospital on the Ave d'Amborovy. The hotel is near the market in the north of town, where you can get taxis-brousses or the No 1 bus to the beach and airport. The hotel has 16 rooms, with toilets and showers, for FMg 8000 per night. Breakfast is FMg 1200.

## Places to Eat

Other than at the *Hôtel de France* and *Nouvel Hôtel*, there are few places at which you can eat out at night. The *Sampan d'Or*, along from the Ritz cinema, is not bad for a Chinese meal. Or there are a number of Muslim restaurants. The *Kismat* down past the Continental Hotel is friendly, but watch their chilli dressing. The Kismat's main competitor is the *Pazika*, at the top of the Ave de la République. Also near the Ritz are the *Taj*, and near the Yaar Hotel is the *Kohinoor*.

For good Indian snacks and drinks, I recommend the *Bhavana Tea* opposite the good Hotel Nassib on Rue Georges. They have nice vegetarian samosas, lassi and natural fruit juices. The surroundings are quaint and pleasant, and the staff are friendly.

There are other salons de thé – opposite the Ritz, next to the market and near the post office.

Two other hotel restaurants which may be worth a visit are the *Boina* and *Kanto*.

## Nightlife

At lunch times in Majunga during the long dry season, sheltered doorways and sidewalks are full of dozing bodies. This does not mean they have had a wild night. But if they did, it would likely be at *Le Ravinala* disco and dancing spot, which is by the docks on the Quai Orsini.

The *Ritz* cinema dominates the Ave de la République and is worth checking on a wet night. The *Hôtel de la Bretagne* on the Ave de la République is a drinking saloon only.

## Getting There & Away

**Air** There are flights six days a week to Majunga from Tana at US$92 one way. The airport is six km north-east of the town, near the coast. Taxis into town charge more than FMg 2200, but there are buses for FMg 150 that serve the nearby beach of Amborovy.

The Air Mad office (tel 24 21), at the river end of Ave Gillon, is open Monday to Friday from 7.30 to 11 am and 2.30 to 5 pm, and on Saturday from 7.30 to 10.30 am.

**Taxi-Brousse & Taxi-Be** The taxi-brousse station is a large park extending along Ave Philibert Tsiranana (named after the first president), near the corner with Ave Gallieni (named after the first French governor).

Competition for business to Tana is fierce. There is the choice of taxis-brousses, taxi-bes or Mercedes truck-buses. The truck-buses, run by Air Route Services, are the most reliable and comfortable, but are often booked out well in advance of the others. Tickets to Tana cost FMg 11,000. As the road to the capital is reasonably good, taxis-bes (which are also known as taxis-familiaux) are the next best option for an extra FMg 1000. Taxis-brousses are cheaper at FMg 8000. They all leave early afternoon and arrive in Tana (at the northern bus station, not the western one) first thing in the morning. Remember to take a change of warm clothing. The drop in temperature is quite sudden and severe as you go from hot Majunga up to the cooler High Plateau. There are also services to Fianarantsoa, and places between, for around FMg 15,500.

**Boat** There are no ferries from Nosy Be to Majunga, but there is one that runs from the town across the river and Baie de Bombetoka to Katsepy Beach. The car ferry leaves from the quay at the bottom of the Ave de la République and costs one-way/return around FMg 400/600 (not including vehicle rates). The crossing takes 30 minutes. The ferry runs twice a day, in the morning and afternoon, but times vary from month to month.

There are small cargo boats operating between Majunga and Nosy Be, and, occasionally, the Comoros. They leave from the Quai Orsini. For information,

contact Ramzana Aly (tel 227 21), Armement Tawakal, BP 60, Majunga. The office is around the corner from the Sampan d'Or restaurant. This Malagasy-Pakistani company runs three ships, mainly carrying rice and sugar. The trips to Nosy Be take, on average, 36 hours and cost around FMg 11,000 per person. You should bring along your own food.

Ramzana Aly is a good contact for general information and assistance and he speaks English well.

### Getting Around

The No 1 bus leaves every 30 minutes, between 6 am and 9 pm, from the Air Mad office on Ave Gillon. It goes out through town to Amborovy Beach, near the airport. Smaller trips around town can be made by pousse-pousse for around FMg 500 a ride.

# Fianarantsoa Province

The central-east province of Fianarantsoa is populated mainly by the Betsileo tribe. The provincial capital, also called Fianarantsoa but usually abbreviated to Fiana, is said to be the intellectual centre of Madagascar. The Betsileo are experts at cultivating rice, laying out and irrigating terraced fields and, with the help of a few Swiss settlers, they've also taken to producing wine.

The barren territory further south of Fiana, around the town of Ihosy, is the home of the Bara tribe. Their origins are Indonesian, like the Betsileo, but the Bara have a dominant African streak.

Their customs contrast greatly with their neighbours, in that the Bara mainly practise polygamy and cattle rustling. A Bara man's worth is judged by how many head of zebu he has, not on how he acquired them. (Zebu numbers have diminished considerably in the past 15 years and the customary thieving has taken on a more serious nature.) If you motor down from Fiana to Ihosy and beyond, you'll come across many herds of zebu being driven along the 'highway'. Often the herders almost outnumber the cattle.

Towards the coast, there are distinct regions populated by five other tribes – the Tanala, Antambahoaka, Antaimoro, Antaifasy and Antaisaka.

## AMBOSITRA

Ambositra means 'place of many eunuchs' and was named after a battle there in which the Merina tribe castrated their defeated enemies. The town is noted for its wood carvers and furniture manufacturing, as well as yoghurt and cheese making. Some travellers, however, said any evidence of these trades was hard to find in the town itself.

You have to take a taxi-brousse a short distance out into the forest to find the 'carving' villages of the Zafimaniry people. The main one is Antoetra. Others include Ambatolahy, Sakaivo, Faliarivo and Ifasina, which is higher up on the Ifasina Massif. They are all linked by good forest walks. It is possible to stay in these villages, with permission from the village chiefs.

There is a Benedictine monastery near Ambositra where for 20 years, a handful of French monks made delicious cheese. They introduced the know-how and turned it into quite a cheese-making enterprise.

The monks left a few years ago, however, taking with them the skill, and the recipe it seems, and their Malagasy converts failed to maintain the craft. Check if there have been any developments – or if the cheese sideline is well and truly in the history file.

there is nowhere to stay. Well, there is. It's called the *Grand Hotel*, but it should be avoided because it's dirty and the meals are expensive. If you must stay, rooms are FMg 7000 per night for a single or double. night for a single or double.

Ambositra is 90 km south of Antsirabe towards Fianarantsoa town on Route National 7. The taxi-brousse fare from Antsirabe is FMg 2400.

## Fianarantsoa

The word Fianarantsoa means 'the town where good is learned' and the town is both the Catholic and the academic centre of Madagascar. This doesn't mean there are universities and magnificent cathedrals galore, but there are some student types around. I was 'hail fellow well met' by two young men complete with long scarves and dandy shoes. They escorted me to my hotel and hung around

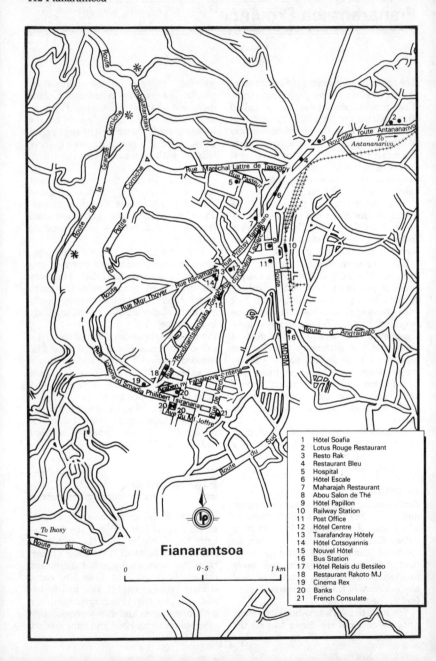

**Fianarantsoa**

| | |
|---|---|
| 1 | Hôtel Soafia |
| 2 | Lotus Rouge Restaurant |
| 3 | Resto Rak |
| 4 | Restaurant Bleu |
| 5 | Hospital |
| 6 | Hôtel Escale |
| 7 | Maharajah Restaurant |
| 8 | Abou Salon de Thé |
| 9 | Hôtel Papillon |
| 10 | Railway Station |
| 11 | Post Office |
| 12 | Hôtel Centre |
| 13 | Tsarafandray Hôtely |
| 14 | Hôtel Cotsoyannis |
| 15 | Nouvel Hôtel |
| 16 | Bus Station |
| 17 | Hôtel Relais du Betsileo |
| 18 | Restaurant Rakoto MJ |
| 19 | Cinema Rex |
| 20 | Banks |
| 21 | French Consulate |

for 15 minutes while I checked in. Whether they were waiting for a tip or to discuss Marx, I never found out.

This town has something for everyone – I think you'll like it. Like Antsirabe, Fiana gets very chilly in the evenings so make sure you have a jumper or jacket. The Malagasy rely on their lambas and blankets.

## Information & Orientation

Fiana town is divided into three parts, which I shall refer to as the high, middle and low district. The high section has all the banks, which is a bugger if you're staying at the Hôtel Soafia. They're open from 8 to 11 am and from 2 to 4 pm on weekdays.

This area leads up the hill to a higher and older part of town where there is a cluster of churches at the summit and picturesque views across Lac Anosy and rice paddies. If you head up there on a Saturday morning you'll probably witness a Malagasy wedding or two.

The middle district is the centre with the post office, railway station and most of the hotels. The most convenient post office is the one opposite the station but there's another up in the bank district. The low district, to the north of Fiana, is the poorer part of town but the most lively at night.

## Vineyards

Fianarantsoa is the wine making centre of Madagascar. Try some Lazan'i Betsileo if you haven't already done so. The vineyards are south of the town en route to Ambalavao. Contact the Papillon hotel and restaurant if you wish to arrange a visit to one.

## Ambalavao

A factory in this town makes *antaimoro* (or *antemoro*) paper, which is dried flowers pressed on papyrus-like parchment sheets. It can be used to decorate menus, books and stationery or for lampshades. There are paper sellers in Fiana.

The Antaimoro tribe are actually based on the coast (see Vohipeno) and are among the most recent arrivals of the Malagasy tribes. They are mostly Muslims, whose ancestors came over from Arab Africa at the end of the 15th century.

There used to be a good market here, but the town is dead now. Speaking of dead, Ambalavao is known as the 'home of the departed', and the famadihana (turning of the corpse) ceremonies are more common here than in most other parts of the country.

Nearby are Ambondrome Crag, the 'valhalla' for the ancestors of the Betsileo people, and Ifandana Crag. Mass suicides took place there in 1811, and it is said that bones are still in evidence. Whatever the case, be careful of local fady (taboos) if visiting these areas.

## Places to Stay

In the upper part of town is the *Hôtel Relais de Betsileo* (tel 508 23). This was a beautiful hotel at one time, but is slowly turning into a dusty museum. Still, there is some finely carved wooden wall panelling and a fireplace in the giant restaurant hall. Rooms are a little overpriced at FMg 9000 for a single or double without a shower and toilet, or FMg 11,500 per night with these 'extras'. The set menu costs FMg 4500.

In the middle or central part of Fiana the *Hôtel Cotsoyannis* (tel 524 86) is an excellent place to stay – one of the best in the country, though it doesn't look much from the outside. You go up a flight of stairs to reception. It is neat, clean, friendly and efficiently managed. A room with a hot shower is FMg 8500 or FMg 7000 without one.

The *Hôtel Papillon* is more renowned as a restaurant than a hotel, although the latter service is also said to be good. Rooms, however, are around FMg 12,000, or FMg 2450 with breakfast.

Rooms at the *Nouvel Hôtel* (also known

Ring-tailed mongoose

as the Hôtel Rakoto Marie Joseph) range from FMg 3500 to FMg 6500, but it's a dive. The *Hôtel Centre* is little better with singles/doubles for FMg 4000/5000 per night. Toilets and showers are communal, but the rooms are large.

Behind the Cotsyannis is the Malagasy *Tsarafandray Hotely* which has cheap rooms.

In the lower part of Fianarantsoa is the *Hôtel Soafia* (tel 503 53), which was opened in 1986 and is a relatively attractive complex. There are some good bargains here with fully equipped single rooms for FMg 9500. Doubles cost from FMg 12,500. Breakfast is FMg 2500 and set meals are around FMg 5500. The Chinese businessman who owns the hotel lives in the big house next door. The development also includes a separate salon de thé, bakery and Alliance Française.

At the other end of the scale and closer to the centre is the shady *Hôtel Escale*. This is a Malagasy wooden den with a warren of seven, low ceiling bedrooms. Singles/doubles are FMg 3000/5000 per night. The restaurant is very cheap. The Escale is bordered by a row of shanty shops selling some amazing items such as zebu shoes, leather and rubber sandals, and large hand-made toys.

### Places to Eat

If you're in Fianarantsoa you have to go to the *Papillon*, which has the dubious reputation of being the best restaurant in Madagascar. It is small and modest by European standards, but intimate and relaxing. The service is topnotch and the prices by no means exorbitant. A la carte choices can break a tight budget, but the choices are tempting. The freshwater crayfish is said to be nice. There is also a set menu for FMg 5500 and a salon de thé section where they sell ice cream specials, though they're not as grand as those of the Honey in Tana.

Near the Hôtel Relais de Betsileo, is the restaurant annexe of the Nouvel Hôtel, but it's as bad as the hotel.

The *Lotus Rouge* Chinese restaurant, near the Hôtel Soafia, is a disappointment. Service and choice was poor with the average price of a dish at FMg 2500. A better choice would be the Chinese *Restaurant Bleu*, or the *Resto Rak* nearby.

Fiana also has a couple of good salons de thé. The *Abou*, at the end of an arcade on

To Antananarivo,
Antsirabe & Ambositra

Sahahoja

Sahatona-Tamboahariva

Vohiposa

Vohimanana
1315 m

Ivanana

Mananjara

Ambohinamboarina

Sahave

Ambohimahasoa

Isaka

Vohidrajiana
1315 m

Tsaratanana

Fanjakana

Kalalao

Tsarafidy

Befeta

Ambondrona

Ranomafana

Ifanadiana

Alakamisy
-Ambohimaha

Ambatovaky

Androy

To Mananjary

Isorana

Nasandratromy

Ivoamba

Maharira
1374 m

Soatanana

Mahatsinjony

Fianarantsoa

Andrainjato

Namorona

Andoharanomaitso

Fandrandava

Talatan' Ampano

1489 m

Mahasoabe

1146 m

Tolongoina

Andronorivato

Alakamisy
-Itenina

To Tular

Asabotsy
-Mahaditra

Taimboro
1842 m

Faraony

Ambatofotsy

Ionilahy

Ambalavao

Sandrananta

Anjoma

Ikongo

Indranana
408 m

Ambohimandroso

Ambondrombe
1936 m

Mahasoa

Sendrisoa

**Around Fianarantsoa**

Antanifotsy

Analafolaka

0        25        50 km

Rue Printsy Ramaharo, serves good, cheap helpings of Indian food. While on Indian food, across the road at the corner with Rue Pasteur, there's the *Maharajah* restaurant. The salon de thé in the Hôtel Soafia compound serves freshly baked cakes and bread.

### Getting There & Away

There are various small-plane flights to Fiana, but the road from Tana is reasonably good (by Malagasy standards). There are plenty of taxis-bes and taxis-brousses to and from Antsirabe (240 km) and Tana (410 km).

The route south to Ihosy, Tulear and Fort Dauphin, however, is an assault course in parts. Usually a lone taxi-brousse leaves for Ihosy each morning, or when it's full. A single fare is FMg 4800. Book the day before you want to leave. (One of the local transport collectives is called SONATRA. They do it *their* way!) If it's broken down, out of petrol or only half full, look around for a Mercedes or 'local authority' truck.

There is a railway from Fiana to Manakara, 170 km away on the coast. It was built in 1927 to service the shipping trade but Manakara didn't have what it took to be a port. The intended links in the rail system from Fiana to Antsirabe and Manakara up the coast to the Tamatave line were abandoned too.

Still, the Fiana to Manakara route is a lovely day trip. There is one train a day each way, leaving Fiana at 7 am and arriving Manakara at 6.45 pm, and leaving Manakara at 12.30 pm and arriving Fiana at midnight. It costs FMg 5300/2900 in 1st/2nd class. Fiana station looks like a giant Swiss mountain chalet.

### Getting Around

There are no pousse-pousses here. You have to catch taxis. Rates around town are FMg 700 to FMg 1500.

### RANOMAFANA

This town, like Antsirabe, has thermal baths. You can take a taxi-brousse the 61 km from Fiana on the road to Mananjary and Manakara. The *Hôtel Station Thermal* (tel 1) has 13 rooms and a restaurant.

### MANAKARA

Most travellers come to Manakara because it's at the end of the train journey from Fiana. You can stay the night at the *Hôtel Sidi*, which has rooms for FMg 13,500 a night with breakfast, or the *Manakara* (tel 211 41), where bungalows on the beach cost around FMg 7000.

### VOHIPENO

Vohipeno is about 45 km south of Manakara on the Matitanana River. This is the heart of Antaimoro country. The tombs of the tribal kings are several km away at Ivato. The women in this area wear a four-pointed hat called a *satruka harefo*.

The taxi-brousse from Manakara costs about FMg 600.

### FARAFANGANA

The great Pangalanes Canal runs from Farafangana straight up the coast to Tamatave. The is not very interesting though. The hotel here is the *Tulipes Rouges* and rooms are around FMg 9000 per night.

Farafangana is 109 km by road to the south of Manakara.

### MANANJARY

Mananjary is a vanilla, coffee and pepper producing community about 177 km north of Manakara by road. The small Antambahoaka tribe that lives here carries out mass circumcision ceremonies every seven years.

Mananjary has a small *Solimotel* (tel 942 50) on the Blvd Maritime.

The southern part of Madagascar is the driest and wildest part of the country. In the centre of this semidesert is the Isalo Massif, a national park and an area of stark beauty and otherworldly qualities. It should not be missed by anyone travelling in this region; it would be like going to Egypt and not seeing the pyramids.

This is also the region of Madagascar's most startling flora – particularly the giant didierea, which grows along the southern coastal stretch between Tulear and Fort Dauphin.

The Tulear region is home for a number of tribes, but principally the Bara around Ihosy, the Mahafaly south of Tulear, and the Vezo clan of the Sakalava on the south-west coast. The latter two are known for their funeral art – particularly the elaborate totem pole decorated tombs of the Mahafaly and the erotic tomb carvings of the Vezo.

## IHOSY

Although the dramatic changes in scenery along the way probably make the trip worthwhile, the 206 km road from Fiana to Ihosy (pronounced 'ee-oosh') is a terror. The journey can take up to nine hours, it's impossible for cars to get through and even 4WD vehicles would have trouble. Some stretches are so badly rutted that taxi-brousse passengers often have to get out to lighten the load or to push.

Trucks are the best way to get there, although Ihosy does have a small airport, three km north of the town, which is used by government officials, construction bosses and the occasional package tour.

### Information

You can change money at the BTM bank next to the market in the middle of town. The post office, near the courthouse, is along from the taxi-brousse station and truck park on the road to Tulear.

Electricity is switched on in the town at 5.30 pm and goes off at 9 pm.

### Places to Stay

There are two hotels in Ihosy. About one km from the centre of town, on the Tulear road, is another in the *Zahamotel* chain (tel 83). The white, single storey hotel has 15 air-con rooms but no character or style. Singles/doubles are FMg 14,000/16,000 per night. Breakfast is FMg 2000 and set meals are FMg 5000. It has money changing facilities.

Preferable for character and price, is the *Hôtel Relais Bara* (tel 17) , opposite the post office. (Formerly the Hôtel Vergère, it's near the roundabout as you enter Ihosy from Fiana.) Rooms are comfortable, clean and separate from the bar, restaurant and reception building. Small rooms are FMg 4000 and large rooms are FMg 6000. The Asian-style toilets are separate and the showers are good. The restaurant is lively at night.

### Getting There & Away

The taxis-brousses to Tulear are few and far between, but there are regular trucks and road construction vehicles heading south. If you get stuck, try hitching from beside the taxi-brousse station. As in every bus station, there are several Malagasy hotelys or snack bars and any truck passing through Ihosy is bound to stop for refreshments. Someone in the 'transport business' will often do the asking and negotiating with the driver for you. Expect to pay the same as you would on the taxi-brousse, about FMg 3000.

### RANOHIRA

Ranohira is 77 km from Ihosy and is the base for the Isalo National Park. The road to Tulear has been undergoing massive reconstruction as far as Sakaraha, 110 km further south-west.

Ranohira is small and there is only one place to stay. This is *Monsieur Berny's* store, bar and restaurant, at a sharp bend in the main road through town.

Monsieur Berny has a few rooms, rather like staff quarters, skirting a yard at the back of the shop. They're a bit rough, with no electricity or running water, but acceptable considering the location. Rooms are FMg 5000 per night.

On the brighter side, Monsieur Berny's manager, Léon, will cook large meals of chicken or zebu fillets 'sur commande' for about FMg 3500. But you have to give a few hours notice. Monsieur Berny also runs a couple of big Mercedes trucks and it may be possible to catch a lift north or south.

## ISALO NATIONAL PARK

This eroded mountain range is a bloody marvellous and magical place. If you have only enough time to go to one place outside Tana in Madagascar, make sure this is it. Very few people manage to do so, there are barely 100 visitors a year and many of them are botanists and zoologists, which makes this place all the more interesting and exclusive.

You can visit Isalo for just a day, or for a week or more of camping and trekking. However, because Isalo is a national reserve, you must have a permit from the good old Direction des Eaux et Forêts. (You can get it at Tana or Tulear.)

This you take to the park rangers in Ranohira. Their office is on the left, as you enter the town from the north, opposite the post office. If you're lucky, you may meet Ferdinand Kasambo, the Chef du Poste du Parc, who has been there for about 20 years.

You'll be asked to sign the visitors' book, giving the purpose of your visit, time of departure and intended time of return. In theory, this is to alert rescue teams should you fail to return on time. In practice, I wouldn't place too much faith in it.

Unless you know what you want and where you're going, or you just want to be alone, then take a guide. There are several to choose from. Ferdinand Kasambo himself is the best guide for short trips, if he can spare the time. Otherwise there is Pierre Claver, the second in command, and then Jean. They charge FMg 2000 to Fmg 4000 a day.

It takes about 40 minutes to walk from Ranohira across grasslands and rice paddies to get up and into the massif at its nearest point to the village. It's like being suddenly transplanted into the middle of a cowboy movie set in Utah. A flat grassy plain is surrounded by wind sculpted rocks and cliffs, seemingly full of eye-holes, noses and beaks; a dozen Mt Rushmore monuments couldn't compete. The French, appropriately, call this *ruiniforme*.

At ground level, there are strange leaves which grow lying flat on the ground, thousands of termite mounds, tiny stalagmite pinnacles, and mini baobab trees which look like inflated rubber gloves or planted human hearts! They produce beautiful yellow flowers.

Running through the middle is a small stream, which at two points runs into little lake gardens. These oases couldn't have been created more perfectly by a Hollywood set builder working on 'Adam & Eve in Paradise'. One in particular, has a natural stone bridge and cave with a waterfall that tumbles into a cool, clean and deep pool, surrounded by overhanging pandanus trees. This spot, where you can swim, is simply Eden. Don't eat the things that look like oranges; they're not. They're inedible *kaboka* fruit.

There are rectangular collections of little holes on some of the flat rock bases, which were made by cattle minders of long ago who would while away the time playing a game, similar to draughts or solitaire, with pebbles. There are also ancient Sakalava tombs in the area and, above all, there is the stillness.

Irish travel writer Dervla Murphy wrote of Isalo in *Muddling Through in Madagascar*:

I've seen the work of erosion in many places but never anything like this. It is, literally, incredible. You don't believe it. You think you're hallucinating...the unique sense of isolation was inexplicable, with Ranohira and Route Nationale 7 only a few miles away...But in the Isalo Massif, though it may sound crazy to admit it, the isolation feels temporal as well as spatial. On levels other than the visual, this is an hallucinatory place. Something very odd happens to time...It is subtly sinister, although – if this can be imagined – enjoyably so.

### Canyon des Singes

Access to this canyon, which is deep in Isalo National Park, involves an interesting walk from Ranohira. Rather than heading directly into the park from the village you walk along the side of the plateau for about two hours to the canyon entrance. The 'canyon of monkeys' (singes) was probably, though incorrectly, named after the sifaka lemurs that live in the area.

### Grotte des Portugais

Some archaeologists believe this cave was used by a shipload of Portuguese sailors who had been shipwrecked off Morombe on the east coast in the 16th century. The cave provided a safe hideaway on their journey across country to the Portuguese base near Fort Dauphin.

Another theory is that the signs of human habitation indicate that the cave dwellers were Arabs, because the structure of the fortress-like shelter suggests Islamic influences. Even Phoenicians are a possibility or the legendary Vazimba people. Like the Redin of the Maldives, the Vazimba are held by the Malagasy, though not anthropologists, as being the first settlers of the country about 1500 years ago.

The cave is quite large, about 30 metres long by three metres high, but it couldn't have been much fun for whoever it was who lived here. There is little water, little to hunt or eat and no soil in which to grow anything.

Getting to the Grotte de Portugais involves a much more ambitious excursion than visiting other parts of Isalo park. It's a 55 km trek from Ranohira that takes at least three days and it's probably best to have a guide.

### Fady

As you might expect of such a mysterious place, there is a fair number of local fady in operation at Isalo. Your guide will demonstrate most of them. The obvious one is the laying of a stone or placing one on an existing cairn to appease the spirits who guard the paths.

### SAKARAHA

This small town is 110 km south of Ranohira, on the new highway, and is the starting point again for taxis-brousses down to Tulear.

From the road you will see huge eroded limestone columns, like buttes, that bare an uncanny resemblance to human figures. One such monument is named the Queen's Head.

If you get stuck for the night in

Sakaraha (God forbid) there is the dowdy *Hôtel Esperance*.

The cost of a taxi-brousse along the new stretch of road from Ranohira to Sakaraha is FMg 2400. It's about the same from Sakaraha to Tulear. The latter road passes several distinctive Mahafaly tombs, cotton fields and some interesting villages where the local people produce firewood and charcoal.

# Tulear (Toliara)

Tulear, the most recent of the Malagasy provincial capitals, came into existence in 1895. The architecture, or rather what is left of it after the racial riots of March 1987, is not particularly elegant. It has a Wild West 'Laredo by the Sea' feel about it, although the beaches are actually mudflats.

The Indo-Pakistani traders control most of the commerce in this town of about 50,000 people, and they bore the brunt of Malagasy violence in the '87 riots. On one street, a Chinese store escaped untouched to continue business while the Indian premises on either side of it were burned down. Most of the heart of the town was gutted.

There is actually not much point in going to the town of Tulear. It is perhaps the least interesting (or most depressing) of the regional centres in Madagascar. It's best seen as the end of a great trek down from Fiana or Ihosy, as a place for starting a trip up to Morombe and Morondava or across to Fort Dauphin.

You may, however, have to spend a few days here waiting for a truck to Fort Dauphin or a visa extension if other reasons do not bring you.

## Information

The post office is near the sea end of Blvd Gallieni and is open from 8 am to noon and 2 to 6 pm on weekdays, and 8 am to noon on Saturdays.

There's a BNI bank opposite the market place on Blvd Delavau. It's open from 8 to 11 am and 2 to 4 pm on weekdays only.

## Regional Museum

The Musée Régional du Cur du Toliara is on the corner of Blvd Philibert Tsiranana and Rue Lucciardi. There's not much to the collection, but as far as Madagascar museums go (which is not very far), it's worth visiting.

There was no fee, guide or caretaker when I visited. I could have walked out with half the exhibits, although I think somebody already had. What there is to see is on the 1st floor and basically consists of tribal artefacts such as spears, statues, wood carvings, musical instruments, and masks of the Mahafaly and Vezo tribes.

There were photographs, but they either became so faded with the sun or were swiped. (Perhaps they were of the Vezo's erotic tomb carvings.) If you wish to know more about the region, you can try around the corner at Tulear University's centre for research into Malagasy art and culture.

## Places to Stay

Tulear favours bungalow-unit hotels. There are two of them on Blvd Lyantey, the town's seaside promenade, overlooking the mudflats. The better of these is the *Hôtel Voanio* which has 16 tidy, wooden chalets with views of the mud, from little verandahs, and good showers for FMg 7000 per night. It is attached to, but not part of, La Cabane restaurant and Zaza nightclub.

At the southern end of the boulevard, past the Hôtel Plazza, is *La Pirogue* (tel 415 37). The bungalows are falling into disrepair, and are popular with the ants, but the owners keep patching them up and you can stay there for FMg 9000 per night. La Pirogue's restaurant and bar serves good, cheap meals.

At the junction of Blvd Lyantey and Blvd Gallieni, is the newest complex in

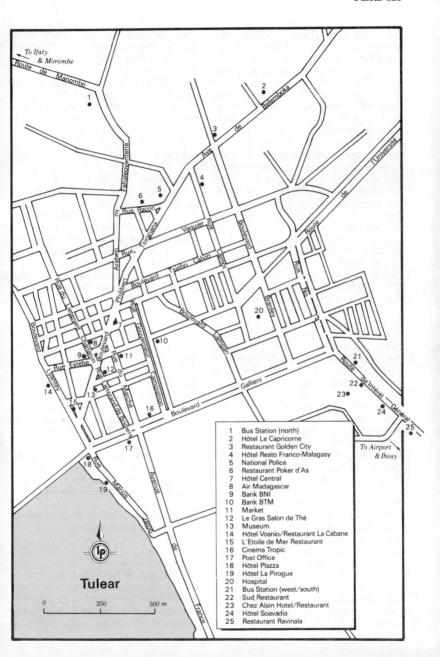

1   Bus Station (north)
2   Hôtel Le Capricorne
3   Restaurant Golden City
4   Hôtel Resto Franco-Malagasy
5   National Police
6   Restaurant Poker d'As
7   Hôtel Central
8   Air Madagascar
9   Bank BNI
10  Bank BTM
11  Market
12  Le Gras Salon de Thé
13  Museum
14  Hôtel Voanio/Restaurant La Cabane
15  L'Etoile de Mer Restaurant
16  Cinema Tropic
17  Post Office
18  Hôtel Plazza
19  Hôtel La Pirogue
20  Hospital
21  Bus Station (west/south)
22  Sud Restaurant
23  Chez Alain Hotel/Restaurant
24  Hôtel Soavadia
25  Restaurant Ravinala

Tulear

0        250       500 m

town, the *Hôtel Plazza* (tel 427 66). Rooms there start from FMg 16,000. An extra FMg 3000 will get you a sea view or air-con, or there are studios at twice that price. The Plazza restaurant is a good place to eat out. The set menu costs around FMg 5000, but it is possible to eat cheaper à la carte. The fried tuna is yummy. Breakfast costs FMg 2500.

At the other end of the market, and town, is the *Hôtel-Resto Franco-Malagasy* on Rue Carnot. There is very little of the 'Franco' about it, with only four tiny, basic bungalows for FMg 4000 per night.

Nearby, around the corner on Ave de Belemboka, is *Le Capricorne*. This hotel, like the Plazza, is in the European-style luxury bracket, and belongs to Jean de Haulme, who also owns most of the hotels in Fort Dauphin. Rooms range from FMg 14,000 to FMg 16,000 without air-con to FMg 20,000 with air-con. Breakfast is FMg 2500 and meals are FMg 5500.

There are a number of small Malagasy places to stay and eat around the western bus station, as you come into town on the Route Nationale 7. The *Hôtel Soavadia* has rooms for between FMg 2000 and FMg 4500 and bungalows for FMg 5500. It is certainly a popular place for food with the Malagasy.

A few hundred metres away, down a lane beside the Sud Restaurant on the same side, is *Chez Alain* (tel 415 27). This is better known as a restaurant, but has three bungalows, set in an attractive garden among palms, for FMg 6500 per night. On the same road, about three km from the town centre near the airport, is the *Hôtel Analamenga*. Rooms there cost FMg 4000 per night.

In the centre of town are two more suspect alternatives. The *Hôtel Central* survived the riots intact, but is surrounded by ruins. It has eight large bedrooms with showers and basins for under FMg 10,000 per night. Breakfast is FMg 1750. When I was there the old Franco-Malagasy owner was managing the place from his sick bed, to which he had been confined for some time. His staff did not speak French, although they strived to please. The hotel was empty. The *Hôtel Tropical* is now a ruin.

Finally, there is the *Hôtel Tanamasoandro* on Rue Gouverneur Campistron. Resort to this only if all else fails.

Many people choose to stay at *Mora Mora* in Ifaty, which is 26 km from Tulear. See the section on Ifaty.

### Places to Eat
The hotels with the best places to eat are the *Plazza, Chez Alain, Soavadia* and *La Pirogue*. In addition, there is *La Cabane*, next to the Hôtel Voanio, which has good seafood dishes for around FMg 2500. *L'Etoile de Mer* across the street has a similar menu and price list.

Around the west bus station, competing with the Soavadia, are the *Ravinala* and *Sud Restaurant*. Up near the north bus station, on Rue Raçon, is the unfortunately named *Restaurant Poker d'As*. For snacks, try *Le Gras Salon de Thé*, behind the museum on Rue Lieterand de Bridiers.

### Nightlife
The Hôtel Plazza is the most popular place in Tulear for tourists, but there are a couple of discos. On the beachfront Blvd Lyantey, are the *Zaza* disco-nightclub, beside La Cabane restaurant, and *Le Calypso* disco, next to the L'Etoile de Mer. They are open each night, but are only worth considering on Fridays and Saturdays. The Zaza is the better of the two.

The *Cinéma Tropic* on Blvd Gallieni is still standing and operating.

### Getting There & Around
Air Mad goes to Tulear four days a week from Tana, twice via Morondava and twice via Fort Dauphin. A single fare costs the equivalent of US$148. The airport is several km out of town, on the main road

Sakalava fisherman cleaning his catch

west. A taxi from the airport to town costs FMg 1800.

If you want to book or confirm a flight out, the Air Mad office (tel 415 85) in town is open Monday to Friday from 7.30 am to 1 pm and on Saturdays from 7.30 to 10.30 am.

There are two bus stations in Tulear. The one for Manombo and Morombe on the route north, is on Araben ny Fahaleovantena opposite the Muslim cemetery. There is one bus a day to Manombo (via Ifaty and Mora Mora), leaving at 7 am.

The other station, for Fort Dauphin, Fianarantsoa and Antananarivo, is at the end of the main road into town near the

junction with the wide Blvd Gallieni. Mercedes truck-buses leave every Wednesday for Fort Dauphin. The journey takes three days and two nights, via Ampanihy, and costs FMg 10,000. KOFIFI run a taxi-brousse to Fiana (FMg 10,000) and Tana (FMg 15,000) twice a week.

Mad Airtours (tel 415 85) run a bus from the Hôtel Plazza in Tulear to Mora Mora. Jean-Louis of Vezo Safari (tel 413 81), offers boat and bungalow excursions to Anakao beach. Approach him directly, rather than dealing through the Hôtel Plazza.

You can get around town by taxi or pousse-pousse.

## AROUND TULEAR
### St Augustin (Anantsoño)

This bay, 35 km south of Tulear by road, was the site of a failed attempt by one John Smart to set up a British colony in 1644. It lasted only 12 years. At Sarodrano, about five km before St Augustin, there are a number of sea and freshwater caves.

### Anakao

This beach village is about 22 km south of St Augustin, across the mouth of the River Onilahy. You can get there only by pirogue from Tulear. Contact Jean-Louis at Vezo Safari (tel 413 81) to arrange a tour. If you bring your own food, you can do the trip for FMg 8000 per person. The reef area is good for swimming, snorkelling and diving. Jean-Louis also promises: 'never any mosquitoes'.

A few km offshore is the island of Nosy Ve. One travel writer said the island was littered with the bones of 16th century pirates, and was one of the world's best scuba diving spots. The reefs, she said, were second only to those of the Red Sea – a distinction that the Maldives and Seychelles also claim.

### Bezaha & Betioky

This is the heart of Mahafaly country. A trip around the countryside gives you the chance to see the funeral art, tombs decorated by *alo alo* totems and other examples of the Mahafaly wood carving abilities.

The place to stay in Bezaha, which is 129 km from Tulear, is the *Taheza Hotel*. There are hot springs in the town.

At Ambatry, near Betioky, there is a spiny forest of didierea.

### Ifaty

There is a marvellous coral reef off the coast at Ifaty and people usually head there to do a spot of diving, often for the first time.

Most tourists and travellers who go to Tulear end up in Ifaty at the Mora Mora village (tel 410 71), which is run by Jacques Ducaud. His subaqua rates are cheap and there are no questions asked about whether you're a member of any professional organisation such as PADI or the like. Because of this, there are a few safety precautions for which you, basically, must be responsible.

Although the air tanks are old and rusty, the water is not too deep (10 metres), the marine life is benign and there have been few, if any, accidents. Double tanks are FMg 14,000 and a snorkelling tour is FMg 6500.

A short way inland from Ifaty is forest land. The fauna and landscape is fascinating, but you would need to take a guide.

**Places to Stay** The place to stay in Ifaty is *Mora Mora* which literally means 'easy easy', the Malagasy equivalent of 'que sera sera' or 'hang loose'; and many do.

There are 10 bungalows which cost FMg 25,000/40,000 for singles/doubles on a half board (breakfast and dinner) only basis.

The *Zahamotel* is a poor alternative, but it's there in case you have to wait for a vacancy at the Mora Mora. Single/double air-con rooms costs FMg 12,000/13,000 per night. Breakfast is FMg 1500 and meals are FMg 4000.

**Getting There & Away** Ifaty village is 26 km from Tulear and there is a taxi-brousse which leaves each day at 7 am from the north station in Tulear. It costs FMg 700.

## MORONDAVA

Morondava is the Sakalava tribe's headquarters. There is nothing special about the town itself, but in the surrounding district you'll find the erotic sculptures on the tombs of Sakalava ancestors. The area is also noted for producing the lamba.

Fifty km south of Morondava, is the small town of Ankevo-sur-Mer, which is a good spot for snorkelling and diving. Belo-sur-Mer, 37 km further south, is another

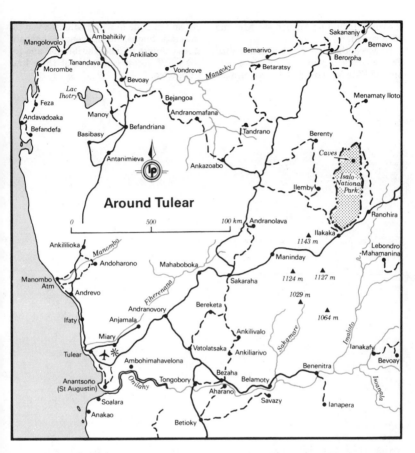

**Around Tulear**

0    500    100 km

lovely beach village. There are no hotels here, but the village chiefs will give shelter to travellers. Remember to take enough food to cover your stay and a small gift (pens, sweets, condensed milk, etc – not fish) as a thankyou.

### Places to Stay

*Les Bougainvilliers* (tel 521 63) is the main hotel in Morondava. It has two rooms and a collection of eight dirty bungalows on the beach for around FMg 11,000 per night. The beach is no good for swimming.

Much better is the relatively new *Medena* hotel which has big rooms with showers for FMg 8000 per night.

### Getting There & Around

There are direct flights four days a week to Morondava. Otherwise you must take a taxi-brousse from Antsirabe or Tana, which takes 1½ days and costs FMg 17,500, or a boat up the coast from Morombe. The boat is not a regular service but it is a beautiful trip. It takes a full day or more, because it delivers food and supplies to each of the villages along the coast, including Ankevo-sur-Mer and Belo-sur-Mer.

In Morondava seek out a man called Farèze who is a guide for the region. For around FMg 5000 per day, he can arrange car and pirogue hire and will take you to the erotic tombs, via an avenue of baobab trees en route to Belo Tsiribihina, and to the CFPF forest centre about three km from town.

# Fort Dauphin (Taolanaro)

Madagascar's south-eastern province is home to two Malagasy tribes, was the site of the first French colony in the 17th century and its capital, Fort Dauphin, is the country's oldest town.

The Antanosy tribe is based north of Fort Dauphin and the Antandroy's territory extends west of the town about half way to Tulear. The Antandroy land is cactus country. The Mexican prickly-pear cactus was introduced by the French from Réunion and was cultivated into natural defence barriers. The Antandroy call it *raketa* and use it for cattle feed. (The large prickles are obvious but beware of the tiny, fine spikes on the 'pear' itself.)

This region also features some unusual species of flora such as the rosy periwinkle (used in treating leukaemia), the insect eating pitcher plant and the triangular rubber palm. Sisal is grown in commercial quantities, for making into rope. There's a factory in Fort Dauphin and a plantation at Berenty.

Uranium was discovered in the area in the 1950s but the French gave up any ideas of exploiting it when richer deposits were discovered in other parts of the world. A Canadian company, however, has recently opened up mineral sands workings.

Fort Dauphin's weather comes under the eastern climatic belt which extends right up the coast beyond Tamatave. The region gets much less rain (less than half Tamatave's annual average) and much more wind. The town is prone to water supply and distribution problems and Fort Dauphin suffers some fierce gales around the middle of the year.

## Fort Dauphin

Where Tulear is the newest town in Madagascar, Fort Dauphin is the oldest. It was named after the Dauphin, the six year old prince who was crowned Louis XIV of France just as the first French settlement was being established in Madagascar in 1643.

The French were not the first to settle the area, however, even though the shipwrecked Portuguese sailors who built a fort near the Vinanibe River were not there by choice. More than 70 of them survived for 15 years in the early 1500s.

The French colonising expedition of 1642, led by a rogue of a governor called Sieur Pronis, originally settled at the bay of St Luce. This site was soon abandoned, however, for the more favourable peninsula 35 km to the south.

A fort was built there and the colony of Fort Dauphin survived for about 30 years before it was decimated by local wars, disease and treachery. It was Pronis who, in 1646, sent 12 mutineers to the then uninhabited Réunion.

The French returned some years later to do some slave trading and make use of the abandoned settlement as a port. At the end of the 19th century it became part of the united French colony of Madagascar.

The port is little used today and Fort Dauphin is a small, isolated town of about 20,000 people. Its attractive location, backed by hills but otherwise surrounded by the sea and good beaches, and its fresh climate make it a popular destination for travellers.

I should mention that much of Fort Dauphin seems to be under the control of a Monsieur de Haulme. He owns four of the hotels in town, the private estate of Berenty 80 km to the west, and a few other bits in between.

## Information

**Post** The post office is near the intersection of Rue Georges Clemenceau and Ave Flacourt. It's open from 8 am to noon and 2 to 6 pm on weekdays, and from 8 am to noon on Saturdays.

**Banks** There are banks on the main road through town, open from 8 to 11 am and 2 to 4 pm on weekdays.

## Beaches

Libanona Beach is one of the best and most convenient beaches in Madagascar. It is clean, pretty, fresh and safe.

The bigger beach on the other side of the Hôtel Miramar point, in the Baie des Galions, looks tempting but is shallow for much of the way out and is used by fishing pirogues.

The large beach to the north, leading up to Evatra is good to walk along, but the sea can be rough and/or polluted.

Talking of pollution, watch your step if walking around the cliffs via the hospital. Stick to the path, because the clifftop grass area is the local toilet! You'll see people passing a lot more than the time up there.

## Pic St Louis

Take the sandy road north and along the beach when it branches at the Panorama Bar. After three km, past a fuel base and military camp, you'll come to a modern looking sisal factory on the left. (You can visit the factory during working hours.) Opposite the entrance gate there is a marked path leading up to the top of Pic St Louis.

The walk up takes about an hour and the going is fine, but bushes overhang the path. The vegetation is benign, but benign all over your face. There is a giant, graffiti adorned rock at the top. Climb onto it for great views over the town, the surrounding countryside and for miles up the coast.

A dawn climb is the ideal, but you would need a torch and a guide. If you like, seek out a Monsieur Jean-Pierre Damy at the

Collège Adventiste (BP 23, Fort Dauphin). He is a Malagasy religious student of very modest means with a young wife and child. He is friendly, helpful and seeks only company in return.

## Evatra

Jean Pierre also will accompany you and arrange a pirogue for this trek north to Evatra. You simply walk for miles along the east beach, Anse Dauphin, from the town's customs yard. You will need a pirogue to get across to Lukar Island, if you cannot wade across. It will take a day of beachcombing there and back.

## Places to Stay

Fort Dauphin has been a base of the Norwegian-American Lutheran Society of Minnesota since 1888. Their church and school stand in the centre of town. Recently, however, the school was closed and converted, with a minimum of alterations, into a hotel.

It is now known as the *Hôtel Mahavoky* and is terrific value. The rooms are big and clean, as are the toilet and (hot) shower blocks. (There are miniature toilets and basins, once needed for the pre-teen boarders.) Rates are FMg 7000 per night.

The choice of meals at the hotel's restaurant is sometimes limited, but the food is good and reasonably priced. The staff are helpful, will arrange free transfers to and from the airport and can organise bike hire. One only hopes this initial enthusiasm doesn't wear off and the demands of guests don't wear them down. If you can't make it out to Berenty, they have a compound of poor lemurs caged up behind the hotel. The hotel is associated with the Restaurant Mahavoky down on Ave du Maréchal Foch.

The *Hôtel Gina* is the best place to eat in town, but the accommodation side has been neglected. They have eight tattered, thatched bungalows ranging from FMg 8000 to FMg 15,000, and one bedroom at FMg 7000. Breakfast is FMg 2000.

Top: Ramena Beach, Diego Suarez (DC)
Left: Waterfall in Montagne d'Ambre National Park (RW)
Right: View of Nosy Lonja from outskirts of Diego Suarez (DC)

Top: 700 year old baobab tree, Majunga (RW)
Left: Street in Soalala, Majunga (DC)
Right: Malagasy twins, Soalala (DC)

Top: Morning wash, Ambalavo, Fianarantsoa (DC)
Left: Thatching the roof of a Merina house, Ambohimanga (DC)
Right: Blind musician outside royal palace, Ambohimanga (RW)

Top: Park Warden Ferdinard surveys Isalo National Park (RW)
Left: A struggling taxi-brousse on National Highway 7 (RW)
Right: Saklava woman wearing mangary pigment, Tulear (DC)

*Chez Jacqueline* on the road to the market and airport is a Chinese restaurant which has six rooms in a plain, dull, but clean concrete block for FMg 7000, including hot showers.

Definitely to be avoided is the *Hôtel de France* near the town square.

One place which may find you before you find it, is the *Maison Age d'Or*. It is simply a small private house on Rue Maréchal Lyautey, down from the cathedral. The owner, Chrisna Hasimbato, lets his two rooms to travellers and cooks up special dinners and other ideas. Monsieur Hasimbato is a Malagasy-Pakistani taxi driver with a part-Chinese wife, two children and some endearing in-laws. He is a character of great wisdom and expectations, though I suspect his religious beliefs get in the way of his entrepreneurial designs.

The family room he offers is a little sparse on the overnight facilities at FMg 4000 a room, but certainly worth it for home-cooked food at around FMg 1500 for lobster and FMg 2500 for a full course meal. You must order well in advance however.

The remaining four hotels in Fort Dauphin are all Monsieur de Haulme's. Two of them *Le Galion* and *Le Dauphin* (tel 212 38) are opposite each other, on Blvd No 1, but run as one. Reception is at Le Dauphin but Le Galion's rooms and outlook seems the better. All singles/doubles cost FMg 24,000/29,000 with air-con, although they were offering considerable discounts in the off season. Breakfast is FMg 3500 and meals are FMg 9500. There is a swimming pool at Le Galion, but it was not 'working' when I called.

The Galion and Dauphin change money and provide a number of day or half day tours to Berenty estate, St Luce (both about FMg 35,000), the Fort des Portugais (FMg 25,000) and Pic St Louis (FMg 15,000), among others.

The five bungalows at the *Hôtel Libanona* look good at FMg 15,000 for one person, FMg 20,000 for two people and FMg 25,000 for three people. Meal prices are the same as the Dauphin and Galion hotels.

The *Hôtel Miramar*, on the point above Libanona Beach, has seven bedrooms. Singles/doubles are around FMg 20,000/ 25,000 per night. It specialises in Chinese food, but watch what you get for your money. The main courses are fine, but they try and charge a fortune for one banana!

### Places to Eat

This is lobsterville. You'll get lobsters cheaper here than anywhere else in Madagascar. The *Hôtel Gina*, next to the closed down cinema, is a must for a meal. The owner is French and does wonders with the lower priced Chinese dishes as well as the Gallic specialities.

*Chez Jacqueline* and *Hôtel Miramar* are also good for Chinese food, but watch you don't get stung by the little extras. A small bottle of lemonade at Jacqueline's costs twice as much as anywhere else in the country.

For a hearty lunch, go to the *Hôtel Henriette*, at the old 'big market' in town (the market has now moved out onto Route 13). This little café is fly and pet ridden, but intimate, friendly, cheap and generous with big helpings of Malagasy food.

The *Chez Rabiy* salon de thé on Rue Général Brulard, near the soccer park, sells nice yoghurt, samosas and brochettes. It has no sign and is hard to find.

The *Hôtel Mahavoky* is also good for meals.

### Nightlife

Fort Dauphin looks like the place where they have a good rage every month rather than every night or weekend. If anything's happening you should see it advertised on posters. If not, try the *Panorama Bar* for discos each weekend. The schools and other societies also run dances:

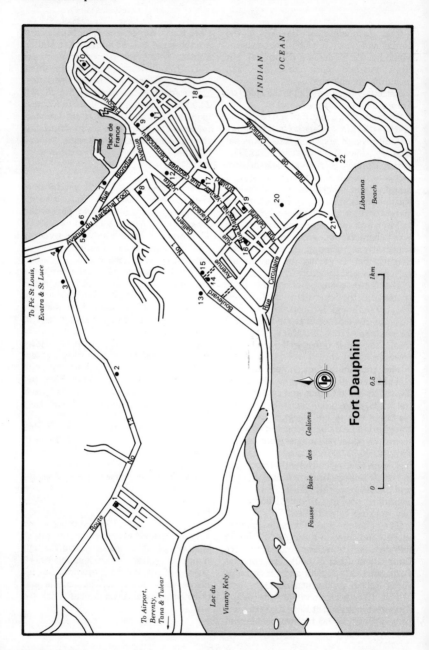

**Fort Dauphin**

| | |
|---|---|
| 1 | Market & Bus Station |
| 2 | Chez Jacqueline Restaurant & Hotel |
| 3 | Hôtel Gina |
| 4 | Panorama Bar |
| 5 | Bank BTM |
| 6 | Restaurant Mahavoky |
| 7 | Customs |
| 8 | Bank BNC |
| 9 | Post Office |
| 10 | Fort Flacourt Army Camp |
| 11 | Hôtel Henriette |
| 12 | Hôtel Mahavoky |
| 13 | Hôtel le Galion |
| 14 | Hôtel le Dauphin |
| 15 | Air Madagascar |
| 16 | Maison Age d'Or |
| 17 | Cathedrale Sacre Coere |
| 18 | Hospital |
| 19 | Chez Rabiy |
| 20 | Stadium |
| 21 | Hôtel Miramair |
| 22 | Hôtel Libanoa |

**Getting There & Around**

There are flights to Fort Dauphin from Tana five days a week (for the equivalent of US$148 one-way), some via Tulear or Mananjary, Manakara and Farafangana.

The airport is four km from town. Some of the hotels have transport waiting to take you to their establishments. Look out for the Mahavoky Hotel one – it's free. (The posh hotels charge FMg 4000 for the airport transfer!) Otherwise, a taxi to town is FMg 1800.

The Air Mad office (tel 211 22) is next to the Hôtel Le Dauphin-Le Galion. It is open Monday through Friday from 7.30 to 11.30 am and 2 to 4.30 pm.

Travelling to Fort Dauphin by road from Tulear, Ihosy or Fianarantsoa is not for the faint at heart. You'll need plenty of time and fortitude. For FMg 15,000, the Mercedes truck-bus to and from Tulear takes *at least* two days and travels via Ambovombe, Tsiombe, Ampanihy and Betioky. The alternative route breaks at Ambovombe and heads north to Ihosy along Route 13, which one travelling survivor

described as 'a perfect reproduction of a dried up mountain torrent'.

There is only one taxi-brousse station in Fort Dauphin and it is at the market on Route 13, out west towards the airport. Few, if any, taxis-brousses go north along the coast towards St Luce and Manantenina as the road is very sandy in parts.

Getting around Fort Dauphin's sandy streets is best done by bicycle. The Hôtel Mahavoky can arrange private hire for FMg 4000 a day.

Monsieur de Haulme's hotels run tours to Berenty Estate and cultural outings to see Antandroy tribal dances and tombs and Antanosy tribal statues and funeral sites.

**AROUND FORT DAUPHIN**
**St Luce**
This was the original site of the first French colony in Madagascar in 1642. Now called Manafiafy, it was abandoned by Pronis and his settlers when they built Fort Dauphin in 1643. It's about 35 km north of Fort Dauphin and getting there is difficult unless you hire a tough taxi or a 4WD.

**Fort des Portugais**
There is not much known about the Portuguese occupation of Madagascar in the 16th century, but they seem to have left more clues than the French did at St Luce.

To get to this island fort, built by shipwrecked sailors near the mouth of the Vinanibe River, you drive or cycle 12 km west of Fort Dauphin along Route 13. At the Chez Mahamanina bar-grocery, turn down a track towards the coast for two km until you come to a small Antanosy village.

The village chief speaks excellent French: he served with the *colons* in WW II. The island is 'governed' now, by the omnipresent Monsieur de Haulme, so you have to show the chief and the island 'warden' some official looking papers they'll accept as authorisation. If not, try money or goods. (Monsieur de Haulme's package tours, arranged through Mad

Airtours, cost tourists FMg 20,000 each per half day!)

The villagers will look after your mode of transport, offer you some food and hire you a few boatmen to take you across the river to the island, one km away. The pirogue trip takes about 15 minutes; finding and hassling with the island's chief can take much longer.

The ruined walls of the small lookout post stand atop a grassy, tree studded knoll. There is a good view across the countryside (rice paddies, zebu, rivers, etc) and out to sea. The island is also a base for some beautiful butterflies. It's not the Hanging Gardens of Babylon, but it's a nice excursion. Expect to pay FMg 2000 for chartering the pirogue and crew.

### Lac Anony

A large lake and beauty spot 15 to 25 km south of Amboasary, which is seven km west of Fort Dauphin.

### Berenty

This is the estate of Monsieur Henri de Haulme. It is 100 hectares of protected forest that is home to a large number of lemurs, including its renowned population of sifakas, ring-tails and makis, as well as fruit bats, and many species of birds.

Berenty estate, north of Amboasary and 80 km west of Fort Dauphin, also features some pretty amazing flora including pitcher plants, spiny forests of didierea, a sisal plantation and some unusual palms. You'll also come across a throng or two of tourists.

You can book tours of Berenty, which cost FMg 5000 for the day, at the hotels Le Galion and Le Dauphin in Fort Dauphin. Unlike the Portuguese fort, you can't get in here without paying but it's probably worth it if you can spare the money.

### Faux Cap

This is the southern tip of Madagascar, just over 200 km from Fort Dauphin. It is difficult to reach unless you have ample resources. If not, you would have to take the Fort Dauphin to Tulear truck-bus and stopover at Tsiombe, 30 km from Faux Cap.

Apart from the desire to stand at 'Land's End', the main attraction of this area is the *aepyornis*, or rather what's left of it. Alas, it has been extinct for more than 2000 years. Its eggshells still cover the sands, however, as if they had been smashed there yesterday.

COMOROS

# Facts about the Country

Early seafaring Arabs called these islands *Kamar*, meaning 'Islands of the Moon'. Hence the name Comoros or, in French, *Les Comores*.

In the Comoros it is the moon which hangs behind the palm trees fluttering in your imagination. There's plenty of sun, but the moon dominates the image of the country, lending it a beautiful and romantic side. But that image is also connected with the dull-to-dark oppressiveness, as often seen through western eyes, of the Muslim faith which strictly governs life on most of the islands. The Islamic moon crescent and stars on seals, insignia and flags are ever present. Then there's the black volcanic nature of the land itself, giving rise to one foreboding brute of a living, smouldering volcano called Karthala. The volcano sleeps with one eye open.

My arrival in the middle of Ramadan, the holy month of fasting set by the moon, didn't brighten matters. The local people were largely subdued and edgy by day, and lively late into the night when they could eat, drink and act more normally.

I wouldn't call the Comorians warm and friendly to visitors in general. It's hard to raise a smile or any excitement out of them, though they're not antagonistic or suspicious. Few are even curious and most just keep a polite distance. There are several reasons for this. One is that after a few generations of French occupation, they're quite used to foreigners walking about. In fact, French government advisers are still attached to most of the Comoros government departments or involved in foreign aid projects.

The Federal and Islamic Republic of the Comoros consists of three islands – Grande Comore (also called Ngazidja), Anjouan (also known as Ndzuani) and Moheli (or Mwali). The fourth island in the group, Mayotte (or Maore), is a *Collectivité Territoriale* (a status between a department and a territory) of France. It is geographically, but not politically, a part of the Comoros.

The Comoros are like a tropical Ireland or Cyprus in that they involve two nations in dispute. The problems are similar, but thankfully not so extreme. The separatism is confusing to outsiders. The Comoros Republic, while still heavily dependent on the French, is struggling to claim Mayotte, and the Mahorais of Mayotte are struggling to strengthen their identity within French rule.

## HISTORY

Legend has it that King Solomon searched the Comoros for the throne of the Queen of Sheba, which was hidden in the crater of Karthala Volcano. Connected with this is the belief that the ancient Israelites were the earliest settlers.

It is more likely that the early settlers came in the 5th century from the opposite direction and were the Malay-Polynesians. These racial origins are particularly noticeable in Madagascar, within the dominant Merina tribe, but not in the Comoros where they have been wiped out by later waves of Arab and African immigrants.

The Muslim islanders today believe the islands were inhabited when the Prophet Mohammed was born, about 570 AD. The ancient Comorians, having been told by Arab sailors of the birth, sent one of their own over to see the prophet, but the founder of Islam died before the sailor arrived. That emissary, Said Mohammed, returned home 10 years later and converted his countryfolk to the faith, which later spread to Madagascar.

For the next 1000 years, the islands were ruled by various rival sultanates, whose wealth was based on the slave and spice trades. The most powerful and numerous

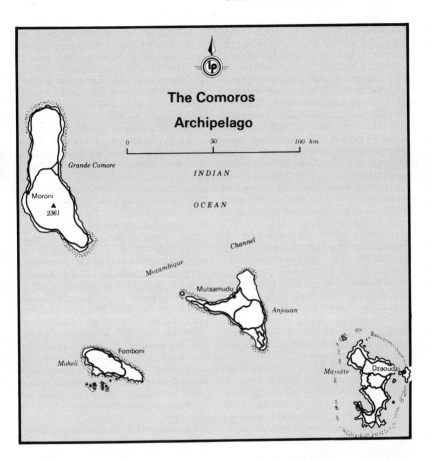

The Comoros

Archipelago

0      50      100  km

*Grande Comore*

INDIAN

OCEAN

Moroni
▲
2361

*Channel*

*Mozambique*

Mutsamudu

*Anjouan*

Fomboni

*Moheli*

*Mayotte*      Dzaoudzi

of the Arab immigrants were the Shirazi from the Persian Gulf. The slave trade, which was not abolished in the Comoros until 1904, brought most of the Africans to the islands.

As with the other Indian Ocean islands, it was the Portuguese who poked their exploring noses in first. Diego Diaz and Ferdinand Suarez, obviously en route to or from Diego Suarez at the northern tip of Madagascar, 'found' Mayotte early in the 16th century. Similarly, the Dutch called in at the end of the century but didn't

stay, as did an Englishman called James Lancaster.

The island sultans were generally left to their own devices. Grande Comore had nine sultans, Anjouan had two and Mayotte and Moheli had one each. Most interference until the 19th century was to come from Madagascar. Mayotte and Moheli in particular were raided regularly by Sakalava and Betsimisaraka pirates from the 'Grande Ile', as Madagascar is referred to.

It wasn't until 1841 that the Sultan of

Mayotte, Sahalave Andriantsoli, ceded the island to the French in exchange for protection, an annual rent of FFr 5000 and a French education for his sons.

The Comoros were important strategically to the French as a counterweight to the British colony and base in Zanzibar, the island off Tanzania. Moheli became a French protectorate in 1886 after the island's capital, Fomboni, had been bombarded periodically by French warships. In 1912, Grande Comore and Anjouan capitulated. All the islands were declared a French colony and later placed under the control of the federal government in Madagascar. They were to remain as such for almost 50 years.

In 1961, after Madagascar's independence, the Comoros gained self-government, but were still ruled by France. Seven years later, there were mass demonstrations led by students, who were no doubt influenced by the Paris riots. The French Foreign Legion and paratroopers put down the civil unrest, but the Comorians were allowed to form political parties; some pushed for independence, others opposed it.

The French held a referendum on independence in 1974. Grande Comore, Moheli and Anjouan voted an overwhelming 'yes'. Mayotte said 'no'. On 6 July 1975, while Mayotte sought protection from the French, the Comorians, led by Ahmed Abdallah, declared unilateral independence from them.

Shortly after, while French nationals were being expelled and their property nationalised, the Comoros were admitted to the UN and the Organisation of African Unity (OAU). France recognised the new government in December '75 and stood back and waited for the fireworks: these started immediately.

In January 1976, Ali Solih took over as president after a mercenary-engineered coup and tried to impose a form of Maoist-Islamic socialism. He put the task of introducing this novel system into the hands of the 'Revolutionary Youth'.

Teenagers took over the administration of the islands and were put in charge of government departments. They burned all the public records and started abolishing traditions which had existed for hundreds of years. The economy went downhill fast, along with the government's popularity.

Matters worsened in 1977 when the Karthala volcano on Grande Comore erupted and when 16,000 Comorian refugees poured in from Majunga, Madagascar, where more than 1000 people had been killed in race riots. (The Comorian refugees were airlifted to safety by the Belgian airline Sabena, and to this day they are known as the 'Sabenas'.)

Meanwhile on Mayotte, the French, taking advantage of the turmoil on neighbouring isles, held another referendum on the question of independence. Ninety-nine per cent of the population voted to stay with France. Phew! *Restez Français pour rester libre* (Stay French to stay free) is still the catch-cry on the island.

During Ali Solih's 30 months of hectic rule, there were four coup attempts. The fifth succeeded, in May 1978, when 50 mercenaries, led by Frenchman Bob Denard, overthrew Solih and his young guard in the name of the new president and original independence leader, Ahmed Abdallah.

Two weeks later, Solih was shot dead, supposedly while trying to escape. Abdallah kept the mercenaries on as a presidential guard, declared the Comoros an Islamic republic and began courting the French again. The new constitution envisaged the eventual return of Mayotte to the fold. The country, however, was expelled from the OAU.

Another coup attempt, in the early stages of planning, was uncovered in 1985. Australian federal police caught three men trying to recruit mercenaries on behalf of Said Ali Kemal, a former Comorian diplomat. Later that year, a coup attempt by 20 of Abdallah's 700 presidential guards was also nipped in the bud.

While Abdallah was visiting France in March 1985, there was another failed coup attempt, this time by presidential guardsmen. Later in the year, about 67 people, mostly members of the banned opposition movement Front Démocratique (FD), were jailed. Many were given amnesty within the following two years.

Abdallah held elections for the country's ruling federal assembly in March 1987, but opposition candidates were only allowed to stand in a minority of seats. He was re-elected but there were allegations of fraud and intimidation tactics by the government and this resulted in many more arrests.

In November, again while Abdallah was in France, 14 former officers of the presidential guard with the help of local troops tried to overthrow him. Three rebels died in an attack on the main barracks, and some civilians were killed, but the mercenary-backed defences won the day.

In April 1988, Nassuf Abdallah, the president's son, founded the Union Régionale pour la Défense de la Politique du Président Ahmed Abdallah, based on Anjouan.

But the mercenaries remain Abdallah's main defence. Bob Denard, whose Congo exploits featured in the Frederick Forsyth novel *The Dogs of War*, had been 'expelled' for the sake of international diplomacy, but he was allowed to slip back, discreetly, to marry a local woman. His house is rented out to a South African.

The republic is back in the OAU, and the same month as the last coup attempt, 128 countries at the UN General Assembly supported Comoros' claim to Mayotte. Only France voted against the motion.

Not surprisingly the Comoros regime is distrusted by its neighbours, but not enough to have denied the republic membership in the Indian Ocean Commission in 1985. The IOC was founded by the Seychelles and Madagascar for economic development cooperation.

The president of the Comoros is elected for six years but, as in the USA, the constitution states he can only have a mandate for two terms.

The president is supported by a chosen council of 11 ministers. Legislative power is in the hands of the 42 member federal assembly. Each island has a governor who is appointed by the president as head of the island's council.

On the other side, Mayotte, as a Collectivité Territoriale, is under the control of the Ministère d'Outre-Mer in France and administered by a préfet. It is guarded by a detachment of the foreign legion.

## GEOGRAPHY

The Comoros lie at the entry to the Mozambique Channel, almost 500 km north-west of the northern tip of Madagascar and about the same distance from the coast of Mozambique in Africa. The four islands of the Comoros archipelago are the tips of a volcanic range of mountains rising from the channel. The total land area is 2236 square km.

The islands were formed well after Madagascar split from Africa during the break-up of the massive Gondwana continent, but not all at the same time. They started to appear about 15 million years ago in the order of east to west. So Mayotte, which is the most eroded, was first and Grande Comore, which is the largest island and contains the only active volcano, was last.

Mayotte, being the oldest, is the only island of the four to have a barrier reef. Anjouan and Moheli only have fringe coral reefs, and Grande Comore has not yet sunk that low.

Moroni on Grande Comore, is 248 km from Dzaoudzi in Mayotte, 136 km from Mutsamudu in Anjouan and 85 km from Fomboni in Moheli.

## CLIMATE

There are two seasons to the tropical climate of the Comoros. The hot and wet season falls between November and April. The rest is the *fraîche*, or cool season, which is the best time to visit.

Temperatures and rainfall vary slightly from island to island. The average coastal temperature throughout the year is 25°C and it rarely moves more than 4°C up or down. On higher land, the mean is 22°C. It is very humid during the hot season.

The islands with the highest relief, Grande Comore and Anjouan, have the greatest variation. That is, it can get quite cool on top of Karthala some nights.

In the hot, wet season the monsoon winds, called the *kashkazi*, blow from the north-west. In the cool, drier season, the islands are swept by the trade winds from the south, known as the *koussi* or *kusi*.

The Comoros are in the cyclone belt. Every three to four years, between November and April, the islands get a bad blow. Anjouan and Moheli were badly hit in December 1980; in January 1983 Cyclone Elinah caused havoc in Moheli; and in April 1984 Cyclone Kamisy ravaged Mayotte, leaving 20,000 homeless and destroying 80% of the crops. Early in January 1987, another cyclone devastated villages and crops.

## FLORA & FAUNA
### Flora
There is plenty of arable land in the Comoros but deforestation, for firewood and building material, and soil erosion have become severe problems. In the 19th century there were three square km of sugar cane plantation on Mayotte. Now there's very little. About 15% of the land remains primitive forest, much of it around Karthala and the Anjouan mountains.

There are palms galore, and they're used of extensively for copra, fibre matting, thatching and basket work. Sisal is also grown and factory-made into rope and cord. There are mangroves and baobab trees. But one tree to look out for is the 20 metre high cycad – it produces sago and can live for 1000 years.

The islands' principal crop is ylang-ylang, which gives rise to the attribution 'The Perfumed Isles'. It takes one ton of the tree's yellow flowers to produce 20 litres of oil to be used in perfume. Every day, the trees are stripped of flowers and pruned so that they do not grow above the picking height. The trees of the ylang-ylang groves are gnarled.

Other perfume plants grown are basil, jasmine, bitter orange, lemon grass and vanilla. The perfume plants were introduced to the islands by a Frenchman called Léon Humblot in the mid 19th century. He was to perfume plants on the Comoros what Pierre Poivre was to spices in the Seychelles, Réunion and Mauritius. Humblot also established cocoa and coconut plantations, but he ran into a long and complicated legal battle with Sultan Ali over the ownership of land on Moheli.

Most fruits and vegetables are grown in the Comoros and there are some fine orchids in the forests 400 metres up the mountainside.

### Fauna
If the Comoros are known internationally for one thing it is for the discovery of the deep sea prehistoric fish the *coelacanth*, pronounced 'seelacant'. The coelacanth, or 'Old Four Legs' as it's affectionately known, was thought to be extinct until one was caught in Comorian waters in 1938. Since then, more than 120 have been caught off Grande Comore and Anjouan. Now, because of the fish's slow reproduction rate, scientists are concerned about it truly becoming extinct.

In 1986, scientists – from the Max Plank Institute for animal behaviour, near Munich – filmed the fish for the first time in its natural habitat among lava caverns and cliffs, 180 metres below the sea surface.

The Comorians call this living fossil the *gombessa*. The *Centre Nationale de Recherche Scientifique* (CNDRS) in

Coelacanthe

Moroni, Grande Comore, has a preserved one on display in the new museum.

The man who originally identified the coelacanth was a South African, Professor J L B Smith, who wrote of his work in the book *Old Four Legs: The Story of the Coelacanth* (Pan Books, 1958).

Another strange fish common to Comorian waters are the flashlight fish, so called because they have an enormous light organ below each eye. They use these to search for food and to communicate. During the day, they swim as deep as 100 metres, but at night come up to within five metres of the surface.

During late afternoon and sunset around Moroni Harbour you can see the incredible sight as hundreds of boats and fishermen try their luck at catching tiny *sim sim*. Like sardines, or the *bichiques* of Réunion, they make good eating.

Marlin and sailfish are also common to the sea here, and with the local marine oddities, the Comoros are gaining greater interest from tourist divers and big-game fishermen, particularly from South Africa.

There are about 700 varieties of shell in the sea still but, unless you're a diver in the know, they are difficult to find. To its credit, the Comorian government has banned the collection and sale of certain seashells, and turtle shells.

On land, the wildlife is not so plentiful or so unusual. The Comoros have little lemurs, called *maki*, wild pigs, giant snails and chameleons in the mountainside forests, but not in any great numbers. Some goats, zebu and sheep are reared for food.

Bird life is equally scarce, and the fruit bat is possibly the most visible flyer. Pigeons, ibis, flamingos, guinea fowl, owls and egrets also drop in, but not in any great number. The good news is that there are no dangerous or venomous creatures.

There are not many dogs around either. I was told that President Solih's young brigands put many to death.

## ECONOMY

The Comorian economy is severely underdeveloped and the country is deep in debt. This can be put down to a lack of natural resources, overpopulation, under-skilled labour, poor harvests and poor communications.

Between 1979 and 1985, France poured almost US$100 million worth of aid into the Comoros, much of it spent on civil aviation, electricity and telecom-munications. The amount represented almost half the foreign aid received by the Comoros. In 1987 French aid totalled around US$22 million.

The islands' economy is still very

dependent on France for skilled labour and development. French government workers assist in running the Comorian government departments, but there is a great lack of doctors and teachers.

Agriculture is the basis of local employment with 80% of the population working on the severely eroded land. 'Perfume plants' cover one third of the arable land. The Comoros supplies 80% of the world's ylang-ylang. However, the industry has suffered from poor climatic conditions, higher distillation costs and competition from Indonesian exports of a cheaper substitute called *canaga*.

Other crops grown for the domestic market are rice, maize, manioc (cassava), sweet potatoes, bananas and citrus fruits. The country has to import 40% of its foodstuffs, including rice, to meet its needs.

Fishing takes place from most coastal towns or villages by outrigger canoes called *galawas*, or by Arab dhows, which have been used for centuries. Fishing is being developed on a local basis with overseas aid. The European Community (EC), realising Comorian waters are rich in tuna, has gained fishing rights for 40 tuna boats from France and Spain in return for development aid.

The government is now concentrating on improving the public health system, food production, housing, water and energy supplies and tourism.

### Tourism
When I was in the Comoros, I wasn't *a* tourist, I was *the* tourist! Only about 6000 people visit the Comoros from overseas each year. Of these, only about 2000 are actually tourists. The 'busiest' seasons are December to January and July to September. After the French, the South Africans are the most frequent tourists.

Comorians are trying to improve the tourist industry with the help of a United Nations Development Programme (UNDP) project. A UNDP report criticised the accommodation prices and services in the Comoros as being noncompetitive with others in the Indian Ocean region. Too right! Although there are several good hotels, the rates are extortionate.

The Comorians are building more hotels, hoping to attract package tourists from South Africa, Italy and France and other tourists visiting Seychelles, Réunion, Madagascar and Mauritius. They are also developing diving as the major attraction, on top of the usual 'tropical paradise' drawcard.

The UNDP calls the Comoros tourist trade 'embryonic'. However, I'd call it stillborn.

### PEOPLE & RELIGION
The majority of people are descended from slaves brought in from the African mainland. These have mixed with people of Malay-Polynesian, Arabic, Iranian and Malagasy tribal origins.

The islands have experienced a recent population explosion. It has increased by 100,000 in the past 10 years to reach almost 500,000, and is expected to break the million mark by the year 2001. Since 64% of Comorians are under age 25 and the largest age group are the under-15s, it would appear there's been more baby booming going on than immigration.

Most aspects of Comorian life are defined by Sunni Islam, which is followed by 99% of the population. There are 1400 mosques at which the faith is practised. Sunni is followed less strictly on Moheli and Mayotte than on Grande Comore and Anjouan.

Generally speaking, the call to prayer five times a day from the minaret is not as loud and dominating as it is, say, in Malaysia. Although the Koran governs life in the Comoros, there are still traces of previous animistic religions in the forms of superstitions and accompanying sorcery. The Maldivians have their *jinis*, while the Comorians refer to their evil spirits or devils as *djins*. There are also several sorcerers (holy men or soothsayers) who will read your fortune in the sand and cast a spell or two.

## CULTURE
### Marriage

Polygamy is still practised, mainly by the wealthy who can afford it. Over 19% of Comorian men have more than one wife.

Marriage customs vary from island to island, but the institution of the *grand mariage* has virtually disappeared due to economic rather than traditional factors. The *grand mariage* was a huge event in a Comorian village or town, and often took three years to organise. It was an 'arranged' affair, usually between an older, wealthy man and a chosen young bride. But it was a very expensive occasion which could, and did, ruin many a family. The public party (called a *toirab*) was great for everyone else though. Ali Solih and his young revolutionaries tried to do away with the ceremony once and for all.

### Dress & Decoration

Even in Grande Comore and Anjouan, some of the more traditional aspects of the Islamic faith have died away. For example purdah, the custom of keeping women in seclusion and dressed in clothing that covers them from head to toe when they go out, is not observed by many women. It has been replaced by the *chirumani* (or *leso*), an all-purpose toga. The town women of Moroni and Dzaoudzi are draped in these brightly coloured and designed wraps which they use like a versatile sari. In the coastal villages, the robes are black and called *bui bui*. In Anjouan, they are predominantly red and white.

One remarkable decorative feature on some young women, which may startle you at first, has no religious significance. I refer to the painted yellow faces that make some Comorian women look as fearsome as Picts decorated with woad, and others ridiculous, as if they'd fallen face first into a bowl of custard. The paste is made from wood, ground on coral and mixed with water, and like any mudpack, is applied for beauty purposes. It is

sometimes caked on with only holes for the eyes and mouth, and other times it is dappled or only spread over half the face. As well as decoration, this make-up is said to be good for the skin and provides protection from the sun.

Most men in the republic's three islands wear the white cotton shirt called *kandou*, and often the white *yamatso* or skull cap. In Mayotte, however, the Mahorais are well into western clothes and fashion. Grace Jones triangle haircuts are the vogue among the younger men and Creole sideburns among the older.

### Homes

The traditional Comorian village homes, made out of coralstone and thatched palm-frond roofs, are gradually being replaced by concrete and corrugated iron shacks.

In the towns, however, there are still ancient crowded compounds of communities (similar to those of the Middle East) with mazes of narrow alleys, gates and steps between the houses. The most important part of these houses is the front door. Often it is a piece of beautifully carved wood standing at odds with the rest of a damp and grey house.

In many villages and towns you will see half built or half destroyed houses. At first, I thought they were cyclone casualties. But they were most likely *maisons des filles*. As soon as a daughter is born, the family starts to build a house for her. She receives it when she marries and gets to keep it if her husband leaves or renounces her. The man who has several wives has several homes – yet none he can call his own.

## ARTS
### Dance

The Comorians like dancing more than anything else, it seems. The Mahorais of Mayotte are the best dancers and the community of Kaoueni near Mamoudzou, the capital, boasts the best dances.

Dancing takes place during all the

Muslim festivals. The most popular dance is the *mougodro*, which has African and Malagasy origins, where all the men, women and children dance in a circle.

Other dances popular throughout the archipelago are the *tam tam*, which uses drums; the *danse de mouchoirs*, which is the handkerchief dance; and the *danse de pilon*, where the women dance around taking turns to pulverise rice with a large stick.

I saw some of these dances at Nosy Be in Madagascar where there is a large Comorian community. They sang and danced nonstop for two nights and days, leading up to the start of the fasting month of Ramadan. They also ridiculed the French in street pageants.

### Crafts

On a more sedate level, Comorian artisans turn out good work on wooden mosaic boxes, Koran holders, furniture and doors, as well as excellent silver work for wedding jewellery.

Clothes for special occasions display some beautiful examples of embroidery. For everyday use, baskets and hats are made out of raffia palm leaves, and in Mutsamudu and Domoni on Anjouan, they make raffia dolls. There is a factory in Anjouan, said to be the only one in the world, which makes furniture out of coconut wood! You can also buy the embroidered *koffia* hats worn by men, and made by their wives. They are cheaper to buy on Moheli (about CFr 25,000) than on Grande Comore.

For more information on Comorian culture there is the Centre National de Recherche Scientifique (CNDRS) museum and library in Moroni, Grande Comore, or the Centre Mahorais d'Animation Culturelle in Mamoudzou, Mayotte. The Mayotte centre also has a library, shows video movies and films each week, hosts art exhibitions, visiting theatre groups and other performers, and runs its own shows and displays.

### HOLIDAYS & FESTIVALS

The main holidays in the Comoros are religious and based on the lunar calendar, so the dates regress each year. The biggest holiday is the *Id-ul-Fitr*. It marks the new moon and the end of the fasting month of Ramadan, which is in the 9th month of the lunar year. Till 1993, Ramadan and Id-ul-Fitr will fall during March and April respectively.

Other holidays are *Id-ul-Adha* or *Kabir*, the Feast of the Sacrifice, which commemorates the willingness of Abraham to sacrifice his son, Isaac; *Maoulid*, the anniversary of the birth of the Prophet Mohammed; *Leilat ul-Miradj*, his ascension to heaven; *Muharram*, the start of the Islamic new year; and *Ashoura*, commemorating the death of Imam Hussein.

The Comoros Republic's national day, commemorating independence, is on 6 July.

In Mayotte, as well as the Muslim holidays there are the main French ones. These are Bastille Day on 14 July, Christmas and New Year.

### LANGUAGE

Arabic and French are the official languages, but the everyday Comorian language is a form of Swahili from East Africa. In Mayotte, it's called Mahorais and there are several different dialects. Some of the more common Comorian/Mahorais words, with the emphasis in capital letters, are:

### Greetings & Civilities

| | |
|---|---|
| welcome | *karibu* |
| good day, hello | *kwezi* |
| good day (in response) | *m'bona* |
| How's it going? | *Jeje?* |
| How's it going? | *Jeje?* |
| fine (in response) | *DJema* |
| thank you | *marAHAba* |
| goodbye | *kwaheri* |
| sir | *monYE* |
| madame | *bueni* |
| mother | *mama* |

| | | | |
|---|---|---|---|
| father | *baba* | rice | *tsohole* |
| grandmother or elderly woman | *koko* | tea | *diTE* |
| | | chicken | *kuhu* |
| grandfather or elderly man | *bakoko* | shark | *papa* |
| | | lobster | *KAMba diva* |
| one | *moJA* | water | *MAji* |
| two | *bilI* | | |
| three | *TRAru* | | |

## Weather

**Getting Around**

| | | | |
|---|---|---|---|
| | | road/street | *paRE* |
| | | market | *baZAri* |
| it's hot | *ina MOro* | beach | *mTSangani* |
| it's cold | *ina baRIdi* | to drink | *hunUA* |
| rain | *VUa* | to swim | *huyeleya* |
| wind | *PEvo* | boat | *marKAbu* |
| sun | *JUa* | to fish | *muLOzi* |
| | | mosque | *mukiri* |

## Time

| | | | |
|---|---|---|---|
| | | countryside or village | *liJU* |
| night | *uKU* | | |
| day | *mTSAna* | town | *mJIni* |
| today | *leo* | post office | *poste* |
| tomorrow | *meso* | | |
| yesterday | *JAna* | | |

Two other useful words are:

## Food & Drink

| | | | |
|---|---|---|---|
| | | paradise | *peVOni* |
| pineapple | *naNAsi* | mosquito | *dUNdi* |
| to eat | *hula* | | |
| it's good | *ya DJema* | | |
| banana | *maSINdza* | | |
| coconut (fried) | *NAdzi* | | |
| coconut (fresh) | *idjavou* | | |
| orange | *trUNdra* | | |
| sugar | *muwa* | | |
| coffee | *kafe* | | |

Little English is spoken and there are no Comorian-English dictionaries or phrase books for sale. The one dictionary, if you speak French, is the *Petit Lexique Franco-Mahorais*, available from newsagencies in Mayotte for FFr 20.

# Facts for the Visitor

## VISAS

The visa system for the Federal Republic of the Comoros and Mayotte is confusing and loosely administered.

All visitors need a visa for the Comoros, but can only get one upon arrival in the Comoros. When you enter the Comoros you will need to show an onward ticket, but will not be asked for a visa. You probably won't even be told you have to go and get one. But you certainly will be asked for it when you leave the country.

To apply for a visa go to the Ministère de l'Intérieur in Moroni, Grande Comore. The visa costs FFr 40 (French francs) or CFr 2000 (Comorian francs) if you are staying longer than two days (ie a stopover). The visa is valid until the departure date on your return or outgoing ticket.

There are no restrictions on any passport holders entering the Comoros. South Africans are permitted entry for business and tourism. Israelis intending to visit, however, would be wise to check first.

There are few diplomatic representatives of the Comoros outside the country. There is an embassy in France – the Ambassade de la RFI des Comores (tel (47) 63 81 78), 15 Rue de la Néva, 75008 Paris. You can apply there for a visa, but write first and check before you send your passport. There are honorary consuls in Belgium (27 Chemin des Pins, Brussels 1180), Singapore (Tong Eng Building, 101 Cecil Street), Japan (Osaka), Senegal (Dakar) and Luxembourg; and an embassy in Egypt (Cairo), and a consulate in Saudi Arabia (Jeddah).

Mayotte has the same entry regulations as France. You need a visa unless you hold a French passport or are a national of the EC. You can apply for a Mayotte visa in Réunion or at the French Embassy next to the Hôtel Karthala in Moroni on Grande Comore. If possible, apply for a Mayotte visa at the French Embassy in your own country. Any other French consulate or embassy has to refer it back to the embassy in your own country in any case, and it will take twice as long.

The application at the French Embassy takes six to eight days to process and costs CFr 3000 or FFr 60. You need one photo. Comorians also need this visa to visit Mayotte, although there have been several instances of people getting into Mayotte without a French visa.

## MONEY

| | | |
|---|---|---|
| FFr 1 = | CFr 50 | |
| UK£1 = | CFr 350 | FFr 7 |
| US$ 1 = | CFr 275 | FFr 5.5 |
| A$ 1 = | CFr 200 | FFr 4 |
| C$ 1 = | CFr 225 | FFr 4.5 |

The Comorian franc (CFr) is tied to the French franc (FFr). The two currencies are interchangeable in the Comoros Republic at that set rate. You can buy food, pay for taxis and hotel bills in either currency. In Mayotte, however, only French francs are in common usage. You have to change Comorian francs at a bank.

There are no import or export restrictions on the currency and no black market.

### Banks

The banks are few but good. There is only one bank in the Comoros Republic and one in Mayotte which change money and travellers' cheques. The Banque Internationale des Comores (BIC) is in both Moroni, Grande Comore, and Mutsamudsu, Anjouan. It is open Monday to Thursday from 7.30 am to 12.30 pm, on Fridays from 7.30 to 11.30 am and closed on weekends. During the month of Ramadan, it closes each day an hour earlier.

The BIC changes most currencies,

including Australian and Canadian dollars, but not South African rand. The bank has an efficient and helpful staff, some of whom speak good English.

The Novotel Ylang-Ylang hotel in Moroni also changes money, but at a lower rate than the bank.

On Mayotte there is the Banque Française Commerciale (BFC). The main office is in Mamoutzou with a branch in Dzaoudzi. They are open each weekday from 7.30 am to 12.30 pm and from 2 to 4 pm. The BFC in Mayotte is just a branch of the head office in Réunion and its powers of transaction are limited. For instance, it has no agency for any credit cards. Neither has the BIC. In other words, the Comoros is a hell of a place to run out of money as I did. Until a kind bank manager helped me out, it was suggested I place myself at the mercy of the préfecture – or the foreign legion!

### Credit Cards
Only the hotels accept credit cards, and then only American Express and Diners Club.

### TOURIST INFORMATION
Unless you bump into a Comorian, it is difficult to get details of the Comoros outside of the archipelago because of the few diplomatic or trade missions. There is no official representative in Madagascar, Réunion or Mauritius, or in any of the East African nations.

You can try writing to the Comoros Embassy in Paris (see the Visa section), to the Société Comorienne de Tourisme et d'Hôtelerie (Comotel), Itsandra Hôtel, Grande Comore (tel 2365), or the Direction du Tourisme, Boîte Postale 433, Moroni, Grande Comore.

Mayotte has several tourist offices but none are particularly active or helpful, particularly to non-French or English-speaking visitors. They are certainly not run along the lines and scale of the Syndicat d'Initiative in Réunion. But you could be lucky. They are:

Office Territorial du Tourisme et de l'Information
    BP 169, Mamoudzou, 97600 Mayotte
    (tel 61 16 04)
Office Mahorais du Tourisme et de l'Artisanat
    BP 42, Dzaoudzi, 97610 Mayotte
    (tel 40 14 48)
Ministère du Temps Libre, Direction du Tourisme
    17 Rue de l'Ingénieur Keller, 75740 Paris Cedex 15, France (tel 57 56 21 60)
Mayotte Représentation à Paris
    1 Ave Foch – 10 Rue de Presbourg, 75116 Paris, France (tel 45 01 28 30)

In France, MVM, Africatours and Jettours (all based in Paris) run package tours to the Comoros. In Italy, the islands are handled by Grand Soleil and Turitalia, and in West Germany by Indian Ocean Tour, Freiburger Strasse 6a, 6082 Morfelden. Thomas Cook and Miller Weadon Travel in South Africa offer tours to the Comoros.

### Embassies

The French Embassy (tel 73 07 53) in the Comoros Republic is next to the Hôtel Karthala in Moroni, on Grande Comore. You have to go there if you need visas for Mayotte.

The US Embassy (tel 73 12 03) is near Itsandra on the road to Hahaya Airport on Grande Comore. Along with a number of other diplomatic missions around the world it has been reduced in size, as a cost-cutting exercise by the US Government, and has no ambassador.

The Madagascar Consulate (and Air Madagascar representative) is opposite the new market, and down towards the town, in Moroni. Visas for Madagascar take 24 hours to process, cost CFr 2500 and require an application in quadruplicate with four passport photos.

## GENERAL INFORMATION
### Post

The postal service in both the Comoros Republic and Mayotte is reliable and not as slow as you might expect.

The post office, near the old market and the BIC in Moroni, is open Monday to Thursday from 7 am to noon and 3 to 5 pm. On Fridays it is open from 7 to 11.30 am only and on Saturdays from 7 am to noon only. (During Ramadan it is open Monday to Thursday from 7 am to 1.30 pm only. Friday and Saturday times remain the same throughout the year.)

There is a poste restante service which charges CFr 150 for each letter collected. There is also a philatelic sales agency in the square opposite the Friday Mosque in Moroni. It has a wide selection of Comoros stamps for sale.

The post offices in Dzaoudzi and Mamoudzou, Mayotte, are open Monday to Saturday from 7.30 am to 5 pm. Postcards cost FFr 1.90 to European countries and FFr 2.70 to Australia and the USA. The lightest of letters (up to 10 grams) are FFr 3.80 for Europe and FFr 4.70 for Australia and the US. They increase 65c for each additional five grams. Aerogrammes cost FFr 3.90 to any destination.

### Telephones

You can make international telephone calls from the post offices in Mayotte or Moroni. At the Moroni post office they charge CFr 1250 per minute for a call to the UK, CFr 1850 to the USA or Australia, CFr 1200 to West Germany, and CFr 800 to France.

### Electricity

Ironically, because of French aid, the Comoros Republic's electricity supply is much more reliable now than that of Mayotte. Moroni's supply is reasonably regular, although Moheli still lacks a proper system. In Mayotte, however, there are blackouts almost daily around the peak times of lunch and dinner, varying between five and 30 minutes. The current is 220 volts and power points take two-pin plugs.

### Time

The time in the Comoros is three hours ahead of GMT.

### Business Hours

In the Comoros Republic, offices are open Monday to Thursday from 8 am to noon and 2 to 4 pm. On the holy day, Friday, they are open from 9 am to noon. Generally shops keep similar hours though some open earlier in the morning, close later in the afternoon and are open a half day or full day on Saturday. Office hours are curtailed during Ramadan, when many shops take a long midday siesta and stay open late into the night.

## MEDIA

### Newspapers & Magazines

There are no daily newspapers in the Comoros. The Comoros Republic gets the sober, but by no means dull, *Al-Watwany* paper twice a month in French and Comorian editions for CFr 200. In 1988, the weekly independent *L'Archipel* began

publication. *Newsweek* and *Time* are also available from the Nouveautés newsagency, near the CNDRS museum and post office square in Moroni, for CFr 1740. In Mayotte, the bright community newspaper *Le Journal de Mayotte* comes out every Friday. It costs FFr 5.

### Radio & Television

There is no TV on Grande Comore, Anjouan or Moheli. But there is Radio Comores. The news is broadcast in French early in the morning, at noon and in the evening. You can also pick up the BBC World Service.

Mayotte has TV between 7 pm and midnight each day.

### HEALTH

The Comoros, for all its economic problems and lack of development, does not strike you as an unhealthy place. You simply have to take a course of prophylactics, as malaria has not been eradicated, and remember not to drink the water indiscriminately.

The water is (probably) OK to drink from the tap in Moroni and in Dzaoudzi or Mamoudzou on Mayotte. Otherwise, drink bottled mineral water, beer, soft drinks, or take the usual precautions of boiling the water or using purification tablets.

### Treatment

If you fall ill or are injured, try to do so in Mayotte where the health system is much more advanced. The hospital is in Dzaoudzi. On Grande Comore there is Hôpital Al Maarouf in Moroni, a Christian mission at Mitsamiouli, and Hôpital d'Hombo in Mutsamudu, Anjouan.

There are two pharmacies in Moroni – the Pharmacie des Comores in the northern Magudju district and the Pharmacie de la Corniche on the Blvd de la Corniche. There is also a chemist in Mutsamudu.

For advice on treatment it is best to call the French Embassy next to the Hotel Karthala, in Moroni, or one of the Comotel hotels.

Alternatively, there are the relief agencies, UN and CARE (USA), an EC development representative and a Canadian project. There are also nursing sisters at the Mission Catholique in Moroni and at Mitsamiouli.

## DANGERS & ANNOYANCES

There are no dangerous creatures on land and no particular danger from sharks and the like when swimming or diving. The greatest hazards to health in the Comoros are the *taxi-brousse* (bush taxi) drivers. They drive much too fast!

The president's mercenary guard should also be kept at a respectful distance on Grande Comore. Be careful when you are taking photographs. Don't take pics at any airport or near the president's residence on the coast road from Itsandra to Moroni. The same applies around the foreign legion and defence establishments on Mayotte. In fairness, I was never bothered or even approached by any soldiers, but you wouldn't want to give them cause to do so.

### Theft

Theft is becoming an increasing problem, in Moroni mainly, but is not a matter for concern as long as you take the normal precautions.

## FILM & PHOTOGRAPHY

As with the books and newspapers, film is also available from Nouveautés in Moroni. It costs CFr 3500 for Kodak Gold (36 exposures) or CFr 2850 (24 exposures). Kodachrome slide film is CFr 7265 (36 exp), including development. However, no printing and developing is done on the Comoros. Film is sent to Paris, which they

say is half the price of sending it to Mayotte.

In Mayotte, film is much more expensive. At the Shoping pharmacy and store in Mamoudzou, for example, Kodak Gold (36 exposures) costs FFr 81.

## ACCOMMODATION

One of the sore points about visiting the Comoros on the cheap is that there are very few budget hotels or *pensions*. It is too risky to throw yourself upon the magnanimity of the local people, who are neither disposed through their faith and recent colonial history, nor tempted by the current trickle of travellers, to help out or exploit foreign visitors.

The cheapest place to stay on Grande Comore is *Le Glacier Restaurant* where rates start at CFr 4000 (FFr 80). The cheapest pensions cost about double that, and other hotels are nearly twice as much again. In Mayotte, the *Bar de Rond* is the cheapest at FFr 150 for a single per night. The others are over FFr 200.

The alternatives are to stay in Anjouan, where there are a few local boarding houses which charge between CFr 1500 and CFr 3000 a night, or to shack up in a thatched beach hut (*paillotte*) or to camp. There are no camping sites or facilities, but neither do there appear to be any restrictions.

## FOOD

Comorian cuisine isn't exactly tantalising. How about rice, fish and coconuts to start with. They're the 'staples' as in many other parts of the Indian Ocean.

There are enough spices and fruits to play around with, but I don't know if the Comorians have come up with anything exclusively Comorian. If they have, you'll be lucky to get a taste. Otherwise, French is still the flavour of the century.

There is a heavy reliance on imported food from South Africa and France to supplement the local produce such as fruits and vegetables, which are cheap in season when the crop hasn't been destroyed by a cyclone. For example, four oranges and six guavas, cost only CFr 100 (FFr 2). Bananas are also a bargain. Look for the pink ones.

There are fresh produce markets daily in Moroni and Mamoudzou. But as in markets anywhere in the Indian Ocean region, when the locals see tourists shopping they think all their Christmases, or the Muslim equivalent, have come at once. If you think the price has been unfairly increased, shop around or find out what the locals are paying.

For imported goods, there are a number of well stocked and reasonably priced supermarkets. In Moroni, about 200 metres around the corner from the Hôtel Karthala, is the Unicoop store. Cheese is CFr 600 to CFr 900, a large Coke or Orangina is CFr 1000 and a Mars bar is CFr 400.

There is a bakery opposite with great cheap cakes and pastries and you can buy bread from street traders for next to nothing.

In Mayotte, there is the SNIE supermarket beside the main market in Mamoudzou and one next to the Ningha nightclub near the ferry pier in Dzaoudzi.

Apart from Moroni, there is a dearth of small, cheap Muslim places to eat. Mamoudzou is especially lacking in such. The French and hotel restaurants are not too pricey with an average meal costing between FFr 50 and FFr 80. You can also get a good, simple meal for around CFr 1000 to CFr 1500 at the local eating places in Moroni. The alternative here is to buy cheap fruit, vegetables and bread from the markets and imported extras from the supermarkets.

## DRINK

As for drink, the Muslim society offers little choice. There may be some coconut toddy in the villages, but that's about all.

Beer, wine and spirits are available from the hotels and the western or Chinese stores. The beer is all imported from South Africa – Carling Black Label

and Castle. It costs CFr 850 from hotels, but CFr 50 from stores. Coffee is drunk more than tea. The standard price of a cup of coffee in a hotel is CFr 450.

## BOOKS & BOOKSHOPS

There is only one newsagency, stationers and bookshop in the Comoros Republic and that's Nouveautés near the CNDRS museum and post office square in Moroni.

It has a wide selection of French-language magazines and some English-language ones including *Time, Newsweek* and *Cosmopolitan*. And, surprise surprise, it also keeps copies of *Playboy* and *Penthouse* behind the counter. There are postcards at CFr 100 each and a limited selection of English paperbacks at around CFr 3000 each. Nouveautés also sells film and maps.

In Mayotte, there are a few similar newsagencies to Nouveautés, but no bookshop as such. The best is Shoping store and pharmacy on the road to the Hôtel Le Baobab. But in Mayotte, all the books and magazines are in French.

### People & Society

I could only find two books on the Comoros in English. One, *Let's Visit the Comoros* by D E Gould (Burke Books, London, 1985), is a general introduction to the islands for secondary students. The other is for more advanced study. This is *The Comoros Islands: Struggle Against Dependency in the Indian Ocean* by Malyn Newitt (Gower, London, 1984).

If you read French, then you may wish to consider *Géographe des Comores* by René Battistini and Pierre Vérin (Nathan, Paris, 1984). It is a colourful and well presented study on the geography and economy of the four islands and is available in Moroni and Mayotte for CFr 3130 or FFr 65.

*Regards Sur Mayotte* is a locally produced soft cover introduction to the island. It costs FFr 20 and is available in Mayotte newsagencies.

*Mayotte – Ile aux Parfums* by Christian Bossu-Picat (Editions Delroisse, Paris) is a souvenir collection of pretty pictures for FFr 200.

## History

A chapter on the Ali Solih regime and the coup which brought the current president to power, is contained within *Africans* (Random House, New York, 1982) by David Lamb, the South African correspondent for the *Los Angeles Times*. The book is not available in the Comoros.

*Comores: Quatre Iles Entre Pirates et Planteurs* by Jean Martin (L'Harmattan, 1984) is a two volume history of the islands covering the 18th century up to 1912. One book costs FFr 276, the other FFr 258.

## Travel Guides

There are no travel guides on the Comoros itself, although it is sometimes included in guides to the Indian Ocean region. However, the enterprising Gilles Gautier has put together an attractive little pocket-guide brochure titled *Karibu* (Les Editions du Baobab, Moroni, 1989).

## Libraries

If you wish to pursue a particular subject the CNDRS cultural and scientific centre, in the Sans Fils district of Moroni, has a new reference library. There are also lending libraries at the Alliance Franco-Comorienne, near the Hôtel Coelacanthe in Moroni, and at the Centre Mahorais d'Animation Culturelle (CMAC) in Mamoudzou, Mayotte.

## Research

For specialist research into the Comoros, the best source outside the country is the Institut National des Langues et Civilisation Orientale of the Centre Océan Indien Occidental in Paris.

## MAPS

Nouveautés in Moroni has a full selection of detailed and accurate Institut Géographique National (IGN) maps. But you cannot buy one for the whole of the Comoros. You have to get two on Grande Comore (CFr 4000), one on Moheli (CFr 2000), two on Anjouan (CFr 4000) and one on Mayotte (CFr 2000). If you wish to obtain these in advance, write to IGN, 136 bis, Rue de Grenelle, 75700 Paris.

## ACTIVITIES

### Diving

Like its neighbours to the north-east, Seychelles and Maldives, the Comoros are promoting diving as the principal attraction.

On Grande Comore, the main school is Jean-Louis Geraud's *Gombessa Plongée* (tel 73 05 75), based at the Hôtel Coelacanthe in Moroni. One dive costs CFr 8000, 10 dives cost CFr 75,000, or one week of unlimited dives costs CFr 70,000. Gombessa (Comorian for coelacanth) caters for up to 12 divers.

The dives take place from the shore opposite the hotel where the depth plunges to 85 metres about 25 metres out. Geraud is hoping to set up a house separate to the hotel where the divers can stay, and use the hotel pool for training.

Further north along the coast at Itsandra, is the school of Jean-Louis Dieu. He has a boat and charges CFr 5000 a dive. You can contact him through the Twamaya Nautical Club (tel 73 04 30) on the beach.

The Maloudja and Novotel Ylang-Ylang hotels also have diving schools. The Orchid hotels at Itsandra, Maloudja, Domoni (Anjouan) and Moheli will be offering diving trips as part of their package tours.

On Mayotte, the subaqua is done through the Village de N'Goudja hotel (tel 40 14 19) on the south-west tip of the island and Hôtel La Tortue Bigotu (tel 61 11 35) in Mamoudzou. The latter charge FFr 160 for a dive with equipment and FFr 1300 for 10 dives, or, there is an introductory dive for FFr 100.

The best diving areas are said to be off the west coast of Grande Comore and about 40 km directly off the east coast from Iconi. There are some good spots on the reef and islands off the south coast of Moheli, but you have to beware of the strong current running between the islands. On Mayotte, the best diving is in the channels of the reef breaks. Because of the rivers the lagoon water around Mayotte is muddy red much of the time, especially during the wet season from November to April.

Spear fishing is forbidden.

### Big-Game Fishing
This is another draw card for wealthy South Africans and French. As with the diving, the Orchid group of hotels and Hôtel La Tortue Bigotu are the main operators. Fully equipped boats cost around FFr 1000 a day between a maximum of four people.

### Swimming & Snorkelling
Good beaches are not as good or as plentiful as you would expect. The best ones on Grande Comore are at Itsandra and Maloudja. On Mayotte, they are at Moya, on the north-east of Pamandzi islet, and at N'Goudja in the south of the island. For snorkelling, try Longoni Bay.

Moheli has good beaches. If you are based in Moroni or Mamoudzou there are hotel swimming pools open to visitors. The Hôtel Coelacanthe in Moroni will let you use the pool for a CFr 500 fee. The pools at the Novotel Ylang-Ylang in Moroni and the Hôtel Le Baobab in Mamoudzou have monthly and annual rates for nonresidents only. But they should let you use it on a one-off basis if you buy a meal or drinks or pay a token fee of FFr 10 to FFr 20.

The Hôtel Le Maloudja near Mitsamiouli, Grande Comore, hires out snorkels and masks for FFr 30 a day.

### Windsurfing & Sailing Catamarans
Most of the beach hotels offer a range of water sports. Hôtel Le Maloudja on Grande Comore rents windsurfers for FFr 100 a day and Hobycat catamarans for FFr 300 a day.

The Twamaya Club (tel 73 04 30) at Itsandra Beach, Grande Comore, has windsurfers for hire at CFr 2500 per half day with instruction CFr 1000 an hour.

**Trekking**

No-one has really looked into exploring the interior of the islands yet. They're all looking around the coast and out to sea. However, recognising that the formidable Karthala Volcano may beckon many curious visitors, Jean-Louis Geraud of the Gombessa Plongée diving school at the Hôtel Coelacanthe, Moroni, is organising tours up the magic mountain (see the section on Moroni).

The Village de N'Goudja in Mayotte organises 4WD vehicle trips into the island for those who don't want to get their feet dirty. Gombessa Plongée and the Novotel Ylang-Ylang, in Moroni, and Hôtel La Tortue Bigotu, in Mamoudzou, also run various boat and sightseeing tours.

**Other Activities**

There is a Franco-Comorian tennis club opposite the Hôtel Coelacanthe in Moroni. It's for members only, but if you brought your racquet . . .

Moroni has a main cinema and smaller video cinemas. The Alliance Franco-Comorienne near the Hôtel Coelacanthe also shows films. In Mayotte, the Centre Mahorais d'Animation Culturelle is responsible for film and theatre shows around the island, although there is also a cinema in Mamoudzou, up the street from La Crêperie restaurant.

The bigger hotels – the Novotel Ylang-Ylang in Moroni, the Village de N'Goudja in Mayotte, and probably the Orchid hotels in the republic put on their own entertainment programme.

**THINGS TO BUY**

Coming back with a souvenir of the Comoros is not easy. There are few local crafts on sale. It's even hard to get shells. Sea turtles are protected, so there are no turtleshell ornaments or jewellery on sale. The retail outlets offer books and postcards and the odd trinket, but that's about all. (See the Arts section in Facts about the Country for other ideas.)

For private purchase, look out for finely carved wooden Koran holders, ceremonial dress silver work, leather, basket work from sisal or raffia, natural-dyed pottery, *koffia* hats and colourful cotton *lambes* or *chiromani* robes.

# Getting There

## AIR
Unless you are fortunate enough to own, charter or crew a yacht, or have contacts in the irregular East Africa, Madagascar and Comoros shipping trade, the only way of getting to the Comoros is by air.

Four airlines operate weekly flights to the Comoros Republic: Air France, Air Mauritius/Air Madagascar, South African Airways and Air Tanzania.

Air France operates flights from Paris to Moroni, via Nice/Jeddah/Dar es Salaam. There is also a Paris to Réunion flight via Marseilles/Moroni/Nairobi. The cheapest Paris to Moroni return fare on Air France is FFr 5790. A Paris to Moroni excursion fare (six to 60 day limit) costs FFr 7505 in the low season and FFr 8360 during the high season (between July and September).

On the shorter hauls, a Réunion to Moroni return fare with Air France costs about CFr 139,500 (or FFr 2790), and an Antananarivo (Madagascar) to Moroni return is around FFr 1600.

Air Mauritius/Air Madagascar share a Boeing 737 Mauritius to Nairobi flight each week, via Antananarivo and Moroni. There are no special fares.

South African Airways operate a weekly Johannesburg to Moroni service, via Lilongwe. The 737 flight takes three hours one way and costs Rand 975 for an economy return ticket.

Air Tanzania have a Dar es Salaam to Mauritius flight via Moroni each Wednesday.

There are also flights, three times a week, between Réunion and Mayotte. Réunion Air Service (Air Mayotte) charges FFr 4300 for a full return ticket, or FFr 3345 for an excursion fare (two to 23 day limit). There are cheaper group fares. The single fare is FFr 2150.

Flights between the Comoros Republic and Mayotte are undertaken by the Air Comores aeroplane (see the Getting Around section). Most people who visit Mayotte do so through Réunion rather than the Comoros Republic. Air Comores used to fly to Mombasa in Kenya, and they are now hoping to start a service to Majunga in Madagascar, but they'll have to buy another plane first.

### Airline Offices
Air Comores (tel 73 95 24), at Iconi Airport, Moroni (the old airfield opposite the Hôtel Karthala), is the representative for Air France. They are open from 7.30 am to noon and 2 to 4 pm. The Air Comores office in Mayotte is on the Blvd des Crabes (the causeway linking Dzaoudzi to Pamandzi Islet), about one km from Dzaoudzi. It is open from 8.30 to 11.30 am only.

The Madagascar Consulate represents Air Madagascar. The consulate is near the new market in Moroni.

In Mayotte, Air Mayotte (Réunion Air Service) has an office at the market square in Mamoudzou. The Air France office is near the ferry pier in Dzaoudzi, but they also have an agency in the Mamoudzou market square.

Remember always to confirm or re-confirm international and domestic flights three days before departure.

### Hahaya Airport – Grande Comore
This new international airport, built with French aid, replaces the airfield at Iconi which now is used for private and presidential flights. Hahaya is 19 km north of Moroni.

### Pamandzi Airport – Mayotte
The runway at Mayotte cannot take jets, so there are no international flights. Air Comores, Air Mayotte (Réunion Air Services) and private hire planes use it. The terminal is small and there are

immigration and customs authorities for flights from the Comoros Republic.

Malaria pills are handed out as you go through, but there are few services for visitors. The Office Mahorais du Tourisme counter was not staffed on the two occasions I was there. It appears they only meet hotel packages from Réunion or France. Taxis are plentiful and take you the few km to the ferry at Dzaoudzi for FFr 2 (FFr 4 on Sundays and holidays). The ferries to Mamoudzou run every half-hour and are free to passengers, but there is a charge for vehicles.

### Arrival

Entry formalities for the Comoros are a breeze compared to those in Madagascar. You are permitted one litre maximum of spirits (even though it's a Muslim country), up to 200 cigarettes and diving equipment. There are no health or monetary controls unless you've recently been to a suspect country.

Passport and baggage checks are cursory. This doesn't mean to say they are lax, it just means that the customs officers are not difficult for the sake of it. With

coup attempts fresh in the memory and always the threat of another, you can be assured somebody will be 'looking after' you, given half a reason, especially when there are comparatively few visitors.

On the negative side, there are no facilities for tourists and travellers. No banks, no hotel reps, nothing. But there are scores of taxi drivers who will attempt to charge you CFr 5000 (FFr 100) to take you into Moroni. This is a ridiculous rate, but it seems that because so many visiting business people, diplomatic or government advisers and whatnot pay it without any qualms, it has become the semiofficial rate.

In fact, the official rate is only CFr 500, but obviously many taxi drivers see this as ridiculously low. You should be able to bargain them down to whatever you like. After all, at most of the arrival times they will have few passengers to choose from and will be going back into town anyway. Otherwise, luggage permitting, walk 100 metres further to the road into town and wait for a taxi-brousse. They cost CFr 250. (See the Taxi section.)

Air Comores run a bus to meet the Air France flight once a week. It costs CFr

1500. Otherwise, it operates for staff only. But ask anyway and they'll probably take you.

## Departure

There is no duty free service available when you leave Mayotte. The most you can expect is a soft drinks counter in the departure lounge. Coke costs CFr 500. There is also no departure tax in Mayotte, but the Comoros Republic stings you for CFr 6000 (FFr 120) for international flights and CFr 500 (FFr 10) for domestic flights, including those to Mayotte.

## AIR

Air Comores runs an extensive – as much as one plane can do in a week – but expensive service between Grande Comore, Anjouan, Moheli and Mayotte. This demand on the 44-seat Fokker F27 means the service is often interrupted by breakdowns, weather conditions and staff illnesses.

There are two flights each week to Mayotte from Moroni and vice versa via Anjouan. They take almost two hours one way and cost CFr 36,400 for a single fare with a CFr 1000 government tax on each ticket. Return tickets are double the price of the one-way fare, but there is a range of special fares, including those for students.

Flights are often full and booked up well in advance. So get in as early as possible. Occasionally, if demand for seats is very high, they will schedule an extra flight. But first they have to get the permission of the French civil aviation authority!

On top of these flights, there are another five flights a week between Moroni and Anjouan, for CFr 21,700 one way, three or four flights a week between Moroni and Moheli for CFr 16,600, and the same between Moheli and Anjouan for CFr 16,600. The Anjouan to Mayotte leg costs CFr 21,700 and Moheli to Mayotte costs CFr 29,200.

There is also one private operator for charter flights. He is Monsieur Henri Bera (tel 73 15 95), based in Moroni, who can take up to four passengers in his light plane. He charges about CFr 45,000 per person for Moroni to Anjouan and CFr 35,000 for Moroni to Moheli.

There are usually taxis-brousses, awaiting arrivals at Moheli and Anjouan airports.

## TAXI-BROUSSE

The taxis-brousses are covered Peugot 404/505 pick-ups. They cover most towns and villages from the island capitals, but the journeys are rough, tiring, often crowded and always too fast. They are cheap, however.

In Moroni, there are two taxi-brousse stations. For destinations to the north and east (Lamachaka, Maloudja, Itsandra, Hahaya Airport, Mitsamiouli, etc) the taxis-brousses gather at the old market, down from the post office.

The station for the southern routes (Iconi, Foumbouni, Singani, etc) is at the southern end of the street from the north station. The maximum fare, say to Mitsamiouli in the far north of Grande Comore, is CFr 450.

brousses go when they are full or as full as they think they are going to get. The waiting and uncertainty of departure can be very frustrating. If you have a plane to catch or you are in a hurry, forget them. Collisions are common and sometimes fatal, especially on Mayotte.

In Mayotte the taxis-brousses for the island gather at the ferry terminal and market square in Mamoudzou and wait for the ferries to arrive. Some have

**air comores**

destinations painted on the side of the vehicle. (Some cross the channel to Dzaoudzi and Pamandzi, but there is no shortage of sedan taxis there which are just as cheap.) Taxis-brousses in Mayotte charge 35c per km. So, for example, Mamoudzou to Longoni Beach is FFr 5.

## TAXI

All the taxis in the Comoros Republic are Renault 4s. In Moroni, there is a flat rate of CFr 150 for anywhere in or around town, as far north as Itsandra and as far south as Iconi. You just flag them down, whether they are carrying passengers or not, and tell them where you want to go. They'll shake their heads if they are not going that way or don't want to go that way. You don't ask how much. It's CFr 150 anywhere, except Hahaya Airport (see the Getting There & Away chapter).

The taxi system is similar on Mayotte. There is a flat rate of FFr 2 during the day for town taxis in Mamoudzou and Dzaoudzi (Pamandzi). This goes up to FFr 4 on Sundays and public holidays, and to FFr 4.50 between 8 pm and 6 am.

## BOAT
### Inter-Island Ferries

There should be a regular ferry between the islands, but it was damaged when it capsized. So if it's running, it's not very safe. It may be possible to hitch a lift on a small fishing boat from Grande Comore across to Moheli. Ask the fishermen at Chindini, on the southern tip of Grande Comore.

The only other ferry is between Mamoudzou and Dzaoudzi. The two car ferries run between 5.30 am and 11.30 pm each day except Sunday, when they start at 7 am. The ferries leave mostly every half-hour. Passengers go free, but there is a charge for vehicles.

### Boat Hire

This is limited. A 14-metre trimaran, the *Trois Rivières*, is available for dive or cruise charter. Call 73 01 14 or contact the organisers through the Hôtel Coelacanthe at Moroni. Two days and three nights on a diving trip costs about FFr 750 per person, if there is a minimum of six people. There are also zodiacs and catamarans for hire at the Le Maloudja and Village de N'Gouja hotels.

## DRIVING
### Car Rental

The main roads on Grande Comore and Mayotte are good, but they're rough in parts on Anjouan and Moheli. Hiring a car in the Comoros Republic is difficult. In Moroni, you can try the northern service station at the crossroads near the government buildings. They have quoted CFr 16,000 a day for a Renault 5 plus the extras and petrol.

The Hôtel Le Maloudja, up near Mitsamiouli, has rental cars for about the same price. There are also the two tour operators CSTS and Royal Transit (see Tours section), whose rates are similar. On Mayotte, the vehicles and service may be better, but the price is the same. Hôtel Le Baobab in Mamoudzou is the best outlet. They have Citroen Meharis and Mini Mokes for FFr 300 a day or FFr 1750 a week, plus extras.

The cost of petrol on Grande Comore is about CFr 300 per litre and in Mayotte FFr 5.

## MOTOR CYCLE

At the Mamoudzou ferry quay is a motor cycle rental 'container' run by Alan Teillier (tel 61 16 98). He has Yamaha 125s for FFr 80 for half a day, FFr 140 for a day, FFr 840 for a week, FFr 150 on Saturdays and Sundays, or FFr 270 for the weekend. He asks for a large security deposit.

## BICYCLE

Bicycles are quite rare in the Comoros. The only place I know which rents them is Hôtel Le Maloudja on Grande Comore. They charge FFr 50 a day or FFr 30 if taken over two days with FFr 10 for each additional day.

## TOURS

There are two local tour agencies in Moroni, neither of which is particularly large or busy. They do some leg work for the few European travel agencies and tour operators, but it's more or less a case of throwing you in the back of a car and taking you around to see a few sights.

Both offices can be found in the Place Badjanani, the square of the Friday Mosque (*Grande Mosquée*). One is Royal Transit (tel 73 00 10), whose boss is Sultan Said Houssein. The other is Comores Services Tours and Safaris (tel 73 15 02). The directors and staff are Saindou Allaoui and Monsieur Chakira. They hire cars and operate transfers to the airport (CFr 5000 per person from the airport to Moroni, which gives taxi drivers ideas! The hotels charge the same).

There are tours for hotel residents at the Novotel Ylang Ylang if you want to make up the numbers. A half day tour around the market, mosque and museum in Moroni costs CFr 3000. A day tour of Iconi, Chindini fishing village, a Chomoni Beach picnic, Lac Salé, Trou de Prophète and Itsandra Fort is CFr 8000. The Hôtel Le Maloudja in Grande Comore also runs island tours at the same rate.

# Grande Comore

This is the largest, and geologically the youngest, of the Comoros islands. It is also known officially by the Comorians as 'Ngazidja', but rarely referred to as such. About 220,000 people live on the island, 22,000 of whom live in Moroni.

The Comoros Republic's capital, Moroni, is on Grande Comore, along with the international airport, Hahaya. The other main feature of the island is Karthala Volcano, which like La Fournaise on Réunion, is still active and bubbling away.

Because of the porous nature of the island's rock base, there are no rivers or waterways. The domestic water supply comes from rainwater collected in cisterns and wells dug on the water table.

The island, which is 60 km long by 20 km wide, is fringed by either volcanic rock, lava, or sandy beaches of various hues. Most of the agricultural land is in the south, and produces mainly bananas, cassava, breadfruit, vanilla, ylang-ylang and coconuts.

# Moroni

Moroni Harbour at sunset must be one of the most beautiful sights in the Indian Ocean. The fading yellow-orange to red-maroon light brings out the best in the coral-chalked ancient Friday Mosque and the surrounding buildings.

At dusk, there are often hundreds of men and boys swimming, or fishing for tiny fish from ship-loading barges. Later at night if there is a good moon, the scene is just as spectacular. During the day, however, Moroni is either drab under cloud, or washed out in the sunlight.

### Information

For details on the post office, bank and other services in Moroni refer to the relevant sections in the Facts for the Visitor chapter. Because there are few street signs, you will have to refer to the town map for locations.

### Things to See

Badjanani and Mtsangani, the ancient part of town around the port and the Friday Mosque, is a claustrophobic clutter of homes and narrow alleys. It's reminiscent of a Greek island village, but more shady and crowded, and you may find it interesting to wander around, just to see where you'll end up. Look out for the elaborately carved doors on many houses.

Visits are not encouraged at the Friday Mosque, but if you really wanted to see inside, I'm sure someone would organise it for you. You would have to be appropriately dressed and go through the ritual feet washing.

By the way, the Comorians don't go in much for street names and signs. All mail goes to post boxes.

The old market beneath the post office, where women in gaily coloured chirumani huddle over piles of fruit and vegetables, is worth visiting.

The Centre National de Documentation et de la Recherche Scientifique (CNDRS), beside the Nouveautés shop, has a new museum, library and video unit. The museum houses butterflies, pottery, jewellery, clothes, jars of lizards and snakes, and the showpiece – a glass display case containing a coelacanth caught by a fisherman off Anjouan in 1985.

The main shopping streets are between the market and the southern taxi-brousse stand and the Route Nationale 1, leading north from the government quarter up to the new market.

### Nightlife

There are films at the *Al Kamar* cinema,

Top: Fishing on Moroni Harbour, Grande Comore (RW)
Left: Old Market, Moroni (GG)
Right: Lac Salé, Grande Comore (RW)

Top: Looking across to Oungoujou peak in South Mayotte (RW)
Left: Village women in traditional dress (GG)
Right: Mudpack for beauty treatment and decoration (GG)

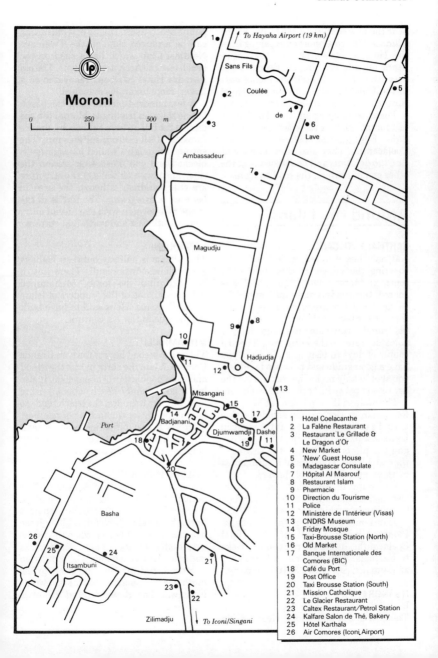

# Moroni

0      250      500  m

To Hayaha Airport (19 km)

Sans Fils

Coulée

de

Lave

Ambassadeur

Magudju

Hadjudja

Mtsangani

Badjanani

Port

Djumwamdji    Dashe

Basha

Itsambuni

Zilimadju

To Iconi/Singani

1  Hôtel Coelacanthe
2  La Falène Restaurant
3  Restaurant Le Grillade &
   Le Dragon d'Or
4  New Market
5  'New' Guest House
6  Madagascar Consulate
7  Hôpital Al Maarouf
8  Restaurant Islam
9  Pharmacie
10 Direction du Tourisme
11 Police
12 Ministère de l'Intérieur (Visas)
13 CNDRS Museum
14 Friday Mosque
15 Taxi-Brousse Station (North)
16 Old Market
17 Banque Internationale des
   Comores (BIC)
18 Café du Port
19 Post Office
20 Taxi Brousse Station (South)
21 Mission Catholique
22 Le Glacier Restaurant
23 Caltex Restaurant/Petrol Station
24 Kalfare Salon de Thé, Bakery
25 Hôtel Karthala
26 Air Comores (Iconi Airport)

near the new market in Magudju, at the *Alliance Franco-Comorienne*, along from the Hôtel Coelacanthe (see the notice board outside the French Embassy for details), or the video saloon cinema next to the Unicoop store up from the Hôtel Karthala. The cost is CFr 250 to CFr 500.

There is dancing at the *La Falène* restaurant, just off the coast road in the Sans Fils quarter before the Hotel Coelacanthe. They also have dancing at *Le Club des Amis* and *La Dérobade* at the other end of town on the road to Iconi.

# Around the Island

## KARTHALA VOLCANO

Karthala last erupted on 5 April 1977, covering the village of Singani, to the south of Moroni. Only the school was spared. But inside a man was trapped for 15 days until rescuers managed to get through the lava. By that time, he had lost his mind. Karthala has the biggest volcanic crater in the world. You'll need a couple of days to visit it, and unless you have a good guide and back-up facilities, you should only make the trek during the dry season between April and November.

The route to the top begins at M'vouni, four km from Moroni. You should be able to find a guide at M'vouni. It takes seven hours to walk up to the top at 2361 metres, and you pitch your tent in the shelter of the crater itself. The summit is surrounded by thick mist for most of the day.

En route to Karthala, in a forest clearing, are the ruins of a chalet called La Convalescence, which was destroyed by fire.

Jean-Louis Geraud, of the Gombessa Plongée diving school at the Hôtel Coelacanthe, intends to run two-day treks to Karthala, with an overnight camp, at an estimated cost of CFr 30,000 per party.

## ITSANDRA

Itsandra is about five km north of Moroni. There is a 200-metre-long clean, white public beach there. Diving or windsurfing can be arranged through the Twamaya Nautical Club which has a shed on the beach (see the Activities section). The old Itsandra Hotel has been renovated to a larger, more luxurious standard.

A few hundred metres from the beach beside the road leading to Moroni (on the crest of the hill up from the beach), are the ruins of a 15th century sultan's fort. The entrance through a walled passageway is blocked and you must walk around the side. The lava rock walls of the structure are still standing, although the area in between is overgrown. The fort is in the shape of a polygon with avenues of entry by the south-east and north-east corners.

## N'TSAOUENI

This village is halfway between Hahaya Airport and Mitsamiouli. There lies, if you can find the tomb, Mohammed Athoumani, one of the founders of Islam in the Comoros. He is said to have built the mosque in the 7th century.

## MITSAMIOULI

This is the second largest town on Grande Comore. It is in the north part of the island and has a population of about 4000. It also has a good, sandy beach, about 1½ km long, but like Itsandra, the beach tends to be a bit public for sunbathing or relaxing. There is a post office in town. A taxi-brousse from Moroni takes more than an hour to get there and costs CFr 350.

## MALOUDJA BEACH

About one km north of Mitsamiouli is perhaps the best beach on the island for tourists. It is looked after by, but separate from, the Hôtel Le Maloudja. Though the beach can be a bit boring when the tide is out, it offers plenty of palms, sand, rocks and safe swimming behind the protection of a small reef. Around the point to the north are two smaller beaches known as Ngalawa. The Royal Orchid Hotel is also here.

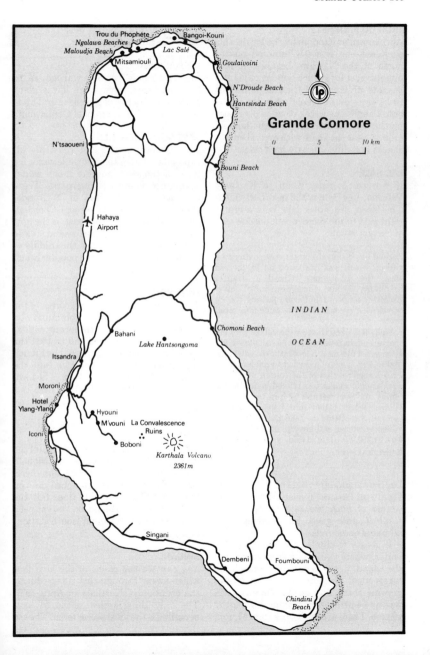

## TROU DU PROPHETE

Also known as Zindoni by the locals, this sheltered bay is a few hundred metres north of the Ngalawa beaches. It is a popular spot for French holiday villas and is quite pretty when the tide is in, but looks like a bit of a 'hole' when the tide is out. There's the wreck of some poor boat in the bay and a very rough 'holiday village' near the shore with several empty shacks charging unjustly high rates.

## LAC SALE

If you can't make it up to Karthala Volcano, Lac Salé is the next best thing. This deep, sea water lake is in a crater right next to the shore, about one km east of Bangoi-Kouni.

Legend has it that the crater once contained a village, which was swallowed up by the sea when the inhabitants refused a stranger hospitality. So now, villagers in nearby Bangoi-Kouni are supposed to offer any passing, thirsty travellers a coconut, lest the same fate befall them.

Well – I walked through the village with my tongue hanging out and won no coconuts at all. However, I did meet a local student called Ali Toihir Abdou who proceeded to render me an embellished version of the tale in which the wandering stranger was offered water by one family and was warned by him to leave the village. When I told him I got no bloody coconut, he offered to take me back to the village to get one, or to have his mate sell me one for CFr 150. 'Too late', I said, 'your village goes under next week.'

Lac Salé is similar to but smaller than Lac Dziani on Pamandzi Islet, Mayotte. The waters of both are said to be rich in sulphur and good for treating skin ailments or wounds.

It is easy to climb up to the rim of the crater, where you get good views around the island, but it is difficult to reach the lake's edge. There are some baobab trees growing there, and on the shore is a sea wall and a little beach leading down to the village. There are bush taxis from Moroni which will drop you off near the crater lake. The fare is CFr 350.

## GOULAIVOINI

From the rim of Lac Salé you can see, to the south-east, what looks like a giant jawbone with a row of jagged teeth. This is the eroded volcanic crater of Goulaivoini.

## EAST COAST BEACHES

The beaches on the east coast are all exposed to the south-west trade winds for most of the year, and are much wilder than their western counterparts. There are nice sandy beaches at N'Droude, Hantsindzi, Bouni and Chomoni. Chomoni, about halfway down the coast, is the best because it is sheltered in a bay and is close to the road cutting across the middle of the island to Moroni. It is a popular beach with the local people too.

## FOUMBOUNI

This town, on the south-east corner of the island, is the third largest community on Grande Comore. It was the former capital of the Sultan of Badjini and in 1884 the German flag was raised there. The French Government's representative on the island at the time, tore it down. The town is now noted for its pottery. There is a restaurant-dance spot here called *Le Baobab*.

## CHINDINI

From this beach on the southern tip of the island, you can see across to Moheli. There are no facilities for visitors there, except for some empty thatched huts on the shore. The beach is fine, but the surroundings are a bit bleak. You can get a taxi-brousse from Moroni (south station) down to Chindini.

## SINGANI

You can see the result of the lava flow which swept through this village during the eruption of Karthala in April 1977. The only thing which seems to have benefited is the local soccer team. The ash has been flattened into a large playing field.

## ICONI

Iconi is the oldest settlement and was the original capital of Grande Comore. It suffered badly from frequent raids by Malagasy pirates in the 16th and 17th centuries.

It is said that the women of Iconi threw themselves off the nearby cliffs rather than face capture. The ancient palace, hill fort and tombs can all be seen.

Iconi is within the CFr 150 Moroni taxi limits. To the right, as you enter the town, you can see the remains of the fort wall along the rim of an extinct crater. It is better to take a guide up (local children are keen), as the path becomes steep and confusing in parts. It's not the Great Wall of China, but there's enough of it to walk along. Inside the crater is a large oasis of palms. The climb up is not for the weak of heart or knees, but those who do make it are rewarded by great views of Moroni and the surrounding craters.

## BAHANI

There is an old French inn on the road crossing the island from Moroni to the east coast. It once provided a cool retreat and a panoramic view for the colonials, and the tourist authorities hope that it will do so again, but this time for tourists. Alas, it is also near the training area for the presidential guard. Be careful when taking photographs.

## HANTSONGOMA

Further east and 350 metres higher into the island's forested centre, is a small lake and the cave of Capitaine Dubois. You will need a guide and several hours to visit this spot.

## PLACES TO STAY

Like any other Indian Ocean country, the Comoros has a number of up-market beach hotels for well-heeled tourists who wish to lie in the sun, lie under a palm tree or bathe in the tropical, turquoise sea. But in the Comoros, there are few cheap alternatives.

### Places to Stay - bottom end

Some small restaurants in Moroni have the cheapest rooms to let. At *Le Glacier* rooms start from CFr 4000 (FFr 80), while *Restaurant Boss* charges CFr 5000. The tourist-class *Le Grillade* (tel 73 17 81), on the Route de la Corniche has new bungalows to let, but the rates are considerably higher.

There are four 'family pensions'. The cheapest is the *Karibu* (tel 73 01 17), in the Sans Fils district. It has nine rooms and rates begin at CFr 7500 a night. They do meals on request.

Then, near the People's Palace, is the *Villa Zilimadjou* (tel 73 16 96), with eight air-con rooms at CFr 12,000/15,000 a single/double. Or there is the smaller *Maina* (tel 73 04 18) in Hankounou, with four rooms at CFr 8000. The *Bouvini* (tel 73 19 57) in Dache, also has four rooms, ranging in price between CFr 9000 and CFr 12,000.

The cheapest hotel by 50% on the others is the *Hôtel Karthala* (tel 73 01 88), opposite Iconi Airport in Moroni. This two storey palace hotel, built in 1940, was *the* place to stay and be seen in before independence, and when Iconi was the international airport.

It has 14 large, clean rooms with bathrooms and hot-water showers. Singles/doubles are CFr 8000/9500 per night, including a continental-style breakfast. There is no air-con or fans, but the rooms are not too hot or stuffy. It is owned by a Frenchman, resident in Paris, and is used mostly by commercial travellers from Africa. It has a bar which serves beer for CFr 800 and small bottles of imported wine for CFr 750, but there is no restaurant. The hotel is rarely, if ever, full.

Around the same price, is a guest house on the new road near the national education institute in the north district of Moroni. It has seven rooms.

In the village north of Itsandra, on the way to Hahaya Airport, there is a house to rent for CFr 3000 a day. Ask for one Hassan Moussa Hantsambou. Any other unofficial room or home should cost between CFr 1500 and CFr 3000 a day.

There is also the possibility of rooms at the *Mission Catholique* in Moroni, but you have to ask the mission priest.

The other alternative is a motley collection of four bungalows or thatched shacks at the Trou du Prophète, near Maloudja Beach and Mitsamiouli. It's called *Dzindani Village des Vacances* and singles/doubles are CFr 5000/7000 per night. Breakfast is CFr 1000 and meals are CFr 2500. The price isn't so bad compared to the hotels, but you get very little for it. The bungalows contain only a bed and a candle and you share the toilet and shower.

### Places to Stay – top end
At the top end there's the costly trio of Comotel, Novotel and Socotel. There are reductions on the rates quoted here if you travel on a package tour with flights and accommodation on a half board basis.

Comotel is a French-owned group of five hotels, which includes the Novotel Ylang-Ylang. Socotel is a joint enterprise between the Comorian Government and the British-managed Orchid hotels.

Three of the Comotel hotels are on Grande Comore. The most popular is the *Hôtel Le Maloudja* (tel Mitsiamouli 323) at Maloudja Beach, 40 km north of Moroni and 20 km north of Hahaya Airport. Built in 1966, it has 30 rooms in bungalows lined along the beach. Singles cost CFr 15,500 (FFr 310) and doubles cost CFr 20,000. Breakfast is an extra CFr 1500. The beach is good for nonresidents and it is a popular meeting place each Sunday for the French community of Grande Comore.

Likewise the *Hôtel Coelacanthe* (tel 73 05 75), is a rendezvous point for Moroni. The rates are the same as Hôtel Le Maloudja. There are 12 air-con bungalows, a saltwater swimming pool, a diving school and nearby tennis courts. The restaurant sometimes has 'special' nights when you can eat heartily for CFr 2000. The swimming pool is open to nonresidents for a CFr 500 entry fee. Generally, however, the hotel is hopelessly overpriced for what it offers in the way of location, comfort, service and facilities.

The biggest and newest of the Comotel group is the 60 room Novotel *Ylang-Ylang* (tel 73 02 40), which is down a long, wide avenue from the Chinese-built People's Palace just south of Moroni. Here singles and doubles are CFr 26,500 (FFr 530) per night. It has all the mod cons you'd expect of a luxury beach hotel, except a beach! It's not particularly attractive either. I'd say the People's Palace up the road looked more welcoming.

Prices for the Comotel group are raised in the high seasons (20 December to 3 January and 11 to 26 April). The weekly half board rate of FFr 1820 goes up to FFr 2100 in the Comotels and from FFr 2450 to FFr 2800 in the Novotel.

The *Royal Orchid Hotel* is just up the shore from Hôtel Le Maloudja along the Ngalawa beaches. It has 150 rooms and lots of water sports.

The *Itsandra Palace Hotel* (tel 73 07 65) at Itsandra is the oldest hotel in the Comoros and is beautifully situated. It has 25 air-con rooms, a terrace restaurant and a small beach. Singles/doubles are about CFr 13,000/16,000 (FFr 260/320), and with breakfast an extra CFr 1000.

## PLACES TO EAT
### Places to Eat – bottom end

Almost all restaurants on Grande Comore are at the hotels or in Moroni. At the bottom end are the local cafés. One of the plainest, but cheapest is the *Caltex* on the south side of town next to, would you believe, a petrol station. You can get an omelette, chips, salad, fruit and coffee for under CFr 1000. They also have good fruit juice. The service is quick and friendly. All they need is a juke box.

Across the road is the less cosmopolitan *Le Glacier* and, down the street towards Iconi Airport and the Hôtel Karthala, is the *Kalfane Salon de Thé*. The tea rooms are attached to a bakery and open at 5 am, but it closes during lunch and in the evenings. You can get good cheap cakes and pastries there and fill your face for CFr 400.

Other cheap, local places are the *Café du Port* between the Friday Mosque and the port petrol station, and the *Boss* restaurant nearby. (BOSS is the South African secret service, but I don't think there's any connection.) There is also the *Al Islam* opposite the pharmacy at the beginning of Route Nationale 1 north, and the *Bambou* and *Tawakal* near the new market.

Out of Moroni are the *Au Terminus* in Voidjou and *Le Baobab* in Foumbouni.

### Places to Eat – top end

The *Hôtel Coelacanthe* occasionally puts on a special cut-price menu on quiet nights. The main dish is around CFr 1500.

Across the road and closer to town there are *Le Grillade* (tel 73 12 15) and *Le Dragon d'Or*. Le Grillade charges about CFr 2000 for a meal. Steaks are the speciality of the house. A few metres away, Le Dragon d'Or, a popular Chinese restaurant, is similarly priced, but more established. It is attached to a small store where you can buy beers at retail price (CFr 500) and drink them on the premises. It is an unofficial bar and gossip corner. You can also buy groceries there.

Hidden up a small lane, between the Hôtel Coelacanthe and Le Grillade and Le Dragon d'Or, is *La Falêne* restaurant. This holds dances on Friday and Saturday nights.

About one km out of Moroni, on the left hand side of Route Nationale 2 as you head south to Iconi and Singani, is the *Restaurant Choidjou*. This open air restaurant, decorated with fairy lights, is said to be the best for Comorian food and is popular with the French community. The fish is excellent, as is the chicken and rice in coconut juice and steak brochettes. Fruit juice is CFr 200 a glass or CFr 1000 for the bottle. The food helpings are big, too big. A meal costs between CFr 3000 and CFr 4000. It would be great if you could get half the food at half the price.

*Chez Babou* (also known as Fakhri Restaurant), at the other end of town on Route Nationale 1 north to Itsandra, is also said to be good value. It specialises in Indian food.

Each of the hotels, apart from the Hôtel Karthala, has a restaurant.

# Moheli

Moheli (also called Mwali or Moili) is the smallest and least developed of the Comoros islands. Some might say it is the wildest and most neglected. The government is in Grande Comore and the president comes from Anjouan, so Moheli tends to be last in line for attention. But because of this, or in spite of it, Moheli is, as they used to say, more 'laid back'. The people are more African-Polynesian than Arab and the Koran isn't such an important book there.

The island is also the most fertile of the three. It has lots of rivers, lots of perfume trees, coconuts and good beaches. Moheli is 50 km long and 20 km wide at its widest point, with a population of 22,000. Fomboni, the capital, is on the central north coast. The only tarred road runs from Nioumachoua on the central south coast 30 km across the island to Fomboni and around the coast to Miringoni. The highest peak in the centre of the island is Mt Mzekukule, at 790 metres.

The small islands off Nioumachoua provide some of the best diving locations in the Comoros. One of them, Ouénéfou, is a former leper colony.

Early in the 17th century, Charles I of England fitted out a vessel the *Seahorse*, and sent it out under the command of Captain Quaid with orders to attack any ship found below the Equator. Captain Quaid based himself at Moheli – and did so until he died.

For the past 50 years or so, the best-known character on the island has been Frenchman René Legrand. He is known by the islanders as the *Tonton aux Etoiles* (Uncle of the Stars), as his passion is astrology.

## AROUND THE ISLAND
### Mwali-Mdjini
At Mwali-Mdjini you can see the remains of an early 19th century village that was destroyed in a raid by Malagasy pirates. The ruined village stands atop a hill on the Nyombeni River near the village of Djwayezi, about five km south of Fomboni, near the airfield.

### Lac Boundouni
If you are aiming for the beach at Itsamia, in the south-east of the island, you should pass Lac Boundouni, a volcanic crater and lake. But you will have to walk.

### Beaches
Moheli is best known for its beaches. There are about a dozen to choose from around the coast. The best are Miremani-Sambadjou, Sambia and Itsamia (see map for locations). You have to walk to reach Miremani-Sambadjou and Itsamia, but Sambia is near where the road leaves the south coast and cuts across to Fomboni.

The other beaches are: just west of Fomboni, from where you can see Grande Comore and Karthala Volcano (the Comotel Relais de Cingani lies on the nearest, but it is not a good beach – the better sites are further west); Kavue Hoani and Domoni on the west point of the island; Miringoni, where the road ends; Miremani-Trandrama, a small, sheltered bay beach lying between two hills just south of Miremani-Sambadjou and best accessible by boat; and Moihani, another bay beach about eight km east of Nioumachoua near the main road, where you can get a good view of the islands.

There are also two beaches at Nioumachoua itself, the better one being the west beach. The village beach is larger, and is the departure point for fishermen and for trips to the islands.

## PLACES TO STAY & EAT
There is a choice of only two places to stay. The cheapest is the local *Hôtel Mlejele* in

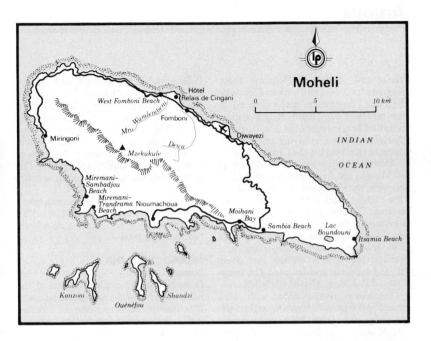

**Moheli**

West Fomboni Beach

Hôtel
Relais de Cingani

Wamlembeni

Fomboni

Mro

Djwayezi

Miringoni

Deua

*INDIAN*

Mzekukule

*OCEAN*

Miremani–
Sambadjou
Beach

Miremani–
Trandrama    Nioumachoua
Beach

Moihani
Bay

Sambia Beach    Lac
Boundouni

Itsamia Beach

Kanzoni

Shandzi

Ouénéfou

0          5          10 km

Fomboni. A double there costs CFr 2000 a night, and meals can be had for CFr 3000.

The Comotel *Relais de Cingani* (tel Fomboni 349) has only 10 rooms and opened in 1984. It offers windsurfing and diving, but has no pool to compensate for its bad beach. Singles/doubles cost CFr 15,500/20,000, without breakfast, according to rates covering all Comotel hotels (except the Novotel Ylang-Ylang).

The *Restaurant à l'Africaine* is an alternative place to eat in Fomboni.

# Anjouan

There are shades of Réunion about Anjouan (or Ndzouani) with its *Cirque de Bambao* (Tsembéhou amphitheatre) in the centre of the island. It is the most beautiful and varied of the islands and is therefore referred to in any promotional sense as the 'Pearl of the Comoros'.

There are not as many good beaches as on Moheli, but Anjouan has a better line in rivers, waterfalls, mountains and lakes. The highest point is Mt Ntingui, at 1600 metres. The triangular island is heavily forested in the centre but it thins out considerably towards the three points. It also produces much ylang-ylang and vanilla, particularly on the east coast around Bambao and Domoni, the home town of President Ahmed Abdallah.

Anjouan is overpopulated with more than 170,000 people – that's more than 400 people per square km. Many of the people are Makoas, the descendants of slaves imported from Mozambique in the 15th century, or Wamatsaha, whose roots go further back to the original Malay-Polynesian settlers. The main centres are Ouani, Domoni and the capital, Mutsamudu. Historically, Anjouan differed from the other islands in that it had only one sultan at a time. The rest had several apiece.

Where Moheli has the 'Uncle of the Stars', Anjouan has the 'Baron of Saint Aubin', a white-bearded colonialist who lives near Mutsamudu. He has been married three times, the second time to a Malagasy lady of noble birth. His father introduced vanilla to the Comoros in 1886 and freed the slaves.

## MUTSAMUDU

The island's capital is the most picturesque town in the Comoros. It has a relatively new harbour, the building of which was financed by the Arab states. Overlooking the town of 15,000 residents is a cannon-laden citadel. It was built with British money by Sultan Abdallah I at the end of the 18th century to help defend the town against Malagasy pirates. The citadel was roughed up badly by a cyclone in 1950, but it has great views. The sultan's palace, next to the Friday Mosque in the centre of town, is still in use by the family. The government wants to turn it into a crafts museum.

Out near the airport, six km from town, to the east of the bay of Ouani, is a 17th century palace. It has long been abandoned but is still in good shape.

## AROUND THE ISLAND
### Domoni

Domoni was the original capital of the island and is now the second largest town. It is surrounded by an ancient fortified wall, built as a protection against Malagasy pirates. You'll find another 13th century palace there which has been well preserved. The mosque is the fifth to take its place on the same foundations.

### Pomoni

This small town is of little interest, except for the fact that it was used by British warships as a coal station.

### Sima & Foumbani

Sima is one of the oldest settlements in the Comoros. The mosque was built in the 15th century in place of one built 400 years earlier.

Foumbani, the site of several volcanic craters is a couple of km east of Sima, on the coast. There is a pebble and grey sand beach and a small hotel.

### Bambao

This village sits in the *cirque* amphitheatre of the same name and makes an interesting contrast from the coastal communities. The palace of Sultan

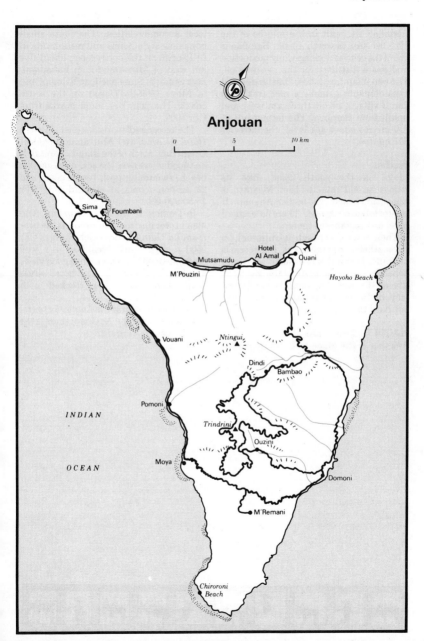

Abdallah III, built in the middle of the 19th century, is worth a look. Bambao is one of the centres of ylang-ylang production and has a distillery for the perfume oil. The two mountain lakes, Dzialandze and Dzialountsunga, make a nice trek from Dindi village, about three km west and uphill from Bambao. The former lies at 910 metres above sea level, the latter at 697 metres.

### Beaches

Moya on the south coast, like its namesake on Pamandzi Islet, Mayotte, is a beautiful beach – the best on Anjouan. It is protected by a reef. There is a small hotel and restaurant there.

There is another beach at Chiroroni, on the southern tip of the island, but access is difficult. Domoni has a black sand and pebble beach to the north of the town, the site of the new Anjouan Orchid Hotel. Hayoho Beach in the north-east is huge, but hard to reach.

### PLACES TO STAY & EAT

Anjouan is the place to head for cheap, local accommodation. There are small bungalow-style hotels and restaurants in M'Pouzini on the north coast, about five km west of Mutsamudu; in Foumbani, near Sima; in Sima itself, at Ntingui; and in Moya (*Hôtel l'Oasis*) on the south coast. The cost per room starts from CFr 5000.

The 'recognised' tourist hotel is Comotel's *Hotel Al Amal* (tel Mutsamudu 365) at Ouani Bay, north of the island's capital. It has good views over the sea, a reasonable beach, swimming pool, tennis court and 25 air-con rooms at single/double CFr 15,500/20,000.

In Domoni is the *Hôtel Karima*, and about three km from the airport is the two-room *La Guinguette*, which charges CFr 9500 a night with breakfast. It's well recommended as it commands good views and has a nice beach. The hotel serves meals and has a bar stocked with Polish beer!

The best restaurant is *La Paillotte* (tel 214) in Mutsamudu. At Ouani there is the *Bel Air* café-restaurant.

# Mayotte

Sea horse-shaped Mayotte is the oldest and the most southerly of the Comoros islands. The hills are not as high as those on Grande Comore, Anjouan and Moheli, and Mayotte is surrounded by a coral reef. The biggest difference, of course, is that this island still belongs to France. Don't, however, make the mistake I did of thinking Mayotte would just be a smaller version of Réunion with the same European standard of living and facilities. It's not. As the inhabitants are fond of pointing out, Mayotte is not just *petite*, it's *petite petite*, and very much a colonial backwater. The island is not a DOM (Departement d'Outre-Mer) or a TOM (Territoire d'Outre-Mer), but a Collectivité Territoriale.

Mayotte is split into *La Grande Terre*, the large central island, and *La Petite Terre*, the small islet of Pamandzi. The small capital on La Grande Terre is Mamoudzou, across the narrow channel from the other main centre, the rock of Dzaoudzi on La Petite Terre. The rock is linked to the rest of Pamandzi by a causeway known as the Blvd des Crabes.

The people of Mayotte are Mahorais (which sounds uncannily like Maoris – is there a connection?). They work in government, banks and other businesses, but ultimately the bosses are French. There is little or no movement towards reintegration with the Comoros Republic, or self rule, and little external military threat. A detachment of the foreign legion is permanently based in Dzaoudzi to discourage any such idea.

The Mahorais seem a lot better off, materially at least, but there appears to be as little or as much integration with the French as there is on Grande Comore. It is certainly nothing like the melting pot of Réunion.

The population of Mayotte is 70,000, of which more than half are under 20 years of age. Although the population is 99% Muslim, the religion is less formally applied or followed on Mayotte.

## Information

For details on the post office, bank and other services refer to the relevant sections in the Facts for the Visitor chapter.

### National Hat Day?

The inhabitants wear an amazing variety of hats – some which defy any fashion, traditional or contemporary. One day on the ferry I saw men wearing hard hats, mop-style wigs, woollen beanies, sombreros, detached anorak hoods, caps with ear flaps – anything they could put on their heads. It must have been National Hat Day. Other novelties included a selection of loud-checked, bell-bottom flares, jester suits and pyjamas.

The women were more traditionally dressed by and large, with an emphasis on large. Many were big and brassy mamas who could spit with the best of them, and frequently did.

As for the French residents, many men were wearing US bowling club shirts. I thought at first bowling was a popular pastime on Mayotte. But no. One clothes shop had imported a large consignment of the shirts and everybody rushed to buy them.

## AROUND THE ISLET
### Mamoudzou

There is little to see in this island capital of 12,000 people, apart from the market, although most of the hotels, restaurants and other facilities are there or across in Dzaoudzi. There are ferries running regularly between the two towns (See the Getting Around section).

### N'Goudja

Close to Kani-Kéli, on the south-west tip of the island, is the beach at N'Goudja, said to be the best beach on Mayotte. It is good for snorkelling and diving. The

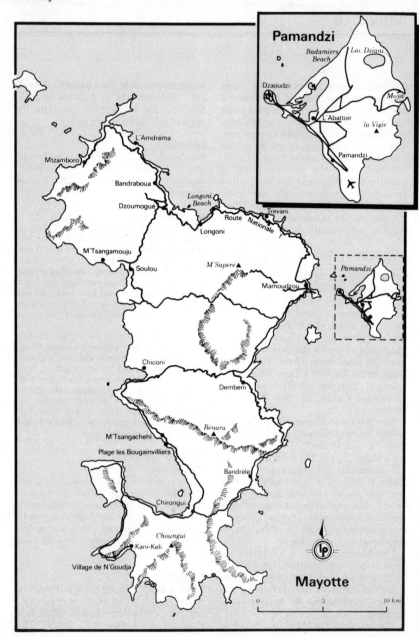

**Pamandzi**

Badamiers Beach

Lac Dziani

Dzaoudzi

Moya

L'Abattoir

la Vigie

Pamandzi

L'Amdréma

Mtzamboro

Bandraboua

Dzoumogué

Longoni Beach

Trevani

Route Nationale

Longoni

M'Tsangamouju

Soulou

M'Sapéré

Mamoudzou

Pamandzi

Chiconi

Dembeni

Bénara

M'Tsangachehi

Plage les Bougainvilliers

Bandréle

Chirongui

Choungui

Kani-Keli

Village de N'Goudja

**Mayotte**

0        5        10 km

Village de N'Goudja hotel is there. The mountain pinnacle, Mt Choungui, in the centre of the sea horse's head in the south, is an extinct volcano. It is steep but only 594 metres high.

## Soulou

There is a beautiful waterfall at this west coast bay beach. Most passing yachts call in to Soulou for a shower and a picnic. It is much more difficult to reach by road. The quickest way is north along Route Nationale 1 from Mamoudzou to Dzoumogué and across country by a secondary road, which meets the coast at the Baie de Soulou.

## Other Beaches

Good beaches around the capital are Longoni, 16 km north of Mamoudzou; Majiméoni, 33 km from Mamoudzou in the Baie L'Amdréma on the north-east tip of the island; and Mtzamboro, 10 km further on around the coast in the north-west – the limit of the main road north.

Longoni is FFr 5 from town by taxi-brousse. There are some good rocks for diving off or snorkelling around. The beach at M'Tsangachehi, on the west coast, may be recommended by some, but I found the water muddy and shallow, especially when the tide was out.

## Pamandzi

If arriving by air, you land at Pamandzi Airport. The island is connected to Dzaoudzi by the Blvd des Crabes causeway. There are 10,000 inhabitants on Pamandzi and a few sights and beaches worth visiting.

Moya cove and Lac Dziani (a crater lake) are close to each other, about a two km walk from the village of L'Abattoir at the end of the causeway.

Moya, which means 'isolated', is pretty and peaceful, except on weekends when it is swarming with families. The sea is much wilder here because there is no reef, but the dangers are minimised by the sheltered bay. To get up to the rim of the crater lake, you have to backtrack to L'Abattoir and cross over to another road. Do not try and walk directly from Moya to Dziani. The undergrowth is too thick and rough.

Lac Dziani is similar to Lac Salé on Grande Comore, but bigger. There is a track up to the crater's rim and you can walk easily down a path to the water's edge. The water is said to be good for treating skin ailments.

You can take a taxi from Dzaoudzi much of the way to Moya or Dziani, but be careful you do not exceed the FFr 2 limit (FFr 4 on Sundays).

Badamiers Beach is more open and sandy than Moya, but is close to naval and fuel bases. You take the same road as for Dziani, but cut off left to the north-west shore.

## Dzaoudzi

This is France's 'Rock of Gibraltar'. Until 1962 it was the island capital, but now it is the administrative and military centre. There is little to do there except walk around the préfecture gardens and hang about with the foreign legion!

## PLACES TO STAY

There is not a great selection of hotels on Mayotte and many are fully booked much of the year.

### Places to Stay – Mamoudzou

The cheapest place I could find to stay in Mayotte, for single rates, was the *Bar du Rond Point*, near the post office in Mamoudzou. This place has been run by the same French family for over 40 years. It is intimate and relaxed, but doesn't stand on ceremony. That is, they won't jump to your every command. At the same time, they don't hassle you for payment.

There are, however, only two tiny bungalows out back to let, both at FFr 150 a night, including breakfast. You have to share the 'trap door' toilet and showers with the family. Home-made 'dish of the

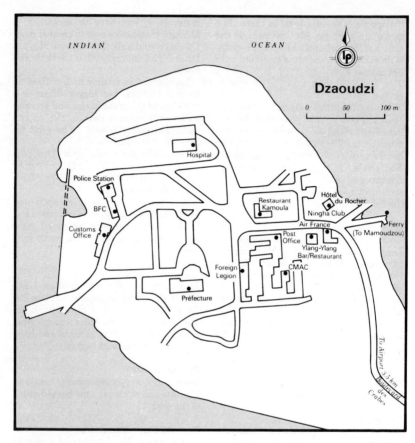

*Dzaoudzi*

INDIAN     OCEAN

Hospital

Police Station

BFC

Customs Office

Restaurant Kamoula

Hôtel du Rocher

Ningha Club

Air France

Post Office

Ylang-Ylang Bar/Restaurant

CMAC

Foreign Legion

Préfecture

Ferry (To Mamoudzou)

To Airport - 3.5 km

Boulevard des Crabes

0     50     100 m

day' meals are FFr 50. There is no menu. The bar has a few regulars, but the restaurant is not a popular eating spot.

Up the hill from the bar, the *Hôtel La Tortue Bigotu* (tel 61 11 35), is also friendly and efficient, but expensive at FFr 280 for a double room with air-con, FFr 25 for breakfast and FFr 100 for a meal. The hotel attracts many big-game anglers and divers, as it runs a range of boat and fishing trips (see the general section on Activities). The hotel has only six rooms and is often full.

The *Hôtel Le Baobab* (tel 61 11 40), a little further south in town, is bigger and cheaper at FFr 250 for a bungalow, including breakfast. The hotel has 12 bungalows in attractive surroundings, a good restaurant, bar and swimming pool. The pool is supposedly for residents or long-term subscribers, but you may be able to cool off for a small fee, or if you buy drinks. Meals are FFr 90. Le Baobab also hires out cars (see the Getting Around section).

## Places to Stay – Dzaoudzi

There is only one hotel on this side of the

water, but several restaurants. The *Hôtel du Rocher* (tel 60 10 10), next to the ferry and only four km from the airport, has recently been upgraded. It has a restaurant and costs around FFr 250/300 for a single/double per night, including breakfast.

### Places to Stay – others

The *Plage Les Bougainvilliers* (tel 61 11 55) on the west coast close to the beach at M'Tsangachehi, has small bungalows for FFr 180 a night. Two-bedroom bungalows cost FFr 300 and three-bedroom bungalows, with kitchens, are FFr 400. Or, you can take a bedroom on a half board basis with singles/doubles FFr 300/400 per day. The hotel was empty when I called and the beach turns into an unenticing mud flat when the tide is out. To get there, take a taxi-brousse from Mamoudzou to Chirongui, via Chiconi for FFr 10. The hotel hires cars for FFr 280 a day to residents (FFr 300 for nonresidents), with a FFr 3000 deposit.

The Bougainvilliers is up against the *Village de N'Goudja* (tel 60 14 19), near Kani-Kéli village in the south-west part of La Grande Terre. The 12 bungalows cost FFr 300 per person per day on a half board basis. It has an excellent beach, diving school and other water sports, as well as boat and 4WD vehicle trips. The holiday village is 50 km from the airport and the transfer cost is FFr 250 each way.

### PLACES TO EAT
### Places to Eat – Mamoudzou

For eating out only, the choice is greater and more reasonably priced than accommodation. Sadly, there are only a few Mahorais places where you can eat. The *Mimosa* snack bar in the market square, Mamoudzou, is one of the few. *La Crêperie*, on the road to Hôtel Le Baobab, is good for both food and service. Soup here is FFr 20, an omelette is FFr 22, meat or fish dishes are FFr 45, and crêpes start at FFr 30. Closer to Le Baobab junction, is the *Restaurant Saidani* (tel 60 12 23). It has good views over the bay, but is run-down in appearance.

In the centre of town, near the ferry, is the *Reflet des Iles*. It has a FFr 70 menu with continental breakfasts at only FFr

Parsons chameleon

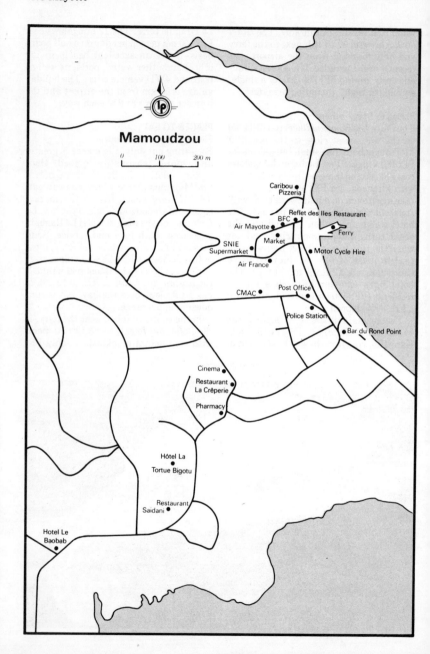

Mamoudzou

0    100    200 m

Caribou Pizzeria
Reflet des Iles Restaurant
BFC
Air Mayotte
Market
Ferry
SNIE Supermarket
Motor Cycle Hire
Air France
CMAC
Post Office
Police Station
Bar du Rond Point
Cinema
Restaurant La Crêperie
Pharmacy
Hôtel La Tortue Bigotu
Restaurant Saidani
Hotel Le Baobab

15. It is open from 8.30 am to 3 pm and 6 to 11 pm. Nearby, on the road north out of town is the new *Caribou Pizzeria* (tel 61 14 18). Pizzas start at FFr 30.

### Places to Eat - Pamandzi

There is a local Mahorais restaurant beside the Cinema 2000 in L'Abattoir, at the other end of the Blvd des Crabes. There is also one on the boulevard between the Air Comores office and the Shoping shop.

Further along towards Dzaoudzi rock, is *Le Lagon* (tel 40 12 45), also known as *Chez Gaston*. It looks like nothing from the roadside but is quite smart, with a terrace overhanging the sea. Dishes start at FFr 50.

On the route out to Moya from L'Abattoir, is the *Moya* restaurant (tel 60 14 23). Many French come here on weekends to play *boules* as well as to eat. It boasts Indian, French and Creole food cooked over a charcoal fire.

In Dzaoudzi, is the *Restaurant Kamoula*, opposite the post office in the Place de France. It is popular with the legionnaires. You can get sandwiches there for FFr 20 and coffee for FFr 5. Near the ferry is the *Ylang-Ylang Bar/Restaurant* (tel 60 12 78), which specialises in Chinese and Vietnamese food.

## ENTERTAINMENT

The only night spot in Mamoudzou, apart from the hotels, is the *Golden Lagon II* (the first Golden Lagon burned down). For film, theatre and other activities, go to the *Centre Mahorais d'Animation Culturelle (CMAC)* (tel 61 11 36), near the post office. It publishes a monthly programme of events which includes video and film shows in Dzaoudzi and Mamoudzou.

In Dzaoudzi there is also a CMAC, again next to the post office. The *Ningha Club*, near the ferry pier, has discos each night, except Monday. Along the causeway, near the Air Comores office, is *Disco 2000*.

# Index

## MAPS

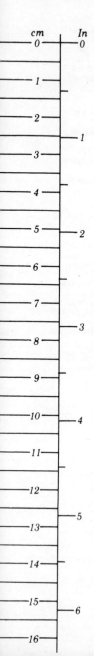

## Temperature

To convert °C to °F multiply by 1.8 and add 32

To convert °F to °C subtract 32 and multiply by ·55

## Length, Distance & Area

|  | *multiply by* |
|---|---|
| inches to centimetres | 2.54 |
| centimetres to inches | 0.39 |
| feet to metres | 0.30 |
| metres to feet | 3.28 |
| yards to metres | 0.91 |
| metres to yards | 1.09 |
| miles to kilometres | 1.61 |
| kilometres to miles | 0.62 |
| acres to hectares | 0.40 |
| hectares to acres | 2.47 |

## Weight

|  | *multiply by* |
|---|---|
| ounces to grams | 28.35 |
| grams to ounces | 0.035 |
| pounds to kilograms | 0.45 |
| kilograms to pounds | 2.21 |
| British tons to kilograms | 1016 |
| US tons to kilograms | 907 |

A British ton is 2240 lbs, a US ton is 2000 lbs

## Volume

|  | *multiply by* |
|---|---|
| Imperial gallons to litres | 4.55 |
| litres to imperial gallons | 0.22 |
| US gallons to litres | 3.79 |
| litres to US gallons | 0.26 |

5 imperial gallons equals 6 US gallons
a litre is slightly more than a US quart, slightly less
than a British one

# Africa on a shoestring

From Marrakesh to Kampala, Mozambique to Mauritania, Johannesburg to Cairo – this guidebook gives you all the facts on travelling in Africa. It provides comprehensive information on more than 50 African countries – how to get to them, how to get around, where to stay, where to eat, what to see and what to avoid.

# Other guides to Islands of the Indian Ocean

### Maldives & Islands of the East Indian Ocean – a travel survival kit

The Maldives are a chain of beautiful atolls lying to the west of Sri Lanka. They offer great diving and a relaxed atmosphere. This new guide also covers Christmas and Cocos Islands, and the Andaman, Chagos, Lakshadweep and Nicobar groups.

### Mauritius, Réunion & the Seychelles – a travel survival kit

Mauritius is a strange blend of Indian, Creole and French cultures – and travel is cheap. Réunion is France's best-kept secret – a superb volcanic island and one of its last colonies. The Seychelles have been discovered by divers, climbers – and beach lovers.

# Other guides from Lonely Planet

### Israel - a travel survival kit
A complete coverage of both the modern state of Israel and the ancient biblical country. Detailed practical travel facts are combined with authoritative historical references in this comprehensive guide.

### Morocco, Algeria & Tunisia - a travel survival kit
A blend of African, Islamic, Arab and Berber cultures make this a fascinating region to visit. This book takes you from bustling souks to peaceful oases and is packed with all the information you'll need.

### East Africa - a travel survival kit
Whether you want to climb Kilimanjaro, visit wildlife reserves, or sail an Arab dhow, East Africa offers a fascinating pastiche of cultures and landscapes. This guide has detailed information on Kenya, Uganda, Rwanda, Burundi, eastern Zaire, Tanzania and the Comoros Islands.

### Turkey - a travel survival kit
Historic Turkey, bridging Asia and Europe, offers a wide range of travel experiences - from the excitement of Istanbul's bazaars to Mediterranean beaches and remote mountains. This widely acclaimed book has all the facts.

### Trekking in Turkey
Western travellers have discovered Turkey's coastline, but few people are aware that just inland there are mountains with walks that rival those found in Nepal. This book, the first trekking guide to Turkey, gives details on treks that are destined to become classics.

# Lonely Planet Guidebooks

Lonely Planet guidebooks cover virtually every accessible part of Asia as well as Australia, the Pacific, Central and South America, Africa, the Middle East and parts of North America. There are four main series: 'travel survival kits', covering a single country for a range of budgets; 'shoestring' guides with compact information for low-budget travel in a major region; trekking guides; and 'phrasebooks'.

## Australia & the Pacific
Australia
Bushwalking in Australia
Papua New Guinea
Papua New Guinea phrasebook
New Zealand
Tramping in New Zealand
Rarotonga & the Cook Islands
Solomon Islands
Tahiti & French Polynèsia
Fiji
Micronesia

## South-East Asia
South-East Asia on a shoestring
Malaysia, Singapore & Brunei
Indonesia
Bali & Lombok
Indonesia phrasebook
Burma
Burmese phrasebook
Thailand
Thai phrasebook
Philippines
Pilipino phrasebook

## North-East Asia
North-East Asia on a shoestring
China
China phrasebook
Tibet
Tibet phrasebook
Japan
Korea
Korean phrasebook
Hong Kong, Macau & Canton
Taiwan

## West Asia
West Asia on a shoestring
Trekking in Turkey
Turkey

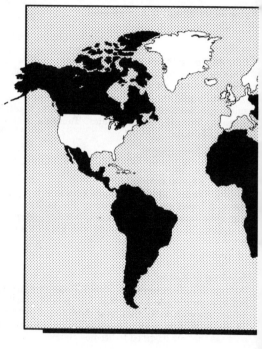

# Mail Order

Lonely Planet guidebooks are distributed worldwide and are sold by good bookshops everywhere. They are also available by mail order from Lonely Planet, so if you have difficulty finding a title please write to us. US and Canadian residents should write to Embarcadero West, 112 Linden St, Oakland CA 94607, USA and residents of other countries to PO Box 617, Hawthorn, Victoria 3122, Australia.

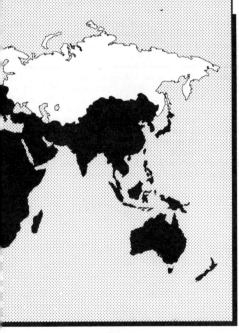

### Eastern Europe
Eastern Europe

### Indian Subcontinent
India
Hindi/Urdu phrasebook
Kashmir, Ladakh & Zanskar
Trekking in the Indian Himalaya
Pakistan
Kathmandu & the Kingdom of Nepal
Trekking in the Nepal Himalaya
Nepal phrasebook
Sri Lanka
Sri Lanka phrasebook
Bangladesh
Karakoram Highway

### Africa
Africa on a shoestring
East Africa
Swahili phrasebook
West Africa
Central Africa
Morocco, Algeria & Tunisia

### Middle East
Israel
Egypt & the Sudan
Jordan & Syria
Yemen

### North America
Canada
Alaska

### Mexico
Mexico
Baja California

### South America
South America on a shoestring
Ecuador & the Galapagos Islands
Colombia
Chile & Easter Island
Bolivia
Brazil
Peru
Argentina

## Lonely Planet

Lonely Planet published its first book in 1973. Tony and Maureen Wheeler had made a lengthy overland trip from England to Australia and, in response to numerous 'how do you do it?' questions, Tony wrote and they published *Across Asia on the Cheap*. It became an instant local best-seller and inspired thoughts of a second travel guide. A year and a half in South-East Asia resulted in their second book, *South-East Asia on a Shoestring*, which they put together in a backstreet Chinese hotel in Singapore in 1975. The 'yellow book', as it quickly became known, soon became *the* guide to the region and has gone through five editions, always with its familiar yellow cover.

Soon other writers came to them with ideas for similar books – books that went off the beaten track with an adventurous approach to travel, books that 'assumed you knew how to get your luggage off the carousel,' as one reviewer put it. Lonely Planet grew from a kitchen table operation to a spare room and then to its own office. It's international reputation began to grow as the Lonely Planet logo began to appear in more and more countries. In 1982 *India – a travel survival kit* won the Thomas Cook award for the best guidebook of the year.

These days there are over 70 Lonely Planet titles. Over 40 people work at our office in Melbourne, Australia and another half dozen at our US office in Oakland, California.

At first Lonely Planet specialised in the Asia region but these days we are also developing major ranges of guidebooks to the Pacific region, to South America and to Africa. The list of walking guides is growing and Lonely Planet now has a unique series of phrasebooks to 'unusual' languages. The emphasis continues to be on travel for travellers and Tony and Maureen still manage to fit in a number of trips each year and play a very active part in the writing and updating of Lonely Planet's guides.

Keeping guidebooks up to date is a constant battle which requires an ear to the ground and lots of walking, but technology also plays its part. All Lonely Planet guidebooks are now stored and updated on computer, and some authors even take lap-top computers into the field. Lonely Planet is also using computers to draw maps and eventually many of the maps will be stored on disk.

The people at Lonely Planet strongly feel that travellers can make a positive contribution to the countries they visit both by better appreciation of cultures and by the money they spend. In addition the company tries to make a direct contribution to the countries and regions it covers. Since 1986 a percentage of the income from each book has gone to aid groups and associations. This has included donations to famine relief in Africa, to aid projects in India, to agricultural projects in Central America, to Greenpeace's efforts to halt French nuclear testing in the Pacific and to Amnesty International. In 1989 $41,000 was donated by Lonely Planet to these projects.

---

## Lonely Planet Distributors

**Australia & Papua New Guinea** Lonely Planet Publications, PO Box 617, Hawthorn, Victoria 3122.
**Canada** Raincoast Books, 112 East 3rd Avenue, Vancouver, British Columbia V5T 1C8.
**Denmark, Finland & Norway** Scanvik Books aps, Store Kongensgade 59 A, DK-1264 Copenhagen K.
**India & Nepal** UBS Distributors, 5 Ansari Rd, New Delhi – 110002
**Israel** Geographical Tours Ltd, 8 Tverya St, Tel Aviv 63144.
**Japan** Intercontinental Marketing Corp, IPO Box 5056, Tokyo 100-31.
**Kenya** Westland Sundries Ltd, PO Box 14107, Nairobi, Kenya.
**Netherlands** Nilsson & Lamm bv, Postbus 195, Pampuslaan 212, 1380 AD Weesp.
**New Zealand** Transworld Publishers, PO Box 83-094, Edmonton PO, Auckland.
**Singapore & Malaysia** MPH Distributors, 601 Sims Drive, #03-21, Singapore 1438.
**Spain** Altair, Balmes 69, 08007 Barcelona.
**Sweden** Esselte Kartcentrum AB, Vasagatan 16, S-111 20 Stockholm.
**Thailand** Chalermnit, 108 Sukhumvit 53, Bangkok 10110.
**Turkey** Yab-Yay Dagitim, Alay Koshu Caddesi 12/A, Kat 4 no. 11-12, Cagaloglu, Istanbul.
**UK** Roger Lascelles, 47 York Rd, Brentford, Middlesex, TW8 0QP
**USA** Lonely Planet Publications, PO Box 2001A, Berkeley, CA 94702.
**West Germany** Buchvertrieb Gerda Schettler, Postfach 64, D3415 Hattorf a H.
**All Other Countries** refer to Australia address.